功能语言学论丛

本书出版由广东财经大学外国语学院重点学科经费及广东省教育厅特色创新项目（教育科研类）（2016GXJK056）资金资助

An Equivalence Study of Projection in the *Lunyu / The Analects* and Its Translations

《论语》及其英译本的投射语言对等研究

胡红辉◎著

·广州·

图书在版编目（CIP）数据

《论语》及其英译本的投射语言对等研究 = An Equivalence Study of Projection in the *Lunyu/ The Analects* and Its Translations: 英文/胡红辉著. —广州：中山大学出版社，2019.12
（功能语言学论丛）
ISBN 978-7-306-06821-7

Ⅰ.①论… Ⅱ.①胡… Ⅲ.①功能（语言学）—研究—英文 Ⅳ.①H0

中国版本图书馆 CIP 数据核字（2019）第 299897 号

出 版 人：	王天琪
策划编辑：	熊锡源
责任编辑：	熊锡源
封面设计：	林绵华
责任校对：	潘惠虹
责任技编：	何雅涛
出版发行：	中山大学出版社
电　　话：	编辑部 020-84111996，84111997
	发行部 020-84111998，84111981，84111160
地　　址：	广州市新港西路 135 号
邮　　编：	510275　　传　　真：020-84036565
网　　址：	http://www.zsup.com.cn　　E-mail:zdcbs@mail.sysu.edu.cn
印 刷 者：	佛山市浩文彩色印刷有限公司
规　　格：	880mm×1230mm　1/32　7.125 印张　300 千字
版次印次：	2019 年 12 月第 1 版　2019 年 12 月第 1 次印刷
定　　价：	35.00 元

如发现本书因印装质量影响阅读，请与出版社发行部联系调换

Acknowledgements

I am grateful to all the people who have helped me in the process of completing this work.

My gratitude goes first and foremost to Professor Huang Guowen. It is he who has led me to the door of Systemic Functional Linguistics and guided me to the research area of linguistic translation studies. His interesting lectures have inspired me greatly and always made me feel enthusiastic in my studies. His fatherly strict requirements and timely instructions during the process of writing will benefit me all my life.

Secondly, I want to extend my heartfelt gratitude to my supervisor, Professor Zeng Lei. During my doctoral study, she has taught me how to be an academic researcher. Her motherly love and patience have accompanied me throughout my study. Without her guidance, this work would not have been completed on time.

I would also like to show my gratitude to all the teachers in the English Department of Sun Yat-sen University: especially Professor Chang Chenguang, Professor Wendy Bowcher and Professor Dai Fan, who have all given invaluable suggestions during the initial stage. I am sincerely grateful for their insightful advice and intelligent comments for the work.

Special thanks should go to Professor Chen Yang, whose illuminating comments and warm support I will always bear in mind.

My thanks should also go to all my teammates on the translation-study group of the *Lunyu* and my classmates in the Functional Linguistics Institute of Sun Yat-sen University: Wu Guoxiang, Chen Ying, Gao Shengwen, Yu Juan, Liang Hongyan, Shang Kangkang, Hu Anqi, Yang Muwen, Hong Dan and others. Their kindness, friendship, constant encouragement and assistance have always been a great source of motivation and inspiration.

I am also deeply indebted to my husband, Zuo Yuhui and my beloved daughter, Zuo Wenqi, for their continuing love and support for me, and for the happy and pleasant family life they have created for me. Without their love and support, the work could never have been completed.

Synopsis

There is no doubt that the translation of the *Lunyu* / *The Analects* (henceforth the *Lunyu*) has been extensively explored and each researcher has made his own contribution to it. However, the prominent linguistic phenomenon of projection in the ancient Chinese work and its equivalence in translation have been less researched. Projection is widely used in the source text (henceforth ST) of the *Lunyu* but has received little attention in the translation studies. The functions served by the projection clause nexus in the source text and target text (henceforth TT) have been only briefly touched upon and are therefore worthy of further exploration.

This book aims to provide a systematic and comprehensive study of projection in three translated versions of the *Lunyu* in line with the framework of Systemic Functional Linguistics (henceforth SFL). In general, this book investigates how the different realizations of projection in different translated versions are related to the different meanings and functions that projection conveys, and examines the different degrees of equivalence that projection can achieve at the level of semantics as well as the level of context. Associated with the aim are four objectives: (1) to describe the distinctive features of the different types and structures of projection in the different translated versions of the *Lunyu*; (2) to analyze the metafunctional features of projection in the translated versions and explore the semantic meanings conveyed by the translators with their different lexicogrammatical choices of projection; (3) to explore the different degrees of metafunctional equivalence of projection in different translated versions; (4) to evaluate the equivalence of projection in the context, both context of situation and context of culture.

This study is descriptive and qualitative in nature. The research method used in this study is in line with the six steps of functional discourse analysis: observation, interpretation, description, analysis, explanation and evaluation. The main findings of this study can be summarized as follows:

First, this study finds that the phenomenon of projection is important in the text of the *Lunyu*. In the different translations, different types and structures of projection have been chosen by their translators, among whom Legge has chosen the most equivalent types and structures of projection while Xu has chosen the most variant types and structures of projection. They have achieved different degrees of formal equivalence of projection as compared to the ST. The cline of formal equivalence from high to low is: Legge's target text (henceforth LT) – Ku's target text (henceforth KT) – Xu's target text (henceforth XT).

Second, this study finds that the different choices among the linguistic forms of projection in different TTs can convey different metafunctional meanings. Through an exploration of the experiential structures of projecting clauses and the different logical meanings conveyed in different types of projection clause nexuses, this study finds that, although the three translated versions can basically convey the ideational meaning contained in the ST, the different TTs achieve differing degrees of ideational equivalence. The cline of ideational equivalence from high to low is: LT – KT – XT.

With an exploration of the speech functions realized by projection and an analysis of different choices in the Mood, Modality, and Person system in different TTs, this study finds that the three translated versions realize equivalent speech functions but convey different interpersonal meanings. LT realizes equivalent interpersonal meaning to the ST, while KT and XT convey some new interpersonal meanings with their different choices of projection. KT and XT are more reader-friendly than the ST.

With an analysis of thematic structures, patterns of thematic progression and cohesive methods in the projection clause nexuses, this study finds that the different TTs have realized different choices in the textual metafunction. Legge has made similar choices to the ST and conveys equivalent textual meaning in his TT. Ku has made different choices in the dialogue part, and Xu has made different choices in the aphorisms as well as in the dialogues. The textual meanings conveyed in these two translators' TTs are accordingly different to those conveyed in the ST. The cline of textual equivalence in the TTs from high to low is: LT, KT, XT.

Last, the different degrees of metafunctional equivalence achieved in the texts have been evaluated in relation to the context. This study finds that different degrees of formal equivalence of projection have resulted in differences of ideational meaning, interpersonal meaning and textual meaning in the TTs, which are reflected in the register as differences in Field, Tenor, and Mode. The variation in the three variables of context of situation shows that translators have reconstructed the context of situation in the TTs. This study finds that Legge has chosen the method of literal translation and basically reconstructed a context of situation similar to that of the ST. Ku and Xu have chosen the method of free translation and Xu has even abandoned the original linguistic forms of projection in the translation. KT and XT have reconstructed a context of situation with different Tenor and Mode but Ku and Xu have realized their translation targets in their context of culture and can still be regarded as successful translations.

The originality of this book lies in three primary aspects. Firstly, it provides a systematic and comprehensive account of projection in the *Lunyu* and its English translations and describes and explains the metafunctional meanings conveyed in the different choices of projection. This broadens the research scope of studies on the *Lunyu* and its translations. Secondly, this book studies the equivalence of projection in the ST and TTs at three levels: the level of lexicogrammar, the level of semantics and the level of context. It proves that judgement of a translation should be formed by combining and analyzing the degrees of equivalence achieved in these three levels. This study also shows that the evaluation of a translation should not be confined to the degree of formal equivalence or metafunctional equivalence it achieves, but should also include an evaluation of the effect of translation in the specific context of culture within which the TTs function. Thirdly, it provides a comprehensive study on the typical linguistic forms of quotation style texts from the perspective of linguistics and translation studies.

内容简介

《论语》作为中国的经典著作,它的英译,一直是语言学、文学等不同流派的学者所关注的研究热点。近年来,从语言学角度研究《论语》的英译也逐渐引起学者们的关注,但对于《论语》中典型的语言现象——投射,以及投射语言的翻译问题,很少有比较系统的研究。对于原文大量存在的投射语言,译者是否选择同样的投射类型和结构,是否能够实现与原文功能的对等,这个问题还鲜有研究。

本研究以系统功能语言学为框架,以功能语篇分析为指导,对《论语》原文及译文中的投射语言展开全面的研究。研究旨在描述不同译文对投射语言类型和结构的不同选择,解释其所体现的不同元功能意义,揭示不同译文在概念功能、人际功能以及语篇功能三方面所实现的不同程度对等,并将其置于语境中,分析其在译文中所构建的不同语境并在文化语境下分析和评估译文投射语言所实现的不同程度对等。研究内容包括:①描写《论语》原文及三个译本中的投射语言类型及结构;②分析不同译本在翻译投射语言时的不同选择所表达的元功能意义;③探讨不同译本在三大元功能方面所实现的不同程度对等;④在情景语境和文化语境中评估不同译本的对等程度,探讨译者的不同选择在文化语境层面的原因。

首先,投射语言现象在《论语》原文及译文中占有很重要的地位,投射语言的对等程度可以反映不同译文的翻译特色。译者在不同译本中选择了投射语言的不同词汇语法形式，选择了不同的投射类型与结构。在本研究的三个译本中，从投射语言和原文的形式对等层面来说，理雅各译本所选择的投射语言类型与结构与原文最为对等，许渊冲译本所选择的投射语言形式与原文相差最大。

其次，不同译本所选择的投射语言形式表达不同的元功能意义。通过考察各译文投射小句复合体中投射小句的不同经验功能结构，不同投射小句复合体类型所体现的不同逻辑功能意义，发现各译文投射语言基本能体现原文投射语言所表达的概念意义，但各译文再现原文概念意义的程度有所差异。基于原文投射语言概念意义与译文投射语言概念意义的对比分析，研究发现各译本投射小句复合体所实现的概念功能对等程度不一，概念功能对等程度由高至低渐变为：理雅各译本——辜鸿铭译本——许渊冲译本。

通过考察各译本投射小句复合体所实现的言语功能，以及投射小句与被投射小句在语气系统、情态系统及人称系统的不同选择所体现的不同人际意义，发现各译本基本实现与原文一致的言语功能，但所体现的人际意义与原文对等程度不一。理雅各译本基本实现与原文一致的人际意义，辜鸿铭及许渊冲译本则添加了以读者为本的人际意义，体现了原文所不具备的人际意义。

通过考察各译本小句复合体的主位结构、主位推进模式以及衔接方式，发现各译本投射小句复合体所体现的语篇功能各有不同：理雅各采用与原文相似的主位结构、主位推进模式及衔接方式，实现了与原文基本对等的语篇功能；辜鸿铭译本及许渊冲译本通过在对话体以及格言体中采用与原文不同的主位推进模式及衔接方式，实现了与原文不同的语篇意义。三个译本与原文的语篇功能对等程度由高至低分别为理雅各译本、辜鸿铭译本、许渊冲译本。

最后，通过在语境中分析和评估不同译本在三大元功能层面所实现的不同程度对等，发现各个译本由于投射小句复合体在词汇语法层面的不同选择，导致不同译本所表达的概念意义、人际意义及语篇意义和原文都有所差异。这种意义的差异体现在语域中，就是语场、语旨和语式的差异，不同译本中情景语境三要素的改变体现了译者在翻译中重构了原文的情景语境，实现了情景语境与原文的不同程度对等。研究发现，理雅各的译本采用的是直译法，基本重现了原文的情景语境，实现了译文从词汇语法形式层面、语义功能层面及语境层面的对等；辜鸿铭的译本和许渊冲的译本，采用意译的方法，许渊冲更是在译本中抛弃了原文投射语言的结构形式，实现了再创作，表达了与原文不一致的人际意义与语篇意义，构建了不同的语旨及语式，但这两个译本在其各自的文化语境之中，实现了各自的翻译目的，依然是成功的译本。

本研究的创新之处在于：①系统描述了《论语》原文及译文中的投射语言现象，对不同投射语言形式的选择所体现的元功能意义做了系统描述和解释，拓宽了《论语》译本研究的范围。②本研究从词汇语法形式层面、语义功能层面和语境层面探讨《论语》英译本投射语言与原文的对等，提出评估译文与原文投射语言的相对对等程度，需要从三个层面综合考察；译文与原文的形式对等程度与语义功能对等程度最终要在文化语境层面得到检验。③本研究对语录体文本中的典型语言所做的翻译研究，为语录体文本的研究提供了语言学与翻译学的借鉴。

序

　　胡红辉是我招收的系统功能语言学方向的第二位博士生。她硕士期间的研究方向是语用学（毕业论文研究的是模糊语言的语用功能）。2010年，作为一名系统功能语言学的门外汉，胡红辉第一次报考了我的博士生，勇气可嘉，结果当然是名落孙山；而后，她知不足而后勇，于当年9月进入中山大学师从黄国文老师做访问学者，认真学习系统功能语言学的理论知识。当时，她已经硕士研究生毕业并从事教学工作近7年，十分珍惜重新学习的机会，如饥似渴地参与系统功能语言学的课堂学习及课外讨论，参加中山大学组织的各种相关学术活动。正是这种求学精神让她得以在2011年中山大学博士研究生入学考试中脱颖而出，进入中大攻读博士学位。

　　胡红辉博士生学习期间的研究兴趣是系统功能语言学途径的翻译研究，并加入了黄国文老师指导的《论语》英译的研究团队。当时，从事《论语》英译本研究的有黄国文老师的好几位博士生。胡红辉作为一位刚入门的新生，所承受的压力确实不小。最后，在我的建议下，她选择了研究《论语》中的投射语言现象。在撰写博士学位论文的几年中，她努力地向老师们、师兄师姐们请教。这种虚心和踏踏实实做研究的态度给我留下了深刻的印象，我想，正是这种态度让她能够完成了博士学位论文的写作并通过了答辩。

　　我很高兴胡红辉根据自己的博士学位论文改写成的《〈论语〉

及其英译本的投射语言对等研究》一书即将出版。该书主要探讨《论语》原文及英译文中投射语言的对等问题。作者运用系统功能语言学理论对《论语》中的相关语料从词汇语法层面、语义功能层面及语境层面进行了系统描述和分析。书中的主要研究发现为不同译文对投射语言类型和结构有不同的选择，这主要是因为译文构建了不同的语境，不同译文在概念功能、人际功能以及语篇功能三方面实现了不同程度的相对对等。可以看出，作者是在文化语境下分析和评估译文投射语言所实现的对等程度，试图构建一个相关语篇的投射语言英译对等程度研究范式。胡红辉的研究表明，语录体文本中投射语言的翻译对等研究，可以体现整个文本原文及译文之间的对等程度，并反映出不同译本的翻译特色。该研究不仅拓宽了语录体文本研究的范围，也为其提供了语言学与翻译研究的借鉴。

胡红辉在中山大学学习六年，这段时期对她的学术生涯意义重大。我一直认为，博士生阶段的学习过程，应该是人生最重要的一个学习阶段，除了学习怎样做学问，同时还在学习与科研中不断丰富和完善自己的人生经历。胡红辉在这六年里，付出了不少，也收获了很多，希望她能够在自己的研究领域里继续钻研，在大部分人认为有点枯燥的科研生活中找到乐趣。

曾　蕾
2019 年 9 月于中山大学珠海校区倚海苑

Table of Contents

List of Figures ··· I
List of Tables ·· II
List of Abbreviations ·· IV

Chapter 1   **Introduction** ·· 1
            1.1   Preamble ·· 1
            1.2   Motivation for the study ························ 2
            1.3   Research objectives and research questions
                     ··· 5
            1.4   Research methodology ···························· 6
            1.5   Data collection ······································ 7
            1.6   Organization of the book ························ 10

Chapter 2   **Literature Review** ······································ 12
            2.1   Introduction ·· 12
            2.2   Previous studies on projection ················ 12
                   2.2.1   Stylistic approaches to projection
                            ··· 12
                   2.2.2   Linguistic approaches to projection
                            ··· 14
            2.3   Previous studies on translation in SFL ······ 18
                   2.3.1   Catford's studies of "equivalence"
                           and "shift" in translation ·············· 18
                   2.3.2   House's model of translation quality
                           assessment ································ 20
                   2.3.3   Bell's descriptive study of translation
                           ··· 21
                   2.3.4   Baker's analysis of thematic structures
                           in translation ···························· 23
                   2.3.5   Halliday's views on translation
                           ··· 24

I

2.4	Previous studies on the *Lunyu* and its translation ········· 26	
	2.4.1 Studies on the *Lunyu* and its translation in various disciplines ········ 26	
	2.4.2 Studies on the *Lunyu* and its translation in SFL ········· 30	
2.5	Summary ········· 33	

Chapter 3 Theoretical Framework ········· 34

- 3.1 Introduction ········· 34
- 3.2 SFL as the theoretical framework of the present study ········· 34
- 3.3 The linguistic parameters defining equivalence ········· 36
  - 3.3.1 Instantiation ········· 36
  - 3.3.2 Stratification ········· 38
  - 3.3.3 Metafunction ········· 40
  - 3.3.4 Axis ········· 45
- 3.4 Translation as recreation of meaning through choice ········· 46
- 3.5 The study of equivalence in context ········· 48
  - 3.5.1 The context-metafunction hook-up ········· 48
  - 3.5.2 Register ········· 50
  - 3.5.3 Equivalence study based on FDA ········· 52
- 3.6 The framework of analysis in the present study ········· 56
- 3.7 Summary ········· 57

Chapter 4 Different Types and Structures of Projection in the *Lunyu* and Its Translations ········· 58

- 4.1 Introduction ········· 58
- 4.2 Different realizations of projection in the ST ········· 58
- 4.3 Clarifying the data of analysis in the ST ········· 61

	4.4	Different types of projection in the TTs ⋯⋯ 63
		4.4.1 Types of projection in the part of aphorism ⋯⋯⋯⋯⋯⋯⋯⋯⋯⋯⋯ 63
		4.4.2 Types of projection in the part of dialogues ⋯⋯⋯⋯⋯⋯⋯⋯⋯⋯⋯ 64
		4.4.3 Types of projection in the asking turn of brief dialogues ⋯⋯⋯⋯⋯⋯ 65
	4.5	Different structures of projection in the TTs ⋯⋯⋯⋯⋯⋯⋯⋯⋯⋯⋯⋯⋯⋯⋯⋯⋯⋯⋯ 65
	4.6	Summary ⋯⋯⋯⋯⋯⋯⋯⋯⋯⋯⋯⋯⋯⋯⋯ 66
Chapter 5	**Ideational Equivalence of Projection in the *Lunyu* and Its Translations** ⋯⋯⋯⋯⋯⋯⋯⋯⋯⋯ **68**
	5.1	Introduction ⋯⋯⋯⋯⋯⋯⋯⋯⋯⋯⋯⋯⋯ 68
	5.2	Ideational metafunction in projection ⋯⋯⋯ 68
		5.2.1 Experiential metafunction in projection ⋯⋯⋯⋯⋯⋯⋯⋯⋯⋯⋯⋯⋯⋯⋯⋯⋯ 69
		5.2.2 Logical metafunction in projection ⋯⋯⋯⋯⋯⋯⋯⋯⋯⋯⋯⋯⋯⋯⋯⋯⋯ 72
	5.3	Degrees of ideational equivalence in projection ⋯⋯⋯⋯⋯⋯⋯⋯⋯⋯⋯⋯⋯⋯⋯⋯⋯⋯⋯ 81
	5.4	Reasons for the different realizations of projection ⋯⋯⋯⋯⋯⋯⋯⋯⋯⋯⋯⋯⋯⋯ 83
		5.4.1 Different interpretations of the ST ⋯⋯⋯⋯⋯⋯⋯⋯⋯⋯⋯⋯⋯⋯⋯⋯⋯ 83
		5.4.2 Translators' meaningful choices ⋯⋯⋯⋯⋯⋯⋯⋯⋯⋯⋯⋯⋯⋯⋯⋯⋯ 85
	5.5	Summary ⋯⋯⋯⋯⋯⋯⋯⋯⋯⋯⋯⋯⋯⋯⋯ 86
Chapter 6	**Interpersonal Equivalence of Projection in the *Lunyu* and Its Translations** ⋯⋯⋯⋯⋯⋯⋯⋯⋯ **88**
	6.1	Introduction ⋯⋯⋯⋯⋯⋯⋯⋯⋯⋯⋯⋯⋯ 88
	6.2	Speech functions realized in projection ⋯⋯⋯⋯⋯⋯⋯⋯⋯⋯⋯⋯⋯⋯⋯⋯⋯⋯⋯⋯⋯⋯ 88
		6.2.1 Equivalence of speech functions realized in projection ⋯⋯⋯⋯⋯⋯ 89
		6.2.2 Shifts of speech functions realized in projection ⋯⋯⋯⋯⋯⋯⋯⋯⋯⋯ 91

6.3　Mood elements in the projecting clause ························ 93
　　6.3.1　Equivalence in Mood in the projecting clause ··········· 93
　　6.3.2　Shifts in the Mood elements of the projecting clause ····················· 94
6.4　Modality in the projected clauses ············ 105
　　6.4.1　Modality realizing different speech functions in projection ············ 105
　　6.4.2　Modality realizing different values in the projected clause ············· 107
　　6.4.3　Understanding of modality in the ST resulting in different choices in the TTs ············ 110
6.5　Person system in projection ················ 113
6.6　Summary ································ 117

Chapter 7　Textual Equivalence of Projection in the *Lunyu* and Its Translations ···················· **119**

7.1　Introduction ······························ 119
7.2　System of Theme in the projection clause nexus ···································· 119
7.3　Thematic structure in projection ············ 122
　　7.3.1　Thematic structures of projection in the aphorisms ···················· 122
　　7.3.2　Thematic structures of projection in the dialogues ···················· 125
　　7.3.3　Textual meaning realized in the thematic structures ············· 128
7.4　Thematic-progression patterns in projection ·· 129
　　7.4.1　Patterns of thematic progression in the aphorisms ···················· 129
　　7.4.2　Patterns of thematic progression in the part of dialogues ············ 130
　　7.4.3　Textual meanings realized by patterns of thematic progression ············ 131

	7.5	Study of cohesion in projection ·············	132
		7.5.1 Cohesion in the aphorisms ·········	133
		7.5.2 Cohesion in the part of dialogues ···	136
		7.5.3 Textual meaning realized in the cohesive methods ··················	141
	7.6	Summary ··	141
Chapter 8	**Equivalence of Projection in the *Lunyu* and Its Translations in Context** ················		**143**
	8.1	Introduction ·······································	143
	8.2	Equivalence in context ························	143
	8.3	Register analysis for the ST and TTs ······	144
		8.3.1 Register analysis of the ST ·········	145
		8.3.2 Register analysis of the TTs ···	146
	8.4	Equivalence study of projection in the context ··	152
		8.4.1 Equivalence study of projection in the context of situation ············	153
		8.4.2 Evaluation of different TTs in the context of culture ················	155
	8.5	Summary ··	159
Chapter 9	**Discussion** ··		**160**
	9.1	Introduction ·······································	160
	9.2	Observation and description of projection choices ··	160
	9.3	The value of a metafunctional analysis of projection ······································	162
		9.3.1 Value of the ideational analysis of projection ·······················	162
		9.3.2 Value of the interpersonal analysis of projection ·······················	165
		9.3.3 Value of textual analysis in projection ···	167
	9.4	Evaluation of translation quality in the context ··	169

| | | 9.4.1 | Purpose of the translators | 171 |

                9.4.2   Literal translation and free translation
                                                                            172
                9.4.3   Role of translators   173
        9.5   Summary   174
Chapter 10   Conclusion   176
        10.1   Introduction   176
        10.2   An overview of the study   176
        10.3   Main research findings   177
        10.4   Implications of the research   180
        10.5   Limitations and suggestions for further
                studies   182
References   184

Appendix I   The courtesy names and given names of
              Confucius' main disciples   201
Appendix II   Translations of the examples given in
              Chapter 4   202

List of Figures

Figure 3-1	Stratification (Halliday & Matthiessen 2004:25)
Figure 3-2	Systems of Interdependency and Logico-semantic relations (based on Matthiessen & Halliday 2009:71)
Figure 3-3	Relation of the text to the context of situation (Halliday & Hasan 1985:26)
Figure 5-1	Transitivity represented as a system network (Halliday & Matthiessen 2004:173)
Figure 7-1	Theme in the clause complex (Halliday 1994a:57)
Figure 7-2	Theme in quotes (Thompson 1996b:161-162)
Figure 7-3	A possible analysis of Theme in the indirect speech (Thompson 1996b:162)
Figure 7-4	Unmarked thematic structure of projection clause nexuses in the *Lunyu*
Figure 7-5	The marked thematic structure of projection clause nexus in the *Lunyu*
Figure 7-6	Unmarked and marked thematic structure in the TTs

List of Tables

Table 2-1	Four types of projection nexus (Halliday 1994a:256)
Table 3-1	Cline of instantiation in context and language (Matthiessen *et al.* 2010:123)
Table 3-2	Patterns of thematic progression (based on Bloor & Bloor 1995:90-92)
Table 3-3	Relationship among the text, register and context (based on Teich 2001:213)
Table 4-1	Different realizations of projection in ST
Table 4-2	Different types of projection in the aphorisms of TTs
Table 4-3	Different types of projection in the TTs of Chapter Twenty, Book Two
Table 4-4	Different types of projection in the asking turn of brief dialogues
Table 4-5	Different structures of projection in the TTs
Table 5-1	Equivalent experiential structures of projecting clauses in the TTs
Table 5-2	The experiential structure of projecting clauses in KT
Table 5-3	Types of projection in the ST
Table 5-4	Types of projection in LT
Table 5-5	Types of projection in KT
Table 5-6	Types of projection in XT
Table 5-7	Equivalence and shifts in the logical metafunction in projection in XT
Table 5-8	The ideational equivalence of projection achieved in the TTs
Table 6-1	Speech functions of projection in the ST and TTs
Table 6-2	Shifts of speech functions in TTs
Table 6-3	Equivalence in Mood in a projecting clause
Table 6-4	Shifts in the choice of Mood elements in projecting clauses
Table 6-5	Different realizations of projecting clauses in Example

Table 6-6	Types and orientation in Modality (Halliday & Matthiessen 2004:620) [6-14]
Table 6-7	Different values of Finite modal operators in English (based on Halliday & Matthiessen 2004:116)
Table 6-8	Different values in the Modal adjuncts or the expansion of the predicators (Halliday & Matthiessen 2004:620).
Table 6-9	Different values realized in the choice of modality in [6-16]
Table 6-10	Different choices from the person system in ST and TTs
Table 7-1	Number of unmarked and marked thematic structures of projection in the aphorisms
Table 7-2	Marked thematic structures in the dialogues
Table 7-3	Shifts of thematic structures in TTs
Table 7-4	Cline of textual equivalence realized in the thematic structure
Table 7-5	Cline of textual equivalence realized in the pattern of thematic progression
Table 7-6	Cohesive methods used in the projecting clauses of the ST and TTs
Table 7-7	Cohesive methods in the dialogues of the ST and TTs
Table 7-8	Cline of texual equivalence realized in the cohesive methods
Table 8-1	Register description of the TTs
Table 8-2	Equivalence and variation in the register of the TTs

List of Abbreviations

SFL	Systemic Functional Linguistics
ST	source text
TT	target text
FDA	functional discourse analysis
SL	source language
TL	target language
LT	Legge's target text
KT	Ku's target text
XT	Xu's target text

Chapter 1
Introduction

1.1 Preamble

The classics, as Calvino (1986:3) points out, are "the books that exert a peculiar influence, both when they refuse to be eradicated from the mind and when they conceal themselves in the folds of memory, camouflaging themselves as the collective or individual unconscious". The *Lunyu* is one of the classics that continue to have great influence upon not only Chinese culture but also many of the myriad cultures spread across the globe. Alfven, who won the Nobel physics prize in 1970, said at an international conference held in Paris that human beings should travel back in time 2500 years in order to learn from Confucius (Gu 2002: 147-148).

The *Lunyu* is regarded as an important way to understand the traditional culture of China and has been rendered into different languages by many translators with disparate backgrounds both at home and abroad. Taking only English translations, up to the present there have been more than 60 translated versions. The first English translation was published in 1691, based on an earlier Latin translation published in 1687. The first complete English version translated directly from Chinese was published in 1861 by Legge (1815—1897), a noted Scottish sinologist whose objective of translation was always "faithfulness to the original Chinese rather than grace of composition" (Legge 1971: vi).

A variety of studies on the *Lunyu* and its translation have been conducted within the frameworks of various disciplines focusing on different research aims (Li & Li 2013; Wang 2006, 2010; Yang 2009), from the perspective of philosophy, hermeneutics and history to the viewpoints of linguistics and translation studies. The perspective taken in this research is that of a linguistics-oriented translation study, focusing on a comparative linguistic analysis of projection in three translated versions of the *Lunyu*, and analyzing the different degrees of equivalence that the three selected translated versions have achieved.

This chapter outlines the reasons for choosing projection in the *Lunyu* and its three translated versions as the focus of this study, and discusses the main research aim and objectives of the study.

1.2 Motivation for the study

The motivation for the current study came from attending the first academic symposium on the translation of the *Lunyu* held on the Zhuhai Campus of Sun Yat-sen University in 2011. During that symposium, many scholars who are experts in the study of the *Lunyu* came together and exchanged their views on translations of the classic Chinese work. This group included experts on philosophy, scholars of translation studies, and specialists in linguistics. Xu Yuanchong, an expert translator of English and French, brought his newly-translated version of the *Lunyu* to the symposium and discussed his views on translating it (Wu 2012). The current researcher's interest in comparative linguistic studies on translated texts was aroused by attending that symposium. It was noted that there are few studies on the grammatical phenomenon of projection that is prevalent in the *Lunyu*. It was decided that Systemic Functional Linguistics (henceforth SFL), as a linguistic theory that has been concerned, among other areas, in the study of translation and comparative text analyses, could serve as the basis for such a study.

Halliday has frequently expounded on the application of comparative descriptive linguistics with regard to translation studies (Halliday 1992, 2001, 2006d, 2009). As Halliday (1992:25) points out, "translation is the guided creation of meaning". In order to interpret and evaluate the translation in question, and to examine the translation equivalence achieved between the source text (henceforth

ST) and the target text (henceforth TT), the researchers should ask "why it is as it is, how it might have been different, and what effect such other choices might have made". Halliday (2001:13) clarifies two groups of professionals who theorize about translation, translators and linguists:

> For a linguist, translation theory is the study of how things are: what is the nature of the translation process and the relation between texts in translation. For a translator, translation theory is the study of how things ought to be: what constitutes good or effective translation and what can help to achieve a better or more effective product. (Halliday 2001:13)

The perspective taken in the present study is that of linguistics. SFL, as a general and appliable linguistics, provides a sound basis for the study of translated texts of the *Lunyu*. A text cannot be judged as effective unless we know what it means. As Halliday (1994a:41) observes, SFL can provide a theoretic support for discourse analysis, which can help analysts understand and evaluate texts, making it possible for them to "say why the text is, or is not, an effective text for its own purposes-in what respects it succeeds and in what respects it fails." The study of the translated texts of the *Lunyu* based on SFL will help to identify and evaluate the meanings conveyed in the different translated versions by studying the choices made by the translators in the different texts. With the guidance of a scientific and systematic theory of language such as SFL, researchers can make a more objective judgment on the translation of the *Lunyu*.

Various studies have explored the *Lunyu* and its English translations from the perspective of SFL. Fang (2006) studies the social-cultural environment of the emergence of the book and discloses its main characteristics as well as the significance of Confucius' values and ethics for the present world with the linguistic analysis of the *Lunyu* at the lexicogrammatical level. Huang (2011) investigates the textual structure of the *Lunyu* from an SFL perspective, with special attention paid to the book's title and chapter headings. Huang (2012b) also discusses the importance of both intralingual translation and interlingual translation in translating ancient Chinese works such as the *Lunyu* into contemporary English. Chen (2009, 2010) discusses the feasibility and appliability of a functional approach to translation studies of the *Lunyu*. There are, however, few studies in the literature to date concerning the phenomenon of projection in the *Lunyu* and its translated texts, something which is prevalent in the text of the *Lunyu* and is a typical characteristic of the quotation style of the text.

Projection has been a topic of interest in many disciplines such as literary studies and stylistics, as well as in linguistics. SFL describes projection as a relationship between clauses, and defines it as "the logico-semantic relationship whereby a clause comes to function not as a direct representation of (non-linguistic) experience but as a representation of a (linguistic) representation" (Halliday 1994a: 250). SFL interprets projection from the perspective of both functional semantics and functional structures (Zeng 2002: 31) and distinguishes different kinds of projection according to whether the structural relationship between the clauses is a paratactic or hypotactic one. In SFL, linguists have also accounted for the interpersonal function expressed through projection and distinguished between the projection of proposition and proposals (Eggins 1994; Hu *et al.* 1989/2008; Thompson 1996b). The study of projection in SFL has developed and deepened in China, extending from the level of clause nexus to the level of discourse (Zeng 2000a, 2000b, 2002, 2003, 2005, 2006a, 2006b, 2007, 2008). There have, however, been few comparative studies on projection in English and Chinese, and few studies on the different realizations of projection in the translated texts, especially in the case of classic Chinese texts and their translations. Can the study of projection in the *Lunyu* and its translated texts based on SFL give new insights to the translation study of the *Lunyu* and broaden the scope of research of translation studies based on SFL? This question is the greatest motivation for the present research.

1.3 Research objectives and research questions

The main aim of this research is to make a comprehensive equivalence study of projection in three translated texts of the *Lunyu* using an SFL framework. In general, this research sets out to investigate how the differing realizations of projection in the different translated texts are related to the different meanings conveyed by projection, and to examine the degrees of equivalence that projection can achieve at the level of semantics as well as the level of context. With a special focus on the study of projection in the translated versions, this book hopes to provide new implications for the translation studies of the *Lunyu* in an SFL framework.

Specifically, translated texts of the *Lunyu* will be observed, interpreted, described, analyzed, explained and evaluated based on the six steps of functional discourse analysis (hence FDA) proposed by Huang (2002a, 2006a). The experiential, logical, interpersonal, and textual meanings conveyed in the ST and the TT will be studied, and equivalence and shifts of projection in ST and TTs will be explored at the level of semantics and context.

Associated with this aim, there are four main objectives to be achieved in this research:

1) To describe the distinctive features of different types and structures of projection in different translated versions of the *Lunyu*;
2) To analyze the metafunctional features of projection in the translated versions and explore the semantic meanings conveyed by the translators with their different lexicogrammatical choices of projection;
3) To explore the different degree of metafunctional equivalence of projection in different translated versions;
4) To evaluate the equivalence of projection in the context of situation and context of culture.

Each of the objectives above is related to a specific research question in the study. The research questions to be answered in this study are as follows:

1) What are the metafunctional features of projection at the level of the lexicogrammar in the different translated versions?
2) How are the metafunctional meanings of projection realized by different types and structures of projection in the different translated versions?
3) What are the varying degrees of metafunctional equivalence of projection achieved in different translated versions?
4) How are the different registers constructed in different translated versions with the different choices of projection and how can the translation quality of projection in different TTs be evaluated in the context of culture?

In this study, we will try to find answers to these four research questions and show how the research objectives can be achieved. The equivalence study of projection will be conducted at the levels of lexicogrammar, semantics, and context. The lexicogrammatical features of projection will be explored and the metafunctional meanings realized by the lexicogrammatical choices will be examined and compared, and the different degrees of metafunctional equivalence achieved by the different translated texts will be analyzed. Based on the study of equivalence at the levels of lexicogrammar and semantics, this study will analyze the different registers constructed in different TTs and the different degrees of equivalence of projection at the level of context.

1.4 Research methodology

This study will be carried out within the framework of SFL. The aim of this research is to provide a comprehensive study of projection in the translated texts of the *Lunyu* so as to shed light upon the phenomenon of projection in translation studies. This study is basically descriptive, comparative and qualitative in nature.

Before evaluating the translated texts, this book will make a discourse analysis of both the ST and the TTs. When researchers analyze discourse linguistically, they usually have two goals: one is "to explain why the text means what it does", the other is to "explain why the text is valued as it is" (Halliday 2001:13). In studying the translated texts, in order to "explain why a text is more, or perhaps less, effective in its context", researchers must first "be able to explain why it means what it is understood to mean" (Halliday 2001:13). In other words, no one can judge whether a translation is good or not unless they know what it means.

The translation analysis in the study also involves the theory of comparative descriptive linguistics. As Halliday (2004) points out, to describe a language meaningfully, it is necessary to base the description on a "consistent and comprehensive theory of language" — descriptive linguistics. In describing the translated texts, we will focus our description on the form of projection at the level of lexicogrammar and then at the level of semantics and context. As Halliday (2004:24) said, "form and context are the principal levels for the statement of meaning; form is the internal aspect of linguistic patterning", and context is the "external aspect", which indicates the relation of the formal items to the situation.

In this study, projection in the translated versions of the *Lunyu* will be analyzed by reference to the three metafunctions at the strata of lexicogrammar and semantics, and the translation quality will be evaluated in the context. The metafunctional equivalence and shifts between the ST and TTs will be described and analyzed, and the equivalence achieved by the different TTs will be evaluated at the level of context.

1.5 Data collection

The data for description and comparison presented in this study come from four sources: the ST and the three TTs which are its translations.

The ST is based on commentaries on the *Lunyu* by Zhu Xi. Zhu was an influential Confucian scholar during the Song Dynasty who wrote commentaries on *the Anlaects, the Mencius, the Great Learning* and *the Doctrine of the Mean (the Four Books)*. These commentaries were widely recognized during his time and are still respected today. The Chinese used in Zhu's commentaries is not punctuated like modern Chinese, which uses quotation marks. However, quotation marks are used in all three of the translated versions of the ST. For the convenience of comparison, the ST of the *Lunyu* is taken from a modern edition given in Yang (2006). The Chinese ST is punctuated based on the understanding of the modernized version's editor, Yang Bojun. This edition also contains an intralingual translation from Classical Chinese to Modern Chinese.

The first translated text analyzed in this study is an English complete translation of the *Lunyu* by Legge (1971). This edition is an unabridged republication of the second revised edition as published by the Clarendon Press, Oxford, in 1893 as Volume I in "The Chinese Classics" series. Legge translated a number of Chinese classics in close collaboration with a Chinese scholar (named Wang Tao) in order to help western missionaries understand Chinese ideas and cultures. His translation has been regarded as a standard, and has had an enormous influence around the world. His translated version of the *Lunyu* has been reprinted many times and has been accorded a high academic value both in the past and at the present (Jin 2009: 45).

The second translated text analyzed in this study is the translation by Ku (1898). Ku was the first Chinese person to translate the Confucian classics into English. He was also the first Chinese person that mastered European science, languages and Sinology. He felt that the interpretations of Western missionaries and sinologists had distorted the meaning of the Confucian classics and thus decided to translate the *Lunyu* himself. Ku was an advocate of monarchy and Confucian values, preserving his queue even after the overthrow of Qing Dynasty. In 1898, Ku published his translation as *The Discourse and Sayings of Confucius*, a version which had great influence in Europe and aroused great interest among scholars within many fields of research. Ku was a talented linguist who commanded excellent skills in speaking and writing in

Chapter 1 Introduction

English, German, French and several other languages. His fluency in English and his familiarity with Chinese culture, his dislike for Legge's translation and his purpose of translation added some special characteristics to his translation of the *Lunyu*, which deserves further exploration.

Another translated text being of vital importance is the translated version by Xu (2005), a well-known literary translator who advocates creative rewriting in his translations. Xu has translated classic Chinese poems into English and French, and has received many awards. He received an award for "lifetime achievements in translation" from the Translators Association of China in 2010, and on August 2, 2014, he won the "Aurora Borealis" Prize at the 20th World Conference of the Federation of International Translators, making him the first Chinese winner of this award. He is in favor of free translation and he has introduced the concept of *Creation for Loss* (Wang 2008) as well as the "three beauties" concept (Chan 2009) to translation theory. He advocates the idea that a translation should be as beautiful as the ST in three ways: semantically, phonologically (rhyme and rhythm) and logically. Xu was in his eighties when he translated the *Lunyu* as *Confucius Modernized, Thus Spoke the Master* (Xu 2005). Such a modernized translation of the Chinese classic translated by the foremost Chinese expert with a unique translation style is certainly worthy of study. Although both Ku and Xu are Chinese translators, they live in different historical periods and their purpose of translation and target readers are also different. That is why the translation of Xu is chosen as the third translated text of this comparative study.

There are up to the present altogether more than sixty different translations of the *Lunyu*. This study has chosen these three particular translations for data analysis specifically because, in prior studies (Hu 2013; Hu & Chen 2013; Hu & Zeng 2012), it is found that the types and structures of projection found in these particular translations vary from one to another.

Due to time and resources constraints, the material to be analyzed includes only the part of the aphorism, that is, the complete dialogues and brief dialogues (which will be explained in Chapter

Four) from Book One to Book Nine in the ST and the corresponding parts in the TTs. The first nine books cover the main types of projection for the purposes of the present study. The part of descriptions in the ST (which contains no examples of projection) and its corresponding parts of translation in the TTs will be excluded from this study.

1.6 Organization of the book

The book is composed of ten chapters. Chapter 1 has offered a general introduction to the motivations of the study, the theoretical framework, the objectives and questions researched, the methodology used and the data collected, and it has also given an introduction to the general arrangement of the study.

Chapter 2 reviews previous studies on projection and on the translation studies within the framework of SFL. Other relevant studies concerning the *Lunyu* and its translation, research into the quotation style of the *Lunyu*, and previous studies of the *Lunyu* and its translation within the framework of SFL are also discussed in this chapter.

Chapter 3 outlines the theoretical background for the study of translation within the framework of SFL, which forms the theoretical basis for this study. It reviews key notions in SFL relevant to the present study, namely, the linguistic parameters defining equivalence: stratification, instantiation, metafunction, and axis. In this chapter, the relevant concepts in SFL related to context and text, register, and theories on projection, are also presented.

Chapter 4 gives a brief introduction to the different types and structures of projection in the ST and TTs. It clarifies the terms used in the present study: projected message, projection clause nexus, and metaphorically realized projection in paragraphs and clauses. The different types and structures of projection in the ST and TTs are then discussed.

From Chapter 5 to Chapter 8, this study concentrates on the description of the texts and the application of SFL theory to analyzing the texts. The descriptions and analyses of projection will be conducted according to the three metafunctions at the levels of lexicogrammar, semantics, and context by studying different lexicogrammatical choices in projection, the different meanings conveyed at the level of semantics, and different influences upon the variables in the context of situation. In these four chapters the ideational, interpersonal, and textual meaning of projection in the translated texts will be inspected and the registers of the different TTs will be explored. In these chapters, the research will move from end-product analysis to a more synthetic and comprehensive analysis of projection in context.

Chapter 9 discusses the main issues related to the equivalence study of projection in the *Lunyu* and its translated texts, as well as the issues raised in Chapters 5 to 8 related to the evaluation of the translated texts based on the analysis of projection from the perspectives of metafunction and of context.

Chapter 10 gives a summary of the whole study and provides a conclusion about the main findings, and implications for current and future research, as well as a reflection on the limitations and insufficiencies of the study. This book concludes by providing some suggestions for follow-up research.

Chapter 2
Literature Review

2.1 Introduction

This chapter begins by reviewing previous studies of projection in different disciplines, as well as prior translation studies within the framework of SFL. Then it will discuss and analyze some other relevant research on the translation of the *Lunyu*, especially on the styles of quotation in it, and the prior studies on the *Lunyu* within an SFL framework.

2.2 Previous studies on projection

Projection, which has been called "reported speech" by linguists from disciplines other than SFL, is an important and "indispensable part in the building up of any human language" (Jacobson 1985:96, cited in Sakita 2002:2). When people want to communicate what is being communicated at the present time, what was said in the past, or what might be said in the future, either by themselves or by some others, they must use projection. Without it, language would be limited in its meaning potential in communication (Coulmas 1985; Sakita 2002). This part will review previous study of projection mainly from the stylistic and linguistic approaches.

2.2.1 Stylistic approaches to projection

The analysis of projection has been a topic of interest for researchers in literary and stylistic studies, which can be traced back to Plato's *Republic* III, in which Socrates is described as making a distinction between mimesis and diegesis. Mimesis, literally "imitation", is used in the sense of direct speech while diegesis, literally "narration", is used for indirect speech. Plato does not give any grammatical definition of direct speech versus indirect speech but this distinction facilitates the emergence of various approaches to the study of projection in literature. In literary works, the writers have always been concerned with this phenomenon and characters' various forms of speech and thought are peculiar features of novels and other literary works.

Stylistics is the "study of the relation between linguistic form and literary function" and as a discipline stylistics applies linguistic concepts to the study of literature (Leech & Short 1981: 1-4). Stylists such as Page (1973) and Leech and Short (1981) have developed the study of projection to cover the various representations of speech and thought in literature.

Page is unsatisfied with the traditional classification of speech into direct and indirect speech and claims that these seemingly simple and clearly-defined categories fail to "accommodate many passages to be found in the work of writers from the eighteenth century onwards" (Page 1973: 24). Page puts forward a more detailed classification of projection in English novels into eight categories: (1) Direct speech: the speech that offers "actual speech" with the "use of quotation marks and other graphological and typographical indications"; (2) Submerged speech: the speech that is "remotest from the original"; (3) Indirect speech: the speech that is "virtual paraphrase"; (4) Parallel indirect speech: the speech that "falls between these two extremes" of indirect speech and coloured indirect speech; (5) Coloured indirect speech: the indirect speech that "preserves many features of the original, including its orthographic variants"; (6) Free indirect speech: the speech which "is characterized by the absence of indication of speaker"; (7) Free direct speech: the speech in which "graphological indications of direct speech" are omitted; (8) Slipping from indirect into direct speech: the speech that "involves a mid-sentence change" from indirect speech to direct speech (Page 1973: 29-35).

Page's classification has been criticized as being too elaborate and complex, with the distinction between different kinds of speech being irregularly arranged (Shen 1991:13-18). Critics have tended to prefer Leech and Short's classification of speech presentation. Leech and Short (1981:324) categorizes the different types of projection under two divisions: "the presentation of speech" and "the presentation of thought". They divide each into five types, according to the interference of the narrator in projection: (1) NRSA / NRTA: it refers to narrative report of speech or thought act and shows the highest degree of interference of the narrator; (2) IS / IT: it refers to indirect speech or thought and shows a lower degree of interference of the narrator than NRSA / NRTA; (3) FIS / FIT: it refers to free indirect speech or thought and shows a lower degree of interference than IS / IT; (4) DS / DT: it refers to direct speech or thought and shows a lower degree of interference than FIS / FIT; (5) FDS / FDT: it refers to free direct speech or thought and shows the lowest degree of interference of the narrator in the five types.

Leech and Short (1981) have discussed the effects of these various presentations of speech and thought in novels. In their opinion, the writers of novels make a conscious or unconscious choice between the various forms available and convey a particular style to the novels. Leech and Short's study of projection, however, focuses its analysis on FIS, FDS and the categories of thought only in literary genres and fails to analyze other genres.

2.2.2 Linguistic approaches to projection

The traditional linguistic approach to projection sees projection as a number of syntactic transformations from direct speech to indirect speech (Baynham 1996: 62): these include pronoun shift, tense shift, mood shift etc. Lyons (1968) shows how traditional linguistics accounts for the features of projection as follows:

> Take for instance a passage such as the following: "The Prime Minister said that he deeply regretted the incident. He would do everything he could to ensure that it did not happen again. On the following day he would confer with his colleagues. He was confident that ... " Once again, passages of this kind are best accounted for in two stages:

first of all, by describing a set of independent sentences in their "direct" form (I deeply regret…; I will do everything I can…; tomorrow I will confer…; I am confident that…) and then, by specifying the secondary grammatical rules that will transpose each of these sentences onto the corresponding "indirect" form when they occur in sequence after a "verb of saying". (Lyons 1968:174)

However, there have been numerous linguistic studies on projection that have extended the traditional understanding of reported speech beyond the syntactic transformation of direct speech into indirect speech, such as Voloshinov's study of projection in discourse (Voloshinov 1978), and Coulmas's study from the perspective of pragmatics (Coulmas 1985). As the current study is in an SFL framework, in the following part, we will mainly review the account of projection in SFL.

Halliday (1994a:250) defines projection as "the logico-semantic relations whereby a clause comes to function not as a direct representation of (non-linguistic) experience but as a representation of a (linguistic) representation" (Halliday 1994a: 250). It is a "resource the grammar offers us for attributing words and ideas to their sources" (Eggins 2004:271). Thompson (1996b: 210) further clarifies the effect of the concept as follows: "the effect of projection comes from this double layer of representation: on the one hand, the language is signaled as, in some sense, not our own; but on the other hand, it clearly differs from the original utterance (even if we quote it verbatim) in that it now incorporated into our present message rather than coming straight from the original source." As Thompson (1996b) explains, projection is a different kind of relationship between clauses from that of expansion, in that the projected clause is always an essential part of the meaning of the whole clause nexus and the meaning of the projected clause may change radically if it no longer stands in a relationship of projection. For example: He repeated, "It's impossible." / It's impossible. The projected clause "It's impossible" in the projection clause nexus realizes different meaning to that of the independent clause of "it's impossible".

Halliday (1994a: 255) distinguishes four basic categories of projection. As Table 2-1 shows, paratactic projection is referred to as "quoting", hypotactic projection is "reporting"; "what is projected verbally" is referred to as a "locution" and "what is projected mentally" is an "idea".

Table 2-1　Four types of projection nexus (Halliday 1994a: 256)

Type of projecting process	Taxis	
	Quote Paratactic 1 2	Report Hypotactic αβ
Locution " verbal	Wording: 1 "2 She said, "I can."	Wording represented as meaning: α "β She said she could.
Idea ' mental	Meaning represented as wording: 1 '2 She thought, "I can."	Meaning: α 'β She thought she could.

Halliday and Matthiessen (2004:443-482) develop the study of projection and identify three aspects involved in the differentiation of projection: (1) the level of projection; (2) the mode of projection; (3) the speech function.

As to the level of projection, projection can be divided into ideas — a representation of the content level of a "mental" clause and locutions — a representation of the content level of a "verbal" clause. As for the mode of projection, combined with the interdependencies between the clauses and the constituency relation of embedding, projection can be divided into paratactic projection of quotes, hypotactic projection of reports and embedding projected clauses. As to the speech function of the projection, the projection can be divided into projected propositions and projected proposals. Halliday and Matthiessen also point out that paratactic projection allows for a greater range of speech functions: we can quote not only propositions and proposals but also minor speech functions such as greetings and exclamations.

According to the above three systemic variables, Halliday and Matthiessen (2004:443-482) recognize the following different types of projection nexus:

(i) Quoting (direct speech, verbal process, parataxis)
   e.g. She said, "Thank God, at least we can do it."
(ii) Reporting (mental process, hypotaxis)
   e.g. She knew that he'd left.
(iii) Reporting speech (verbal process, hypotaxis)
   e.g. He says it needs mending.
(iv) Quoting thought (mental process, parataxis)
   e.g. "The gods must watch out for Kukul," he thought to himself.
(v) Quoting offers and commands
   e.g. I said to Peter, "Don't say anything."
   "You could still apply for it, you know — the managership," Andrew was suggesting helpfully.
(vi) Reporting offers and commands
   e.g. The doctor ordered that all the books and toys must be burned. (verbal reporting of commands)
   He threatened to blow up the city. (verbal reporting of offers)
   She wanted him to go. (mental reporting of proposal)
(vii) Free indirect speech (paratactic, report)
   e.g. Someone once asked Adrian what was the name of his first wife.
(viii) Embedded locutions and ideas
   e.g. the assertion that Caesar was ambitious. (embedded locution)
   The thought of being a queen encouraged her. (embedded idea)
(ix) Facts
   He's trapped by the fact that the river flows south.

Zeng (2000a, 2000b, 2002, 2003, 2005, 2006a, 2006b, 2007, 2008) further develops the study of projection in China. She not only probes projection from the perspective of lexicogrammar and semantics, but also studies projection from the perspective of discourse and investigates how projection functions in discourse analysis. In her study of projection, Zeng characterizes projection not only at the level of clause complex, but beyond the clause complex level as well. Zeng (2006a) identifies the different types of projection in discourse including projection clause nexus, projection clause and projection group or phrase.

Zeng's (2006a) classification of projection describes the different realization of projection at different levels. Her study of projection extends Halliday and Matthiessen's study of projection into the level of clause and has shown how the projection clause and projection group merge into the text. Her study expands and deepens the study of projection in the clause level and the level of discourse.

Other accounts of projection based on SFL can be found in Thompson (1996b), Eggins (1994) and Hu *et al.* (1989/2008). The concept of projection provides SFL with a much broader and more usable way of studying the representation of speech and thought than the traditional understanding of "reported speech" (Thompson 1994). The study of projection is far from complete. The analysis of projection needs to be carried out in texts of various genres, such as the genre of classic Chinese texts and their translations.

2.3 Previous studies on translation in SFL

Translation has long been a subject of interest to translators, linguists, and language teachers, and even to electronic engineers and mathematicians (Catford 1965: vii). Numerous studies on translation have been conducted by researchers from a number of points of view. The following discussion mainly reviews the literature relevant to the present study — the study of translation within the framework of SFL.

2.3.1 Catford's studies of "equivalence" and "shift" in translation

Catford, who takes "the theory of translation" to be a "branch of Comparative Linguistics" (Catford 1965: 20), studies translation within the framework of SFL. Catford attempts to set up a linguistic theory of translation which may be "drawn upon in any discussion of particular translation problems (Catford 1965: vii). His definition of translation is "the replacement of textual material in one language (SL) by equivalent material in another language (TL)" (Catford

1965:20).

He further explains why he uses the term "textual material" in his definition instead of "text" because that term underlines the fact that "in normal conditions it is not the entirety of a SL text which is translated, that is, replaced by TL equivalents" (Catford 1965:20). He goes on to explain the "key term" in the theory of translation—equivalence. He distinguishes between "textual equivalence" and "formal correspondence" as follows:

> A textual equivalent is any TL text or portion of text which is observed on a particular occasion ... to be the equivalent of a given SL text or portion of text. A formal correspondent, on the other hand, is any TL category (unit, class, structure, element of structure, etc.) which can be said to occupy, as nearly as possible, the "same" place in the "economy" of the TL as the given SL category occupies in the SL. (Catford 1965:27)

From this definition we can see that "textual equivalence" is determined based on particular SL and TL texts, while "formal correspondence" is more "generally" (Munday 2001:60) based on the systems of the SL and TL. When "textual equivalence" deviates from "formal correspondence", "shifts" occur. By "shift" Catford means "departures from formal correspondence in the process of going from the SL to the TL" (Catford 1965:73). He illustrates two types of shifts: level shifts and category shifts. "Level shifts" are defined as taking place when "a SL item at one linguistic level has a TL translation equivalent at a different level": level shifts from grammar to lexis, or from lexis to grammar, are the only possibilities in translation. "Category shifts" include the changes of rank (unit shifts), changes of structure (structure shifts), changes of class (class shifts), and changes of term in system (intra-system-shifts).

Catford's research on "translation equivalence" and "shifts" has been praised as a "wonderful contribution" (Matthiessen 2001:43) to the systematic study of translation within linguistics. It also represents one of the most important attempts to study translation within the framework of SFL. However, his analysis of translation has been criticized for relying on examples that are "idealized (i. e. invented and not taken from actual translations) and de-contexualized" and for not investigating "the whole text, nor even above the level of sentence" in his study of equivalence and shifts (Munday 2001:62).

2.3.2 House's model of translation quality assessment

From the mid-seventies, House took a comparative-linguistic approach to the study of translation in designing a model of translation quality assessment (House 1977, 1997). House regards translation as "the replacement of a text in the source language by a semantically and pragmatically equivalent text in the target language" (House 2001:136). In a revised model brought out in 1997, House compares a ST and its TT on the following three levels: the level of Language / Text, Register (Field, Tenor, Mode) and Genre to assess whether the TL is semantically and pragmatically equivalent to the SL.

In her studies, House distinguishes two kinds of translation: overt translation and covert translation. As she points out, STs requiring an "overt translation" have an "established worth in the source language community" and may be "either tied to a specific occasion in which a precisely specified source language audience is / was being addressed or they may be timeless source texts", such as the translation of a political speech made by Winston Churchill after the Second World War, which is tied to a particular source culture, time and historical context, or the translation of various works of literature, which are tied to their source culture (Munday 2001:93). She further explains that a "covert translation" is covert because it is "not marked pragmatically as a translation text of a source text" but may be "created in its own right" (House 2001:140), and the ST is not particularly linked to the ST culture or audience, such as the translation of a tourist information booklet, or a letter from a company chairman to shareholders. The function of a covert translation, as stated by House (1997:114), is to "recreate, reproduce or represent in the translated text the function the original has in its lingua-cultural framework and discourse world".

House's model of translation quality assessment focuses on text. Seeing translation as "a linguistic-textual phenomenon" (House 2001:155), House states that the "primary concern for translation critics" is "linguistic-textual analysis and comparison" (House 2001:155). She argues that the two basic functional components of translation criticism are linguistic analysis and value judgments, the latter of which would be useless without the linguistic analysis, description and explanation based on research (House 2001:156).

House's (1977, 1997) model of translation quality assessment is the first complete translation quality assessment model in the history of translation criticism (Si 2005:84), but there has been criticism of her model. Some researchers have doubted the feasibility of the model by questioning "whether it is possible to recover authorial intention and ST function from register analysis" (Gutt 2000:46-49, cited in Munday 2001:101).

2.3.3 Bell's descriptive study of translation

According to what Manfredi (2014) says, Bell adopts an "SFL model within a cognitive theory of translation, in an attempt to describe the process of translating" (Manfredi 2014:13). Bell (2001) makes a distinction between translation as process, translation as product, and translation as a concept:

1) translating: the process (to translate; the activity rather than the tangible object);
2) a translation: the product of the process of translating (i.e. the translated text);
3) translation: the abstract concept which encompasses both the process of translating and the product of that process. (Bell 2001:13)

Bell emphasizes the importance of studying the translation process by stating that "it is the process which creates the product and it is only by understanding the process that we can hope (if we see ourselves in such a role) to help ourselves or others to improve their skills as translators" (Bell 2001:22). He gives a text-linguistic or social-linguistic explanation for the steps of the process of translation. In his view, translators must understand both the source language (henceforth SL) and the target language (henceforth TL) so as to make meaningful choices in selecting appropriate ways of preserving the semantic and stylistic characteristics of the ST and convey the message in translation. As Bell puts forward in his definition of translation:

> Translation is the expression in another language (or target language) of what has been expressed in another, source language, preserving semantic and stylistic equivalences. (Bell 2001:5)

Bell (2001) suggests adopting a descriptive rather than a prescriptive approach to the study of translation process, claiming that the purpose of translation studies is:

> To reach an understanding of the processes undertaken in the act of translation and, not, as is so commonly misunderstood, to provide a set of norms for effecting the perfect translation. (Bassnett 1980:37, cited in Bell 2001:22)

Bell suggests an objective description of the steps taken by the translators when they are transforming the ST into the TT in the translation studies and tries to set up an objective model for describing translation issues (Wang & Zhang 2001:F26).

As Bell (2001:10-12) defines, prescriptive translation theory is a "normative approach" to the study of translation which sets up a series of "maxims consisting of do's and don'ts" in translation. Bell argues that prescriptive translation theory is like the "rules of etiquette", which tells what people ought and ought not to do in particular circumstance of translation and seeks to constrain the activity of translation. Descriptive translation theory, following Bell, is a set of rules which helps people to understand the translation process. It is "constitutive" instead of being prescriptive and it defines rather constraining the activity of translation.

Bell made " [...] one of the more comprehensive attempts at modeling translation and related phenomena in an overall SFL-based framework" (Steiner 2005: 486). Bell's descriptive approach to the study of translation based on SFL and text linguistics is in accord with the approach taken in the present study of translations of the *Lunyu.*

2. 3. 4 Baker's analysis of thematic structures in translation

Baker (1992:4) states that translation, as a "young discipline", should "draw on the findings and theories of other disciplines in order to develop and formalize its own methods". Baker (1992) uses theories from text-linguistics and pragmatics to explore the key term in translation, equivalence, at different levels: at word level, above word level, at the level of grammar and text. Baker follows this bottom-up approach in her study for pedagogical reasons: as she says, "This book attempts to explore some areas in which modern linguistic theory can provide a basis for training translators and can inform and guide the decisions they have to make in the course of performing their work" (Baker 1992: 5). She discusses problems translators may meet in the process of translation due to lack of equivalence and provides some strategies for translators to deal with the problems.

Although Baker takes a bottom-up approach to the study of translation, she emphasizes the key importance of equivalence at the text level. As she says: "the ultimate aim of a translator, in most cases, is to achieve a measure of equivalence at text level, rather than at word or phrase level" (Baker 1992:112). She draws on Hallidayan and Prague linguists' approach to thematic structure and information structure, and argues that it is essential for translators to understand the effect of thematic choices in a particular language and so be aware of the meaningful choices made in the SL and TL so as to make use of the "thematization devices" available in each language in the process of translation (Baker 1992:129). Translators, as Baker (1992) argues, must be sensitive to the various systems of thematic structure and information structure in the languages they work with, because a failure to appreciate this can result in translation shifts at text level.

Baker's text analysis in the areas of thematic structure,

information structure and cohesion in the translation text shows the potential and value of thematic analysis in studies of translation.

2.3.5 Halliday's views on translation

2.3.5.1 SFL approach to translation

Halliday's study of translation began from his interest in machine translation. Halliday (2004, 2006d) studied the application of linguistics to machine translation and argued for the importance of descriptive and comparative linguistics in translation. Halliday (1992, 2001, 2009) studied issues in the linguistic study of translation and clarified the unique characteristics of linguistic studies of translation and its difference from translators' study of translation.

Halliday (2001) clarifies the different purposes of translation theory from linguists and translators:

For a linguist, translation theory is the study of how things are: what is the nature of the translation process, and what is the relation between texts in translation. For a translator, translation theory is the study of how things ought to be: what constitutes good or effective translation and what can help to achieve a better or more effective product. (Halliday 2001:13)

Linguists' theory of translation is declarative (or indicative) and tends to look at translation systemically, whereas translators' theory of translation is imperative and tends to look at translation instantially (Halliday 1992, 2001). To linguists, the theory of translation is "explanatory and descriptive, and not concerned with guiding principles for those who are translating or interpreting" and it is an "understanding … of the relationships that are set up between languages in translation, and of the processes that are involved when those relationships come to be established" (Halliday 1992:15).

Halliday's systemic functional view of translation regards translation as the "guided creation of meaning" (Halliday 1992:15) and thinks that the purpose of the linguistic study of translation is to set up a model of how this guided creation of meaning is achieved. In his model of interpreting and evaluating the translation text, Halliday studies the conditioning effect of context in establishing the most likely equivalence in translation. In his view, in order to interpret the problem of equivalence, in order to investigate in relation to the translation text "why it is as it is, how it might have been different, and what effect such other choices might have made" (Halliday 1992:25), linguists must "take account of three distinct aspects of the context": "the immediate grammatical environment of the words", "the discourse semantics" of the words and their "construction by the text", and "the situational and cultural context" (Halliday 1992:24) of the text as a whole.

2.3.5.2 Equivalence value in translation

Halliday (2001) defines "equivalence" in translation in respect of three vectors: stratification, rank, and metafunction. He argues that there may be differential values of equivalence according to the different conditions in a specific instance of translation.

As for stratification, he observes that "equivalence at different strata carries differential values": the higher the stratum is, the more value it carries. For example, semantic equivalence is valued more highly than lexicogrammatical and contextual equivalence the highest of all. As for "rank", Halliday states that equivalence at a higher rank carries higher value. For example, clause complex equivalence is valued more highly than clausal, clausal than phrasal and so on. As far as "metafunction" is concerned, Halliday argues that ideational equivalence carries the highest value, as he says:

> As a general rule, "translation equivalence" is defined in ideational terms; if a text does not match its source text ideationally, it does not qualify as a translation, so the question whether it is a good translation does not arise. (Halliday 2001:16)

Halliday argues that in judging if a translation is good, different values attached to equivalence at different ranks, different strata and different metafunctions should be considered. High values are usually given to equivalence at some higher rank and higher stratum, which implies that some variations are allowed in terms of shifts at a lower rank. For example, if contextual equivalence is achieved, semantic or lexicogrammatical equivalence need not be. If the clause complex equivalence is achieved, clausal or phrasal equivalence need not be. As to metafunctions, since the ideational equivalence is a must-be, without which the translation cannot be regarded as a translation (Halliday 2001:16), equivalence in the interpersonal and textual realms should be highly valued and investigated. As Halliday defines: "a good translation is a text which is a translation (i. e. is equivalent) in respect of those linguistic features which are most valued in the given translation context" (Halliday 2001:17). The present study aims to investigate the equivalence of the *Lunyu* with its translation texts by reference to the three vectors Halliday puts forward here, in order to investigate the metafunctional equivalence of SL and TLs at the strata of context and lexicogrammar, in relation to the projection clause nexus.

2.4 Previous studies on the *Lunyu* and its translation

There have been a number of studies on the *Lunyu* within various disciplines (Li & Li 2013; Wang 2006, 2010; Yang 2009). A review of a few such studies will be conducted as follows: first, some of these studies will be reviewed, including the research on some extracts of the ST, on the quotation style of the *Lunyu* and its translations. Because the present study is specifically based on SFL, those studies on the translation of the *Lunyu* in SFL will also be reviewed.

2.4.1 Studies on the *Lunyu* and its translation in various disciplines

Studies of the *Lunyu* have aroused great interest of research in different disciplines. The studies reviewed in this part include research conducted concerning some extracts of the ST, the quotation style of the ST and its translation as well.

Some scholars have used an analysis of some extracts of the ST to study Confucius's views on specific issues. For example, Chang (1997) studies Confucius' views on words and speaking from the perspective of language and social psychology. By studying the text of the *Lunyu*, Chang (1997) finds four principles characterizing

Confucius' views on words and speaking: words define and reflect moral development; beautiful words lacking substance are blameworthy; actions are more important than words; and appropriate speaking relies on rules of propriety. Wu (2009) explores Confucius' ambiguous attitude toward speech by analyzing Confucius' statements about *yán* (言 "speech") and *nìng* (佞 "skillful words"). He finds that although Confucius recognizes the basic importance of speech, he dislikes skillful words and speech and prescribes gentlemen to be cautious and slow in speech.

Some scholars study the extracts of the ST in order to throw light on the personality of Confucius. Harbsmeier (1990) and Olberding (2007) are two examples. Harbsmeier (1990) studies some extracts in the *Lunyu* and concludes that Confucius is a man of humor, with his light-heartedness, self-irony, informal tone, linguistic playfulness, the informal camaraderie between teacher and disciples, and "down-to-earth" style of behavior. Olberding (2007) analyzes the personal style of Confucius as shown in the text and studies its educative function.

Other scholars have also studied certain extracts or key concepts in the ST: for example, Pfister (1986) studies the key concept of *dé* (德 "power") and its philosophical implications; Hsieh and Jen (1991) analyze the concepts of *jūnzǐ* (君子 "great man") and *xiǎorén* (小人 "small man") in the *Lunyu* and groups the specific descriptors of great man and small man into four condensed descriptive categories. They take a transformation approach and clarify the understanding of human behavior presented in ancient Chinese texts; Lim (2012) studies Chapter Twenty-five of Book Six in the sense of Confucian aesthetics, by which Confucius "represents moral values by using image thinking". Xiao (2007) systematically studies the communicative and hermeneutic practices shown in the ST of the *Lunyu*.

Some other researchers have examined the ST from the perspective of literary criticism in relation to the typical quotation style of the *Lunyu*. Some of them point out that the *Lunyu* cannot be regarded as a pure literary work but rather as a record of quotations concentrating on teaching. Some of them argue that the first book of quotation style is the *Lunyu* (Xia 2013: 112). Xia (2013) has studied the formation of the quotation style of the *Lunyu* and argues that *Lunyu* not only records the aphorisms said by Confucius and the dialogues between Confucius and his disciples, but also records Confucius' behavior. Xia argues that the compilation of the *Lunyu* by the disciples and followers of Confucius and the current style of the text is the result of a process of adding, deleting, transferring and recreating on the part of the compilers, which has led to the co-existence of records of aphorisms, dialogues and behavior. Some argue that the style of quotations and dialogues is an important way of conveying Confucius' ideas and thoughts in literature, education, aesthetic life etc. (Yuan 2008) Some studies the quotation style of the *Lunyu* and the Chinese cultural characteristics conveyed by the style. According to Liu (2011), the quotation style, with its typical form zǐ yuē (子曰 "the Master said"), comes out of the historiographer culture and flourishes with the development of private educational institutes. The quotation style of the *Lunyu* indicates a direct judgment without any argument and a unidirectional education with a lack of any questioning spirit from the disciples. By studying the expression style of weī yán dà yì (微言大义 "deep significance with simple words") of the *Lunyu*, Guo (2007) finds that imperative and instructive statements prevail in the *Lunyu*, as a result of the prestigious status of Confucius held in the eyes of his disciples. He argues that in the process of compilation Confucius has been recreated in the image of an immortal and intelligent saint who absolutely controls the process of saying and talking, resulting in the present style of the *Lunyu* in which readers can only read the words of Confucius' instructions with only a few arguments between Confucius and his disciples. Wu (2011) has studied the similarities and differences between the *Lunyu* and *The Dialogues of Plato*. Wu points out that while both have a colloquial style, the difference in style lies in the following parts: Firstly, in *Lunyu*, readers can only perceive the monologue of Confucius in most situations, while in *The Dialogues of Plato*, readers can perceive the dialogues of Plato's Master, Socrates with his students. Secondly, in the dialogues of *Lunyu*, there are no arguments between Confucius and the disciples, but *The Dialogues of Plato* is opposite.

As for studies concerning the translation of the *Lunyu*, previous studies come mainly from reviews of the latest translations. Durrant (1981) reviews the translation of the *Lunyu* by D. C. Lau. Durrant criticizes D. C. Lau's translation for not referring to any "earlier translations or explaining what unique contribution his translation makes to the ever-expanding field of LY studies", for not providing any explanation with footnoting, for unnecessary verbiage, and for the impropriate translation of key terms in the *Lunyu*. According to Durrant (1981: 114), translators have a tendency to neglect the "terse, even cryptic nature" of the original text and fail to capture the "hardy, concrete" style of the *Lunyu*, tending to reduce the characteristics with "prolixity and imprecision". Cheang (2000) reviews four translations of the *Lunyu* translated by Roger T. Ames and Henry Rosemont, Jr., E. Bruce and A. Taeko Brooks, Chichung Huang, and Simon Leys, respectively. According to Cheang, every translation is an act of interpretation. Readers of the translation can hear the translator's voice as well as the original voice of the text. Thus, in the translation of Leys, Confucius speaks in "urbane and equable tones", in Brooks' translation, Confucius speaks like an "aging warrior" and "fussy pedant", Huang's Confucius speaks like a "nineteenth-century schoolmaster: humorless and dogmatic, speaking without expectation of being spoken to in return", while in the translation by Ames and Rosemont, Confucius has no sense of individuality. Cheang also analyses each of the different translators' views of the authenticity of Confucius' sayings. Schaberg (2001) reviews the latest seven translations of the *Lunyu* from the perspective of translation styles, and lexical choices for the key terms. With basically negative comments on the current translations, the writer calls for the introduction of a kind of translation that "combines linguistic, philosophical and historical competence in equal measure, that appeals without pandering, and that does justice to the work's intellectual force without seeking to denature or dilute it" (Schaberg 2001: 139). Littlejohn (2005) reviews the translation by Edward Slingerland and regards as the merits of Slingerland's translation its providing "straightforward and readable translation" and "helpful appendixes" as well as citing the traditional commentators.

Some other scholars have shown interest in the commentaries on the *Lunyu* (Makeham 2003). Makeham (2003) investigates the philosophical issues in the commentaries and the commentators' philosophical agendas and explains "how the commentarial genre has functioned as a medium for philosophical expression" (Makeham 2003:4). Makeham (2006) examines the problems translators and interpreters may be confronted with in the process of interpreting ancient Chinese texts. He gives a heuristic model for understanding the relationship between author, reader / interpreter and text.

2.4.2 Studies on the *Lunyu* and its translation in SFL

As discussed in the previous section, the present study is conducted in the framework of SFL. The following review will focus on studies of the *Lunyu* and its translation which also fall within the framework of SFL.

The first Chinese scholar to study the *Lunyu* in an SFL framework is Fang (2006), who conducted studies over the ST of the *Lunyu*. She examined the characteristics of the social, historical and ideological contexts in which the *Lunyu* came into being, as well as the features of lexicogrammar that realize these contextual features. Based on Halliday's accounts of the levels of language and their relationship of realization among the levels, Fang studies the context of culture and context of situation of the *Lunyu* and their realization at the level of lexicogrammar.

Some other scholars have conducted a series of studies concerning the *Lunyu* and its translation in SFL. Three symposia have been held on the translation of the *Lunyu* (Wu 2012; Xiao & Li 2013; Yang 2014). Huang (2011, 2012a, 2012b, 2013) has examined different translations of the *Lunyu* in the framework of SFL. He argues that the study of the translation of ancient Chinese texts should begin with discourse analysis to analyze the relationship between the meaning and forms of the text (Huang 2011:90). He analyzes the generic characteristics of the *Lunyu* and studies the textual structure of the *Lunyu* based on SFL with special attention paid to the translation of book titles and chapter headings (Huang 2011). He carries out a grammatical analysis of some examples in the translation of the *Lunyu* and studies the methodology of translating ancient Chinese works (Huang 2012a). He finds that most translators prefer "free translation", and argues that one shortcoming of the free translation of ancient Chinese texts is that it may convey to the readers only one interpretation of the original text. He also analyzes extracts from translations of the *Lunyu* and studies the process of translating the ancient Chinese works into modern English (Huang 2012b). He finds that in the process both intralingual and interlingual translation are involved; in other words, translating ancient Chinese into modern Chinese, and translating from modern Chinese into modern English respectively. Huang suggests that the translators should base their translations on previous studies of the *Lunyu* and existing intralingual translations to help convey appropriate meanings in the translated texts. Huang advocates the application of SFL to the study of the *Lunyu* and its translation and tests the appliability and feasibility of SFL in studying the translation of ancient Chinese works into English with his analysis on the ST and TT. The methodology used in the present study is the same as that used in Huang's study.

Other scholars' studies of the *Lunyu* and its translation within the SFL framework are also worthy of mention. Chen (2009, 2010) uses an FDA model in studying the feasibility and appliability of SFL in the study of the *Lunyu* and its translation. She concludes that the six steps of FDA — observation, interpretation, description, analysis, explanation and evaluation — are appliable in the study of the *Lunyu* and its translated texts. She also argues that the purpose of her study is to evaluate the appropriateness of the meaning expressed in the translation based on a comparative study of the form and meaning of the translated texts. Other researchers (Hu 2013; Hu & Chen 2013; Hu & Zeng 2012) have studied the ideational meaning, the interpersonal meaning and textual meaning of the projection clause nexus in the *Lunyu* and its English translations. Some researchers have studied the register equivalence of the *Lunyu* and its different translated texts (Gao 2012). Some analyze and describe cohesion in the *Lunyu* on the phonological, lexical, syntactic and rhetorical level based on Halliday and Hasan's theory of cohesion (Wang 2013). Some have used Appraisal theory to compare the interpersonal meaning in the *Lunyu* and its English translations (Han 2008; Lang 2009; Yu 2013). Others, for example Qi (2011), have studied the *Lunyu* and its English translation from the perspective of the three metafunctions of language to see whether the translation has achieved equivalence of the ideational meaning, interpersonal meaning and textual meaning with the ST.

The topic of reporting clauses in the *Lunyu* has begun to arouse scholarly interest. Du (2009) has made a comparative study of reporting verbs in the *Lunyu* and its translations and studies the motives of the translators through their choice of reporting verbs. Huang (2013) analyzes reporting clauses in Chapter Fourteen of the *Lunyu* and its English translations with the aim of showing that "even the analysis of a single example from the *Lunyu* can provide implications for translation studies within SFL framework" (Huang 2013: 256). Through an analysis and description of the lexicogrammar of the translations, the roles taken by participants in the dialogue, the different choice of reporting verbs, and the different realization of the relationship between reporting clause and reported clause, Huang argues that a comparative study of different translations from an SFL perspective can offer a great deal to the study of the translated versions of the *Lunyu* and other classic Chinese works.

However, studies on the *Lunyu* and its translations still need further investigation. Huang (2013) also suggests that certain areas should be the focus of further study from an SFL perspective, such as the analysis of the text from the perspective of three-metafunctions, and analysis concerning cohesion devices and coherence achieved in the text. The prevailing projection in the *Lunyu* lacks a comprehensive study on its translations from an SFL standpoint.

2.5 Summary

This chapter has reviewed studies on projection from different disciplines, studies of translation within the SFL framework, and previous studies on the *Lunyu* and its translation. It is clear that the study of the *Lunyu* has aroused great scholarly interest both at home and abroad. A great number of studies have been conducted within the framework of SFL, but there have been only a few systemic functional translation studies on projection in the *Lunyu*. The appliability of SFL in the translation studies needs to be developed from different perspectives, which is the primary reason this book has chosen the study of projection as its research focus.

Chapter 3
Theoretical Framework

3.1 Introduction

As the present study is a translation study based on SFL, this chapter will be devoted to an outline of the basic linguistic parameters used to define equivalence in SFL so as to pave the way for the equivalence study of projection in the *Lunyu* and its translated versions. It will begin by introducing SFL as a general and appliable theory and then the parameters of equivalence in SFL will be introduced. The chapter will end by constructing a model in order to conduct the equivalence study of projection in the translated texts of the *Lunyu*.

3.2 SFL as the theoretical framework of the present study

The present study has chosen SFL as the theoretical framework based on a number of considerations. First, SFL is a general and appliable linguistics. As Huang (2007) observes, SFL is a general linguistics which attempts to develop theories explaining general universal regularities of language. Halliday has also called himself "a general linguist" (Halliday 2006e). SFL is a general linguistics which studies how language functions in society, and its research target is the natural human languages, including Chinese, English, French, German, Russian, Italian, Japanese and so on (Huang 2006b, 2007). According to Halliday (2006e: 13), it is important for a linguist to have a clear picture of what language in general is and how it works, not just of a particular language. As a general linguistics, SFL can not only be used in the study of particular languages, but also in comparative study of different languages, such as of the source and target language in translation, which is the focus of the present study.

Halliday (2006e) also states that SFL is appliable as follows:

> appliable rather than applicable, because the word "applicable" refers to one particular purpose, whereas "appliable" means having the general property that it can be put to use in different operational context. (Halliday 2006:19)

To Halliday, one of the main purposes of establishing SFL is "to create a theory for solving a range of problems faced by potential 'consumers' of linguistics" (Coffin 2001: 94, cited in Huang 2006b: 2). Here, the "range of problems" includes various issues concerning language and its usage and certainly includes the issue of translation studies. According to Huang (2002b), there have been numerous studies applying SFL in the translation studies, and the marriage of SFL and translation studies has become an important focus of research in a number of Chinese universities (Huang 2002b: 287).

The second reason to choose SFL as the theoretical framework is because of SFL's "functional" and "semantic" theory of language. SFL is basically "functional and semantic rather than formal and syntactic in orientation" (Halliday 1994b:4505; Halliday 2006a:433). It studies the "text" rather than the "sentence"; it focuses on "use" and "usage" rather than "grammaticality" (Halliday 2006b:433). It is "a functional grammar...that is pushed in the direction of the semantics" (Halliday 1994a: F45) and it is "meaning-oriented".

To systemic linguists, language is a "resource for making meaning", organized according to systems, each of which represents a set of choices (Halliday 1994a; Huang 2007). Translation means re-construing meaning in one system into meaning in another system. "Translation" is not a passive reflection of the original, but a creative act of re-construing the meanings of the ST as meanings in the TT (Matthiessen 2001: 64). The functional and semantic approach to language in SFL fits well with the requirements of the present study. Below the primary notions of SFL related to the study of equivalence in translation will be introduced in turn.

3.3 The linguistic parameters defining equivalence

As a general and appliable linguistic theory, SFL defines and studies translation from a linguistic viewpoint. Based on the understanding of language as a meaning-making system, SFL regards translation as a semantic transformation of the ST into the TT (Matthiessen 2001:73). In understanding equivalence in translation, SFL introduces six relevant linguistic parameters: "stratification, instantiation, rank, metafunction, delicacy, and axis" (Halliday 2009: 19). As Halliday remarks:

> These six dimensions — stratification, instantiation, rank, metafunction, delicacy and axis — are critical to any comparison of two or more different languages and hence to the process of translation, because they are the parameters that define equivalence (and therefore also non-equivalence, or shift). (Halliday 2009:19)

The linguistic study of equivalence can be conducted on any of these six dimensions. But as Halliday admits, it is impossible to "give an overall measure of equivalence" in these six dimensions because equivalence is "of so many different kinds". The different linguistic parameters for equivalence relevant to the current study will be introduced below.

3.3.1 Instantiation

Instantiation is a "move between the system and the instance" (Halliday 2005a: 352). As Halliday (2005a, 2006c) points out, language as system and language as instance are the same phenomenon seen by different observers from different perspectives. Language as system is an abstract potential and a pattern formed by the instances. Spoken and written texts are instances of language in use. Halliday explains the relationship between instance and system using the analogy of weather and climate:

the instance-observer is the weatherman, whose texts are the day-to-day weather patterns displaying variations in temperature, humidity, air pressure, wind direction and so on, all of which can be observed, recorded and measured. The system-observer is the climatologist, who models the total potential of a given climatic zone in terms of overall probabilities. What appears to the former as a long-term weather pattern becomes for the latter a defined climatic system. (Halliday 2006c:82)

In other words, instantiation is the relation of system to text. Text is the instantiation of systemic potential and system is the text potential that is instantiated in text. The instance keeps the potential alive, reinforcing it and challenging it and changing it. Text and system form a "complementarity" (Halliday 2008:83).

The cline of instantiation is one of "the global dimensions in the organization of language in context" (Matthiessen et al. 2010:122). The importance of the cline of instantiation lies in its defining the "domains of observation, analysis, description and theory in scientific engagement with language" (Matthiessen et al. 2010:123). Systemic functional linguists observe and analyze texts in their context of situation: at the instance pole of the cline of instantiation, they examine instances and based on the analysis of these instances, they can move further along the cline of instantiation towards the potential pole, to the a text type or the register, until they reach the whole semiotic system being studied. The cline of instantiation in context and language is shown in Table 3-1 below.

Table 3-1 Cline of instantiation in context and language (Matthiessen et al. 2010:123)

	Potential	Sub-potential	Instance type	Instance
Context	context of culture (cultural potential)	Institutional (sub-cultural) sites	situation types	contexts of situation
Language	language system (meaning potential)	register	text types	Texts (acts of meaning)

Translation, as Matthiessen (2001:87) observes, is located at the instance pole of the cline of instantiation as we translate texts in one language into texts into another: we do not translate one language into another language. When texts are usually translated as instances of the overall linguistic system they instantiate, the translation of an instance always "takes place in the wider environment of potential that lies behind the instance" (Matthiessen 2001:87).

3.3.2 Stratification

In SFL, stratification refers to "the way a language is organized as a hierarchy of strata" (Halliday 2009:17-18). The strata in the organization of language are semantics, lexicogrammar, phonology (graphology) and phonetics; context is interpreted as a stratum above language (Matthiessen *et al.* 2010:205). Following Hjelmslev (1943) and Martin (1992), the stratal organization of language includes two general planes: the content plane and the expression plane. Stratification takes place in the content plane as well as the expression plane. The content plane can be further stratified into the strata of semantics and lexicogrammar. The expression plane can be further stratified into the strata of phonology and phonetics. Patterns of experience and social relationships are transformed into meaning: that is the stratum of semantics. The meaning is further transformed into wording: that is the stratum of lexicogrammar. (Halliday & Matthiessen 2004:25)

Realization is "the relationship among the strata", linking one stratum with another (Halliday & Matthiessen 2004:26). For example, the stratum of semantics is realized by the stratum of lexicogrammar and the stratum of lexicogrammar is realized by the stratum of phonology. In other words, meanings are realized as wordings, wordings realized as sounds (Halliday 2005a:352). Halliday and Matthiessen (2004:25) provide a model of stratification as in Figure 3-1.

Chapter 3   Theoretical Framework

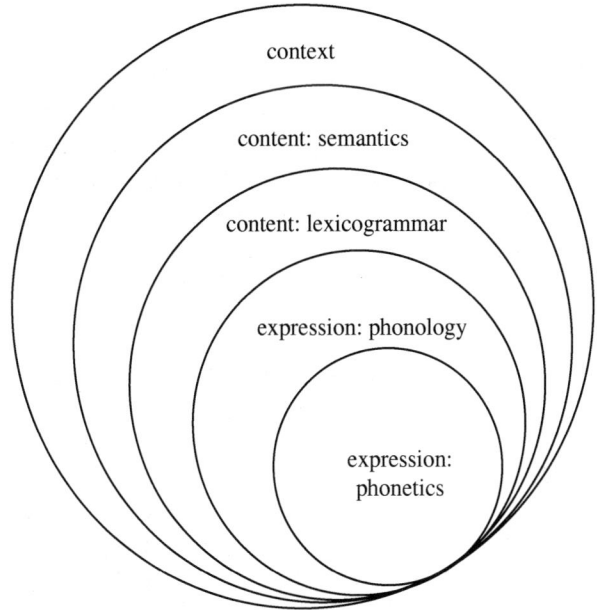

Figure 3-1   Stratification (Halliday & Matthiessen 2004 : 25)

In the current study of the *Lunyu* and its translations, we focus our study on the strata of context, semantics and lexicogrammar. As observed by Matthiessen (2001:89), "while translation can be located at one end of the cline of instantiation, it cannot be located only at one stratum along the hierarchy of stratification". Translation takes place along the strata of lexicogrammar, the strata of semantics and the strata of context. The relationship between translation and the hierarchy of stratification is "largely a question of what we try to keep as constant as possible and what we allow to vary" (Matthiessen 2001:89), because "the nature of translation changes depending on where we locate translation along the hierarchy of translation" (Matthiessen 2001:89). In the usual case, a "free" translation aims to translate texts at the strata of semantics and the strata of context and keep the meaning constant at the stratum of context, while a "literal" translation aims to keep constant the patterns of wording at the stratum of lexicogrammar. This phenomenon will be further illustrated in Chapter 4.

3.3.3 Metafunction

Metafunction is an important dimension of SFL theory. It is "one of the basic concepts" around which SFL theory is constructed (Halliday 1994a:35). In SFL, language is conceived as a "source of meaning potential" (Halliday 1994a:16), and the different "modes of meaning construed by the grammar" are referred to as "metafunctions" (Matthiessen & Halliday 2009:52). The notion of metafunctions refers to the "highly generalized functions" (Halliday & Matthiessen 2008:7) that language evolved to serve: the ideational metafunction, which is further divided into the experiential and the logical metafunction; the interpersonal metafunction; and the textual metafunction. These can be regarded as "the functional components of the semantic system of a language" (Halliday & Hasan 1985:29).

The three metafunctions in SFL are of equal status, none of them is regarded as more important, and each is manifested in every act of language use. They operate simultaneously in the clauses. Any text in a language represents a combination of choices from the grammatical systems that realize all these three functions, i.e. Transitivity, Mood and Theme.

In analyzing the meaning of the clause, we should take account of all three dimensions together to get complete understanding of the meaning. The three modes of meaning are simultaneously embodied in the structure of the clause. Each contributes "equally to the meaning of the message as a whole", and each of the three types of meaning is "typically expressed by a different aspect of the wording of the clause" (Thompson 1996b:30). The "matching of particular types of functions or meanings with particular types of wording" (Thompson 1996b:30) makes SFL an appliable theory in the sense of "exploring how meanings are created and understood" (Thompson 1996b:30).

In the present study, we will examine the ideational metafunction, the interpersonal metafunction and the textual metafunction in the ST and TTs of the *Lunyu* in order to investigate the degree of equivalence achieved between the ST and the different TTs.

3. 3. 3. 1 Ideational metafunction

The ideational metafunction refers to the "grammatical resource for **construing** our experience of the world around us and inside us" (Matthiessen & Halliday 2009: 54, original emphasis). There are "two modes of construing experience within the **ideational metafunction**" (Matthiessen et al. 2010:132, original emphasis), one of which is referred to as experiential metafunction and the other is the logical metafunction.

The experiential metafunction refers to the function of language used to construe human experience. The system of grammar that realizes the experiential metafunction is the Transitivity system, which "construes" the "experience of change in the form of a **process configuration**" (Halliday & Matthiessen 2008: 512, original emphasis). It is about "the type of process expressed in the clause, with the participants in this process, animate and inanimate, and with various attributes and circumstances of the process and the participants" (Halliday 2005b:7).

The logical metafunction refers to the function of language used to "set up logical relationships between one clausal unit and another" (Halliday 2006b: 17). The systems which come under the logical metafunction are those of Taxis and Logico-semantic relationships. The system of Taxis construes the degree of interdependency between clauses in terms of two variables: parataxis, where the relation between two elements of equal status; and hypotaxis, the relation between two elements of unequal status, a dependent element and its dominant.

The system of logico-semantic relationships construes two kinds of logical relationships between clauses: one of which is "expansion", in which "the two processes are of the same order of experience and the second one is interpreted as in some respect expanding on the first"; the other of which is "projection", in which "the second process is construed as belonging to a different order of experience: it is projected, by the first one, on to the semiotic plane" (Halliday & Matthiessen 2008:520).

The system of interdependency and the system of logico-semantic relations is shown in Figure 3-2 below.

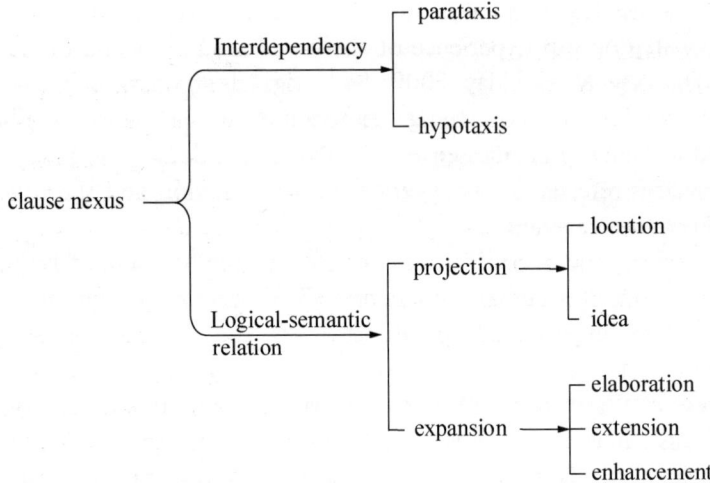

**Figure 3-2 Systems of Interdependency and Logico-semantic relations
(based on Matthiessen & Halliday 2009: 71)**

3.3.3.2 Interpersonal metafunction

The interpersonal metafunction refers to "the interaction between speaker and addressee(s) — the grammatical resources for **enacting** social roles in general, and speech roles in particular, in dialogic interaction; i.e. for establishing, changing, and maintaining interpersonal relations" (Matthiessen & Halliday 2009: 53, original emphasis). The main sytems of grammar realizing the interpersonal metafunction are Mood and Modality.

In the interactive event, there are two basic speech roles: giving and demanding; and two basic types of commodity being exchanged: goods and services or information. The clause takes on the different forms of a proposition or a proposal depending on the commodity that language is used to exchange. These two variables, taken together, define the four primary speech functions of language: offer, command, statement and question.

Chapter 3 Theoretical Framework

Mood[①] is the main grammatical system that realizes the different speech functions in language. It constructs the clause either as a "proposition" (statement or question) or as a "proposal" (offer or command), each of which is assigned either positive or negative polarity. The elements in the Mood structure, which consists overall of Mood and Residue, realize the interpersonal metafunction of a clause. The Mood consists of the Subject and the Finite. Subject is a nominal group that is responsible for "the functioning of the clause as an interactive event" (Halliday 1994a:76) and "the validity of the information" in a proposition rests on the Subject chosen. The Finite is part of a verbal group which not only expresses the primary tense of the clause but also realizes the modality and the polarity features of the clause (Halliday 1994a:75). The variable selection and order of the Subject and the Finite realizes different types within the system of Mood.

Modality is another important system expressing the interpersonal meaning of a clause. The system of modality constructs the validity of clauses located between positive and negative poles. The validity of propositions is defined along the dimensions of "probability: ' possibly / probably / certainly ' " and " usuality: ' sometimes / usually / always ' ", collectively known as modalization. The validity of proposals is defined along the dimensions of " obligation: ' allowed to / supposed to / required to ' " and "inclination: ' willing to / anxious to / determined to ' ", collectively known as modulation (Halliday & Matthiessen 2004:147).

Other grammatical resources that construct the interpersonal meaning include "expressions of attitudes" and "numerous forms of personal address and reference (kinship terms, personal names, honorifics, endearments, insults and the like) (Halliday & Matthiessen 2008:527). The vocatives and person system can also construe

---

[①] This "Mood" refers to "the primary interpersonal system of the clause — the grammaticalization of the semantic system of SPEECH FUNCTION" (Halliday & Matthiessen 2004:113). It is written as MOOD in Halliday & Matthiessen (2004:113) to distinguish from the Mood referring to "an element of the interpersonal structure of the clause (Mood + Residue...)"

interpersonal meaning in the clause, as will be discussed in Chapter 6.

3.3.3.3 Textual metafunction

The textual metafunction of language refers to "language used to create a coherent text" (Halliday 2006a: 435). The textual metafunction of language has an "enabling role" in language, without which neither ideational nor interpersonal metafunction would make sense.

The textual metafunction of language encompasses the systematic resources a language has for creating coherent texts, coherent with both "the context of situation and other instances of text" (Halliday & Matthiessen 2008: 528): in relation to the clause this includes the system of Theme, involving choices relating to the ordering of elements in the clause, while in relation to the text this includes the system of Cohesion, including reference, ellipsis, conjunction and lexical cohesion.

The thematic choice in a clause or clause complex is a very important factor in developing the textual meaning of a text. The Theme system offers the choices "about what meanings to prioritize in a text, what to package as familiar and what as new, what to make contrastive"(Eggins 2004:320) and contributes to the "communicative effect of the message" (Eggins 2004: 299) in the development of a text.

Patterns of thematic progression also realize textual meanings in discourse. Researchers in SFL have studied the thematic structure and summarized in their research the main patterns of thematic progression (Bloor & Bloor 1995: 89-94; Eggins 2004: 324; Huang 1988: 80-85; Zhu & Yang 2001: 96-115). Following Bloor and Bloor (1995: 90), there are four main patterns of thematic progression in the texts: the Constant Theme pattern, the Linear Theme pattern, The Split Rheme Pattern, Derived Theme pattern.

Table 3-2 Patterns of thematic progression (based on Bloor & Bloor 1995: 90-92)

Patterns of thematic progression	Features of the pattern
Constant Theme pattern	Common Theme is shared by each clause
The Linear Theme pattern	The Rheme of one clause is taken up as the Theme of the subsequent clause
The Split Rheme pattern	The Rheme of a clause has two components, each of which is taken in turn as the Theme of a subsequent clause
The Derived Theme pattern	where two or more independent Themes alternate within the text

Cohesion is another textual lexicogrammatical resource. The different methods of creating cohesion in text include " (i) conjunction, (ii) reference, (iii) ellipsis and (iv) lexical organization" (Halliday & Matthiessen 2004:533). The study of the kinds of the cohesive methods in a text can show the characteristics of the different texts.

3.3.4 Axis

The "hierarchy of axis" refers to "the distinction between **paradigmatic organization** and **syntagmatic organization**, the distinction between choice and chain, in simple terms" (Matthiessen et al. 2010:61, emphasis in original).

The syntagmatic organization of language is modeled as "structure": what comes together with what. The paradigmatic organization of language is modeled as "system": what could have come instead, what are the other options that might have come but did not. SFL linguists give priority to the paradigmatic relations of language. For SFL linguists, the underlying organization at each level of language is paradigmatic and each level is "a network of paradigmatic relations, of Ors — a range of alternatives" (Halliday 1978:40).

The two axes of system, or paradigmatic organization, and structure, or the syntagmatic organization, are complementary in language. As Halliday (2009:19) puts it, the meaning of any element in language is the product of relations on both the axes. But, as Halliday (2009:19) observes, the paradigmatic axis is what defines the "translation potential" because it involves relations with things that are not present in the particular instance.

In our present study, we will focus on both axes of structure and system, but with more emphasis put on the paradigmatic organization of language. We will try to find the reasons underlying the choices made by the translator among the system of translation potentials.

3.4　Translation as recreation of meaning through choice

Translation, as defined by Matthiessen (2014: 271), is the "**recreation of meaning in context through choice** — choice in the interpretation of the original text and choice in the creation of the translated text."

Choices are made by translators from the meaning potentials of both the ST and the TT in the process of translating. Different translators are likely to make different choices among the alternatives in the meaning potential and hence to convey different meaning in the target texts. The different choices made in the target texts can reflect the different interpretations by the translators of the ST. Different choices made by translators in the process of translating will lead to "shifts in meaning" (Matthiessen 2014: 271) but as Matthiessen puts forward, the shifts are "a matter of degree" (Matthiessen 2014: 271). Some shifts are fairly small while other shifts can be massive.

In SFL, people understand texts in terms of their overall understanding of the following different modes of meaning: logical meaning, experiential meaning, interpersonal meaning, and textual meaning. From this point of view, Matthiessen (2014:277) explains how translators interpret the meanings contained in the ST and reconstrue them in the TT:

> In terms of **logical** meaning, translators choose how to interpret logical-sematic relations used in forming "coherent" source texts, and they choose among the

options in the target language to reconstrue them in the translation they are producing.

In terms of **experiential** meaning, translators choose how to interpret events as configuration of elements (processes, participants and circumstances) and target "chunks" of experience made up of events such as episodes and procedures, and they choose among the options in the target language to reconstrue the **experiential** meanings in the translation they are producing.

In terms of **interpersonal** meaning, translators choose how to interpret propositions, proposals and the assessments associated with them in the exchange of meaning embodied in the source text, and they choose among the options in the target language to **re-enact** the interpersonal meanings in the translation they are producing.

In terms of textual meaning, translators choose how to interpret messages and the sequences of messages that create the flow of information in the source text, and they choose among options in the target language to **re-present** the textual meanings in the translation they are producing.

A translated text, according to Matthiessen (2014:277-278), is a combination of choices made from the logical, experiential, interpersonal and textual systems. All these choices are made "in the environment of other linguistic choices, and also in the environment of the **context** in which the source text operates and in which the text being translated will operate" (Matthiessen 2014:279).

When we examine the choices made by translators among the metafunctional modes of meaning, we will find various degrees of equivalence and shifts between the metafunctional meanings of the ST and the target texts. We can analyze whether "the translated text is experientially equivalent, logically equivalent, interpersonally equivalent, and / or textually equivalent" (Huang 2013:265). In the present study, the different degrees of equivalence achieved will be analyzed and compared in the context of different target texts.

3.5　The study of equivalence in context

3.5.1　The context-metafunction hook-up

The terms "context of situation" and "context of culture" were first introduced by the anthropologist Bronislaw Malinowski. Malinowski regarded context of situation as "the environment of the text" and context of culture as "the whole cultural history behind the participants" (Malinowski 1935, cited in Halliday & Hasan 1985: 6-7). He claimed that these two notions play important parts in the adequate understanding of the texts. The linguist J. R. Firth developed this concept of context and claimed that "all linguistics was the study of meaning and all meaning was function in a context" (Halliday & Hasan 1985:8). Firth extended the notion of context of situation to the "more general issue of linguistic predictability" (Eggins 1994:51-52): from describing the context, people can predict what language will be used; and from the language used, people can predict the context in which the language is used.

Following the tradition of Firth, Halliday correlates "the organization of language itself (the three types of meanings it encodes)" and "specific contextual features" (Eggins 1994:52) and points out the relationship between them:

> There is a correlation between the categories of the situation and those of the semantic system, such that, in general terms, the field is reflected in the experiential meanings of the text, the tenor in the interpersonal meanings, and the mode in the textual meanings. We could express this the other way round by using a complementary metaphor and saying that experiential meanings are activated by features of the field, interpersonal meanings by features of the tenor, and textual meanings by features of the mode. (Halliday & Hasan 1985:29)

What Halliday refers to as "context of situation" is the immediate context in which the text is produced: such as the relevant elements concerning the setting in which the text takes place, the relationship between the participants etc. The context of situation is described in terms of the three variables in it: Field, Tenor and Mode. The Field is realized in the experiential meanings, which are realized in the lexical choices in the vocabulary, in the transitivity structures in the grammar, etc.; the Tenor is realized in the interpersonal meanings, which are realized in the lexicogrammatical features of mood, modality and person etc.; the Mode is realized through the textual meanings, which are realized and reflected in the lexicogrammatical features of theme, information and cohesive relations etc. The reasons why people make specific choices in the text can also be explained by the study of context of situation: this is the so-called "the context-metafunction hook-up hypothesis": the high probability of correlation between features of context and the linguistic metafunction (Hasan 1995: 223, cited in Bowcher 2013: 320). As Figure 3-3 shows:

SITUATION Feature of the context	Realized by	TEXT Functional component of semantic system
Field of discourse (what is going on)		Experiential meanings (transitivity, naming, etc.)
Tenor of discourse (who are taking part)		Interpersonal meanings (mood, modality, person, etc.)
Mode of discourse (role assigned to language)		Textual meanings (theme, information, cohesive relations)

Figure 3-3   Relation of the text to the context of situation
(Halliday & Hasan 1985:26)

There is a two-way relationship between language and situation in that "the situation in which linguistic interaction takes place gives the participants a great deal of information about the meanings that are being exchanged, and the meanings that are likely to be exchanged" (Halliday & Hasan 1985:10), and at the same time, "the meanings that are being made by the language will give the participants a great deal of information about the kind of situation they are in." (Halliday & Hasan 1985:55)

In Halliday's model of context (Halliday 1978; Halliday & Hasan 1985), context is a complete level above language that includes the context of situation and the context of culture, which stand for the two poles of the continuum of instantiation. The context of situation is located at the instantial point and represents the immediate situation in which the text takes place; while the context of culture is located at the potential point and represents a more abstract level of context which potentially controls the use of language. Context of culture, following the terms of Eggins, is a context that gives "purpose and meaning" (Eggins 1994:30) to a text.

We can understand the relationship between the context of situation, the context of culture and the text from the following statements by Halliday 1991 cited in Matthiessen (1993:271)

> I have suggested that the context for the meaning potential — for language as a system — is the context of culture... The context for the particular instances — for language as processes of text — is the context of situation. And just as a piece of text is an instance of language, so a situation is an instance of culture. So there is a proportion here. The context for an instance of language (text) is an instance of culture (situation). And the context for the system that lies behind each text (language) is the system which lies behind each situation — namely, the culture...

3.5.2 Register

The language we use varies according to the situation. Register in SFL is defined as the "clustering of semantic features according to situation type" (Halliday 1978:68) and variation "according to use" (Halliday & Hasan 1985:41).

Halliday proposed that the register is determined by "the semiotic features of the situation", and the three variables in the context of situation are realized in actual texts:

Chapter 3   Theoretical Framework

The semiotic features of the situation activate corresponding portions of the semantic system, in this way determining the register, the configuration of potential meanings that is typically associated with this situation type, and becomes actualized in the text that is engendered by it. (Halliday 1978:117)

Register, is "an intermediate level" between the "semiotic properties of the context" and the "semantic properties of texts" (Halliday 1978: 110). The notion of register is "a form of prediction" (Halliday 1978: 32): by identifying the register, we can identify "the context from which they come and the linguistic features which are typical of that context" (Thompson 1996b:36).

In SFL, the context of situation is correlated with language by the mechanism of "functional diversification: field and the ideational metafunction correlate, tenor and the interpersonal one, and mode and the textual one" (Halliday 1978, cited in Matthiessen 1993:229). A register is thus multifunctional — as Matthiessen (1993: 229) states: "any register is simultaneously ideational, interpersonal, and textual".

The ideational aspect of a register construes a Field: Field is concerned with "what is happening", "the nature of the social action that is taking place: what is it that the participants are engaged in, in which the language figures as some essential component" (Halliday & Hasan 1985:12). Field can also be regarded as the focus of the activity in which the text is involved or the social activity type of the text (Eggins 1994). It is realized in the transitivity system that realizes the ideational meanings of the text as well as in lexical choices.

The interpersonal aspect of a register construes a Tenor: Tenor is concerned with "who is taking part" and "the nature of the participants, their statuses and roles: what kinds of role relationship obtain among the participants, including permanent and temporary relationships of one kind or another, both the types of speech role that they are taking on in the dialogue and the whole cluster of socially significant relationships in which they are involved" (Halliday & Hasan 1985:12). Poynton has proposed that Tenor can be divided into "three different continua: **power, affective involvement,** and **contact**" (Poynton 1985, cited in Eggins 1994: 64). The roles and statuses of the participants can be seen "as a complex of these three simultaneous dimensions" (Eggins 1994:64).

The textual aspect of a register construes a Mode: Mode is concerned with "part the language is playing, what it is that the participants are expecting the language to do for them in that situation: the symbolic organization of the text, the status that it has, and its function in the context, including the channel (is it spoken or written or some combination of the two?) and also the rhetorical mode, what is being achieved by the text in terms of such categories as persuasive, expository, didactic, and the like" (Halliday & Hasan 1985:12).

Register can both be placed along the continuum of potentiality and instantiation. Viewed from the instantial point, a register can be regarded as "a generalization about recurrent patterns across instances"; while viewed from the potential point, a register can be regarded as a "variation within this potential" (Matthiessen 1993: 271). The relationships among the text, register and context can be seen in Table 3‑3:

Table 3-3 Relationship among the text, register and context (based on Teich 2001:213)

Stratification	Instantiation		
	System	**Subsystem / Instance type**	**Instance**
context	culture	institution / situation type	situation
semantics	semantic systems	register / text type	texts (meanings)
lexicogrammar	grammatical systems	register / text type	texts (items)

3.5.3 Equivalence study based on FDA

"Equivalence" is a "central concept" in translation studies (Chesterman 1989) which has been regarded as the ultimate purpose and "a clear aim" of translation (Yallop 2001:241). However, there is no absolute equivalence or absolute non-equivalence in the translation: the issue of equivalence is always "a matter of 'more or less'" (Halliday 2009:24). Yallop (2001:242) explains that there is no ultimate guarantee of equivalence in a world in which everything is unique; what we encounter in translations are merely similarities.

FDA — functional discourse analysis — refers to the kind of discourse analysis based on the theoretical methodology of SFL (Huang 2001, 2002a, 2006a; Chen 2009, 2010). It is similar to the term "systemic text analysis" (Eggins 2004) but has a wider coverage than systemic text analysis. The FDA approach has been used in translation studies and testified the appliability of SFL in the study of translations (Huang 2006a, 2011, 2012a, 2012b, 2013; Chen 2009, 2010; Hu 2013). The FDA approach to translation studies has the following six steps: observation, interpretation, description, analysis, explanation and evaluation (Huang 2001, 2002a, 2006a).

The activity of translating takes place at the level of discourse (here text) and the analysis and judgment of equivalence of translating should also be based on the level of discourse (text). In translation the ST and TT stand in a comparative relation, the comparison of which depends on a description and analysis of the texts. To understand the meaning conveyed by the translators in the TTs with their different choice in translation is the first step in the present translation study of *the Lunyu* and its translations. This is in accordance with the first level of achievement in the functional discourse analysis. As Halliday (1994a:F41) points out:

> In any piece of discourse analysis, there are always two possible levels of achievement to aim at. One is a contribution to the understanding of the text: the linguistic analysis enables one to show how, and why, the text means what it does. In the process, there are likely to be revealed multiple meanings, alternatives, ambiguities, metaphors and so on. This is the lower of the two levels; it is one that should always be attainable provided the analysis is such as to relate the text to general features of the language — provided it is based on a grammar, in other words.

In order to understand the meanings conveyed by the different choices of translators in their translations, the present study conducts a linguistic analysis of the texts along the dimension of "metafunction", which is "critical to any comparison of two or more different languages; and hence to the process of translation, because they are the parameters that define equivalence" (Halliday 2009:19). The theory of metafunctions in SFL can be used to explore how meanings are created and understood in the text as they "allow the matching of particular types of functions or meanings with particular types of wordings" (Thompson 1996b:30).

As Matthiessen (2001:96) observes, at the content levels of language (lexicogrammar and semantics), the organization of language according to three simultaneous metafunctions is critical to translation. To maintain equivalence between the ST and TT in translation, the basic requirement is to achieve the ideational equivalence. The value accorded to interpersonal equivalence and textual equivalence is variable according to the context. For example, in some contexts, maintaining the interpersonal relationships of power and distance in the original text may be highly valued in the translation so as even to override the demand for exact ideational equivalence (Halliday 2001:16). Analyzing the different choices translators make in expressing the ideational, interpersonal and textual meanings of the original text is thus of great importance in studying the effectiveness of the translations.

The second step of the present FDA approach to the translation studies of the *Lunyu* is to study the differential value that different kinds of metafunctional equivalence have in the context of situation and the context of culture, in order to evaluate whether a translated version is or is not an effective translation. That is in accordance with the higher level of achievement in discourse analysis:

> The higher level of achievement is a contribution to the evaluation of the text: the linguistic analysis may enable one to say why the text is, or is not, an effective text for its own purpose — in what respects it succeeds and in what respects it fails, or is less successful. This goal is very much

harder to attain. It requires an interpretation not only of the text itself but also of its context (context of situation, context of culture), and of the systematic relationship between context and text (Halliday 1994a: F41).

The three different strands of meaning: the ideational, the interpersonal and the textual meaning in a text can be related predictably and systematically upwards to context and downwards to lexicogrammar. To be related upwards to the context, one of the types of meaning is associated with one variable in the situation. To be related downwards to lexicogrammar, each type of meaning is realized through the associate lexicogrammatical pattern — as pointed out in section 3.5.1 and 3.5.2, there is a hook-up relationship between text and context. The present study will conduct an equivalence study of projection in relation to both text and context so as to gain a comprehensive understanding of the equivalence achieved in different translated versions of the *Lunyu*. It will study the different lexicogrammatical structures of projection in order to gain an understanding of the different levels of formal equivalence of projection achieved in different TTs. It will also analyze the different degrees of metafunctional equivalence achieved in the TTs. Based on the discourse-analysis study on the different choices made by translators, the study will evaluate the translation quality concerning projection in the context of culture.

What criteria should be employed to determine whether or not a TT is a good translation? Different researchers may give different answers. As House (1997: 1) posits: "evaluating the quality of a translation presupposes a theory of translation. Thus different views of translation lead to different concepts of translational quality, and hence different ways of assessing it." The present study evaluates the appropriateness and effectiveness of a translation in the specific context of culture. The TTs must meet the basic requirement of a high degree of ideational equivalence to the ST, but may vary in interpersonal metafunction and textual metafunction. This study will investigate the different degrees of metafunctional equivalence the translations achieve and explain the reasons for variation in the context of culture.

Below, the model of analysis will be introduced concerning the study of projection in the *Lunyu* and its translations based on functional discourse analysis approach of translation studies in SFL.

3.6 The framework of analysis in the present study

This section will illuminate how the analysis of projection in the *Lunyu* and its translated texts will be conducted under the theoretical guidelines of SFL.

This study will be conducted from the instance end of the instantiation cline — specific texts realized in particular linguistic forms, to the systemic end of the instantiation cline — the meaning potential embedded in the context. As Halliday (2009: 24) points out, we can use linguistic analysis to help us explore the effectiveness of a translated work: "to take two or more translated versions of the same text where you feel that one is clearly better than another, and observe what emerges from the analysis." The linguistic analysis of the texts, as Halliday (1994a: F41) points out, can help people to "say why a text is, or is not, an effective text for its own purpose — in what respects it succeeds and in what respects it fails, or is less successful". Evaluating translated versions of a text requires "an interpretation not only of the text itself but also of its context (context of situation, context of culture), and of the systematic relationship between context and text."

The ST and TT will be studied in terms of the meaning potentials and the expression forms. The linguistic forms realizing the three modes of meaning of projection in the ST and the different TTs will be compared to reveal how the meanings in the ST are realized in the linguistic forms and how they are reconstructed in the TTs. We investigate the linguistic structures realizing the functions of the projection clause nexus and study the meanings conveyed in the structures from the perspective of the three metafunctions.

In describing and analyzing the meanings and linguistic forms realizing those meanings, we investigate the meanings realized at the rank of clause complex. A comparison and analysis of the shifts and equivalence of the projection clause nexus will be conducted in

Chapter 3 Theoretical Framework

Chapter 5, Chapter 6 and Chapter 7. These three chapters study the ideational equivalence, the interpersonal equivalence and textual equivalence of projection in the *Lunyu* and its translations. Chapter 4 introduces the key terms of projection used in this thesis and analyzes the main types and structures of projection in the ST and TTs.

Having conducted these analyses, in Chapter 8 this study will move on to the stratum of context to compare and analyze the different registers constructed in the ST and TTs and try to analyze how the differences and variables in context may result in changes in the three register variables. Chapter 9 will bring all the issues discussed in the current study together and discuss the issue of evaluating the translation quality of the three translated texts of the *Lunyu*. Chapter 10 will bring the whole study to a conclusion.

On the whole, the present study of projection in the *Lunyu* and its translated versions involves three interrelated procedures from three strata: lexicogrammar, semantics, and context. On the strata of lexicogrammar, the systems realizing the three metafunctions, e. g. the system of Transitivity, the system of Mood, the system of Theme, will be studied.

3.7 Summary

This chapter has described and introduced the parameters defining equivalence within the SFL framework. The theory of equivalence based on FDA in text and context was also introduced. Finally, a model for studying projection in the *Lunyu* and its translated versions was constructed. In the following chapters, the description and analysis of projection in the *Lunyu* and its translated versions will be conducted at the levels of lexicogrammar, semantics, and context.

Chapter 4
Different Types and Structures of Projection in the *Lunyu* and Its Translations

4.1 Introduction

In the previous chapter, the theory connected with the present study was introduced and a model was constructed for conducting the present study within the framework of SFL. In this chapter, the conceptions of projection used in the present study will be clarified, and the different types and structures of projection in the *Lunyu* and its translated texts will be discussed.

4.2 Different realizations of projection in the ST

In Section 3.5, we outlined the three systems involved in the differentiation of projection proposed by Halliday and Matthiessen (2004). i.e. the level of projection, the mode of projection and the speech function of projection. Halliday and Matthiessen (2004) account for the different types of projection clause nexus based on the assumption that projection is congruently realized by a nexus of two clauses with projection understood as one of the two logico-semantic relations between clauses in a clause complex (Halliday 1994a). But in discussing ideational metaphor, Halliday and Matthiessen (2004:638-646) mention that there are cases in which "a projection sequence" is not realized congruently by a clause nexus but realized metaphorically by "a simple clause" and either or both of the figures is "down-ranked from clause to group / phrase". In the

Chapter 4 Different Types and Structures of Projection in the Lunyu and Its Translations

case of projection, "a sequence of projection can thus be realized not only by the manifestation of projection in the clause nexus, but also by its manifestation in the clause or the group / phrase" (Halliday & Matthiessen 2004:646).

In Section 2.2.2, we have reviewed how Zeng (2006a) has expanded and deepened the study of projection at the clause level and the level of discourse. Zeng finds that, in real texts, we often find not only projection clause nexuses, projection clauses, projection groups but also projection paragraphs or projection texts (Zeng 2006a:132). Zeng (2006a) identifies the different types of projection in discourse including projection clause nexus, projection clause and projection group or phrase. By projection clause nexus, Zeng refers to projection that enters into paratactic or hypotactic clause complexes. By projection clause, she refers to embedded clauses functioning as Qualifiers in nominal groups, or as a projecting signal for the projection clause. e. g.

> The film is so dull and wordy that it bears out in every frame Powell's assertion that Pascal "knew as much about directing as a cow does about playing the piano".

In her classification, projection clause includes embedded locutions, embedded ideas, and facts. By projection group or phrase, Zeng (2006a) means that the projected message introduced into the text is not a clause, nor an embedded clause nor a nominalization, but appears "as a noun, or a verb, or a phrase or a group that is projected into the clause and thus would be coded as a Verbiage or a Phenomenon in a transitivity analysis" (Zeng 2006a:144). e. g.

> (1) They have declared an end to violence. (2) His last school report has been good though — "an excellent head for figures" the maths teacher had written.

In the present study of projection in the *Lunyu*, we have found that projection is not always congruently realized as clause complexes. In some cases, the projected message is not congruently realized as a clause, but as a paragraph, or as a nominal group. The study refers to these projections as the metaphorical realization of projection in paragraphs and in clauses. Table 4-1 shows the different realizations of projection in the ST.

Table 4-1 Different realizations of projection in ST①

Congruent realization of projection in clause nexus	Zǐ yuē : "fùmǔ wéi qí jí zhī yōu." 子曰："父母唯其疾之忧。"(ST:2/6)[4-1]
Metaphorical realization of projection in paragraph	Zǐ yuē : "xué ér shí xí zhī , bú yì yuè hū ? Yǒu péng zì yuǎnfāng lái , bú yì yuè hū ? Rén bù zhī ér bú yùn , bú yì jūnzǐ hū ?" 子曰："学而时习之，不亦说乎？有朋自远方来，不亦乐乎？人不知而不愠，不亦君子乎？"(ST:1/1)[4-2]
Metaphorical realization of projection in clause	Zǐyóu wèn xiào 子游问孝 (ST:2/7)[4-3]

This book analyzes the grammar of projection mainly at the level of the clause nexus. The metaphorical realization of projection in paragraphs is analyzed as the paragraph consisting of several projection clause nexuses with the projection clause nexus following the first one as the one omitting the same projecting clause. For instance, while studying the metafunctional meaning conveyed in the following paragraph:

[4-2] Zǐ yuē : "xué ér shí xí zhī , bú yì yuè hū ? yǒu péng zì yuǎnfāng lái , bú yì yuè hū ? rén bù zhī ér bú yùn , bú yì jūnzǐ hū ?"
子曰："学而时习之，不亦说乎？有朋自远方来，不亦乐乎？人不知而不愠，不亦君子乎？"(ST:1/1)

We only take the first projection clause nexus as our research target:

Zǐ yuē : "xué ér shí xí zhī , bú yì yuè hū ?"
子曰："学而时习之，不亦说乎？"(ST:1/1)

Likewise, we regard the following projected clauses yǒu péng zì yuǎnfāng lái , bú yì yuè hū ? rén bù zhī ér bú yùn , bú yì jūnzǐ hū ? (有

---

① The translations for the examples in this chapter can be seen in appendix II.

朋自远方来，不亦乐乎？人不知而不愠，不亦君子乎？) as two projection clause nexuses with the projecting clause *Zǐ yuē* (子曰 "the Master said") omitted and it is out of the scope of present research.

As the current study is confined to the framework of projection set up by Halliday and Matthiessen (2004) at the rank of clause complex, the metaphorical realization of projection in a clause will also be ruled out here.

4.3 Clarifying the data of analysis in the ST

The style of the *Lunyu* has long raised the interest of numerous researchers. Chen (2006) points out that the *Lunyu* is an extract from the records of Confucius' disciples of the sayings and actions of Confucius and dialogues between the disciples and the Master. He also points out that the compilers of the *Lunyu* extracted the essence from the original records of the disciples and compiled the *Lunyu* in the form of aphorisms and dialogues in a summarized and concise style. Hou (2008) classifies the three kinds of "literary structure" of the *Lunyu* as "pure quotations, the summarized dialogues (with recapitulated questions) and the relatively integral dialogues (with complete questions and answers)". Xia (2013) classifies the whole text into three types: aphorisms, dialogues and descriptions. Xia states that the typical style of the *Lunyu* is that it records not only the aphorisms of Confucius and his disciples and the dialogues between them, but also records the descriptions of their actions.

In the current study, we will rule out the descriptions of actions, as proposed by Xia (2013), and focus instead on the aphorisms and dialogues of Confucius and his disciples. The ST cited is taken from Yang (2006). The data of analysis in the ST is classified into the following two types.

1) Aphorisms[①]:

[①] According to Wikipedia, the free dictionary, "aphorism" refers to a saying that expresses a general truth or principle. The term is later used to refer to a statement of philosophical, moral or literary principles.

We choose the term "aphorism" to refer to the part of text in the ST which contains pure quotations by Confucius or one of his disciples, with only one speaker in one chapter. Aphorisms are either congruently realized by a projection clause nexus as in [4-1], or metaphorically realized by a paragraph consisting of one projecting clause and one paragraph of a projected message as in [4-2]. As stated in 4.2, we only choose the first projection clause nexus in a paragraph as our research target. In part of some aphorisms, there is a conjunction of sayings with descriptions. For example:

[4-4] *Jì rú zài , jì shén rú shén zài. Zǐ yuē:"wú bú yù jì , rú bú jì."*
　　祭如在，祭神如神在。子曰:"吾不与祭，如不祭。"(ST: 3/12)

In the present research, we will rule out descriptions such as *Jì rú zài , jì shén rú shén zài* (祭如在，祭神如神在) and study only sayings of Confucius.

In the aphorisms, the logico-semantic relation between the projecting clause and the projected message is that of quoting (direct speech, verbal process, parataxis).

2) Dialogues:

The term "dialogues" in the ST refers to those parts in which there is a dialogue between two or more speakers. The dialogue consists of two or more turns of speech including questions and answers. In the case of complete dialogues, each turn of questions and answers is realized either congruently by a projection clause nexus or metaphorically in a paragraph as example [4-5] shows, the projection in the first turn of asking is realized as a projection clause nexus, and the projection in the second turn of answering is metaphorically realized as a projection paragraph.

[4-5] *Āigōng wèn:"dìzǐ shú wéi haòxué?"*
　　哀公问:"弟子孰为好学?"
Kǒngzǐ duì yuē:"yǒu Yán Huí zhě haòxué, bù qiān nù, bú èr guò. búxìng duǎnmìng sǐ yǐ. Jīn yě zé wú, wèi wén haòxué zhě yě."
　　孔子对曰:"有颜回者好学，不迁怒，不贰过。不幸短命死

Chapter 4   Different Types and Structures of Projection in the Lunyu and Its Translations

矣。今也则亡，未闻好学者也。"(ST:6/3)

Projection in the asking turns of brief dialogues is metaphorically realized by a clause. As the current research focuses on the study of projection at the rank of clause complex, the metaphorically realized projection in clause and in paragraphs will be ruled out of the research scope here. Projection in the answering turns of brief dialogues is realized as a projection clause nexus or a projection paragraph as shown in examples [4-5] and [4-6]. The projection clause nexus is realized as quoting (direct speech, verbal process, parataxis).

[4-6] *Zǐxià wèn xiào .*
子夏问孝。
Zǐ yuē : "sè nán. yǒu shì , dìzǐ fú qí láo ; yǒu jiǔ shí , xiānshēng zhuàn. céng shì yǐ wéi xiào hū ?"
子曰："色难。有事，弟子服其劳；有酒食，先生馔。曾是以为孝乎？"(ST:2/8)

[4-7] *Mèng Wǔbó wèn xiào.*
孟武伯问孝。
Zǐ yuē : "fùmǔ wéi qí jí zhī yōu ".
子曰："父母唯其疾之忧。"(ST:2/6)

4.4   Different types of projection in the TTs

In the study of the translated versions of the *Lunyu*, projection is realized by the following different grammatical types, which will be studied in relation to the aphorisms or dialogues to which they belong.

4.4.1   Types of projection in the part of aphorism

In the aphorisms, the projection clause nexus in the ST is realized by quoting. The projected message is the sayings of Confucius or one of his disciples. In the translated versions, quoting (direct speech) is realized by different types of projection in different translated versions, as shown in Table 4-2:

Table 4-2　Different types of projection in the aphorisms of TTs

Types of projection	Example
Quoting (direct speech, verbal process, parataxis)	The Master said, "The study of strange doctrines is injurious indeed." (LT:2/16)
Free indirect speech	To antagonize a different view, said the Master, would reveal one's own weakness. (XT:1/1)

4.4.2　Types of projection in the part of dialogues

In the complete dialogues and answering turns in the brief dialogues, projection in the ST is realized as quoting (direct speech, verbal process, parataxis). In the translated versions, projection is realized either as quoting (direct speech, verbal process, parataxis) or as reporting (verbal process, hypotaxis), or by an independent circumstantial clause embedded within a projection clause nexus. As Table 4-3 shows, in the TTs for Chapter Twenty, Book Two, the projection in the asking and answering turns is realized by different types.

Table 4-3　Different types of projection in the TTs of Chapter Twenty, Book Two

Types of projection	Examples
Reporting speech	Chî K'ang asked how to cause the people to reverence their ruler, to be faithful to him, and to go on to nerve themselves to virtue. (LT:2/20)
Quoting	The Master said, "Let him preside over them with gravity; — then they will reverence him. Let him be filial and kind to all; — then they will be faithful to him..." (LT:2/20)
Hypotactic enhancing *When-* clause	When Ji Kang Zi asked how the people could be induced to be respectful and faithful, the Master replied, "..." (XT:2/20)

As Table 4-3 shows, the first turn of Legge's translation is realized as reporting while the second turn in Legge's translation is realized as quoting. In Xu's translation, the first turn is realized as a hypotactic enhancing *when-* clause with an embedded reporting clause in it.

4.4.3 Types of projection in the asking turn of brief dialogues

In the brief dialogues in the ST, the asking turn is metaphorically realized by a clause with the projected message realized as a noun phrase. The answering turn is realized as a projection clause nexus. In the translated versions, the answering turn is mainly realized as quoting like the ST, while the metaphorically realized projection in the asking turn of ST is realized by different types of projection as shown in Table 4-4:

Table 4-4 Different types of projection in the asking turn of brief dialogues

Types of projection	Examples
Metaphorical projection in clause	Mèng Wǔbó wèn xiào. 孟武伯问孝 (ST:2/6)
Metaphorical projection in clause	Mang Wu the elder asked about filiality. (Pound:2/6)
Projection clause nexus	Mǎng Wû asked what filial piety was. (LT:2/6)
Hypotactic enhancing *When*-clause	When the son of Meng Yi Zi asked about filial duty, (XT:2/6)

4.5 Different structures of projection in the TTs

The main type of projection in the ST is the projection clause nexus realized as quoting, with the structure " projecting clause ^ projected clause". The other structure takes the form of "projecting clause ^ projected clause ^ omitted projecting clause ^ projected clause" in the metaphorically realized paragraphs①. In the old Chinese texts, there are no punctuation marks. In order to clarify the

---

① Although our basic research target is projection at the level of clause nexus, in some cases, we need to study the whole projected message in the projection paragraph, and thus we have the structure of "projecting clause^projected clause ^omitted projecting clause^projected clause".

source of the projected message, writers of the old Chinese texts frequently use the projecting clauses and put them in front of the projected message. In the ST, readers can see the projecting clauses "Subject +*yuē* (曰 "say") before each projected message, and the message can be a word, a clause, a clause complex, or even several clause complexes.

In the different translated versions, the structure of projection is realized in different linguistic forms as shown in Table 4-5 below.

Table 4-5 Different structures of projection in the TTs[①]

Structures of projection	Examples
P-ing C ^ P-ed C	The Master said, "Is it not pleasant to learn with a constant perseverance and application?" (LT:1/1)
P-ed C ^ P-ing C ^ omitted P-ing C ^ P-ed C	A man should live an honest life, said the Master. It is by luck that a dishonest man can escape punishment. (XT:6/19))
part of P-ed C ^ P-ing C ^ the other part of P-ed C	A good man, said the Master, would rarely say what he does not believe, or pretend to appear better than he is. (XT:1/3)
minor P-ed C ^ P-ing C ^ omitted P-ing C ^ P-ed C ^ omitted P-ing C ^ p-ed C	"A significant question!" said the Master. "In ritual performance, it would be better to be thrift than lavish; in mourning service, it would be better to be deep in grief than minute in observance." (XT:3/4)
P-ing C ^ P-ed C ^ omitted P-ing C ^ P-ed C	…, the Master said, "Filial sons of today only take care their parents are well fed. But even dogs and horses are well fed now. What is the difference if their parents are fed without reverence?" (XT:2/7)

4.6 Summary

Projection in the ST can be differently realized in different types

---

[①] In Table 4-5, Table 7-2 and Table 7-7, "P-ed C" stands for "projected clause", "P-ing C" stands for "projecting clause".

Chapter 4 Different Types and Structures of Projection in the *Lunyu* and Its Translations

and structures of linguistic forms in different TTs. Whether the different types and structures of projection chosen by the different translators can convey an equivalent meaning to the ST is a topic worthy of study. In the following chapters, the different meanings conveyed by the different types and structures of projection in different translated versions will be studied from the viewpoint of the three metafunctions, with the aim of examining whether the translation can achieve ideational equivalence, interpersonal equivalence, and textual equivalence as conveyed through the translators' choice of different types and structures of projection.

Chapter 5
Ideational Equivalence of Projection in the *Lunyu* and Its Translations

5.1 Introduction

From this chapter on, equivalence in projection in the *Lunyu* and its translations will be conducted by comparatively examining the ideational, interpersonal and textual meanings realized by the different choices made by the translators at the level of lexicogrammar. In the present chapter, the ideational meanings conveyed in the ST and TTs will be analyzed and compared. The study of ideational equivalence of the ST and TT will be conducted from two perspectives: experiential equivalence and logical equivalence.

5.2 Ideational metafunction in projection

As discussed in Section 3.3.3.1 above, the ideational metafunction of language is further divided into the experiential metafunction and the logical metafunction. The system of grammar that realizes the experiential metafunction is that of Transitivity. The systems which come under the logical metafunction are that of Taxis and Logico-semantic relations. The study of ideational aspect of projection in the ST and TTs will be conducted in the two parts: the study of experiential metafunction in the projecting clauses; the study of logical metafunction in the projection clause nexus.

5.2.1 Experiential metafunction in projection

The experiential metafunction is realized in the grammatical system of Transitivity, which construes the world of experience into a set of process types. The different process types form a system from which people can choose to construe their experience as shown in Figure 5-1.

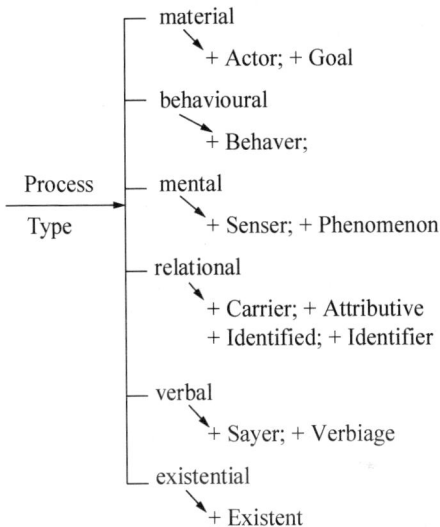

Figure 5-1 Transitivity represented as a system network
(Halliday & Matthiessen 2004:173)

Projection is one of two kinds of logical relationships construed in language, in which one process is used to construe another process as belonging to a different order of experience. The types of processes that can be used to project another process are verbal and mental processes. The elements of the experiential structure of the clause include three components: a process, the participants involved in the process, and the circumstances associated with the process (Halliday & Matthiessen 2004:175-176). The configuration of these three components construes the different experiential meanings.

In the projection clause nexuses in the aphorisms of the ST, the

Process used to project another Process is a verbal Process, usually with only one participant — the Sayer. In the experiential structure of the projecting clauses, there is usually no Target for the action of speaking and there are no adverbial groups or prepositional phrases to realize the Circumstance(s) of the process. The typical realization of the projecting clause in the ST *zǐ yuē* (子曰 "the Master said") and the elements of experiential structure in the projecting clause include the Sayer participant realized by *zǐ* (子 "the Master"); and the verbal Process realized by *yuē* (曰 "say").

In the dialogues in the ST, the Process in the projecting clause is also realized by a verbal group, but with some differences from the typical realization of projecting verbs by *yuē* (曰 "say") in the aphorisms, for example: *wèn* (问 "ask"), *wèn yuē* (问曰 "ask and say"), *wèi* (谓 "call, tell"), *yǔ* (语 "tell"), *shǐ zhī yuē* (矢之曰 "swear him say"), *gào zhī yuē* (告之曰 "tell him say"), *duì yuē* (对曰 "reply say"), etc. In a few cases, there are two participants in the verbal process. For example, in Chapter Six of Book Three, the projecting clause is *zǐ wèi Rǎn Yǒu yuē* (子谓冉有曰 "the Master tell Ran you say"). In this case, there are two participants in the verbal process: *zǐ* and *Rǎn Yǒu*. Generally, there is also no Circumstance in the experiential structure of projecting clauses in the dialogues.

The *Lunyu* was compiled by the disciples of Confucius to record what the Master has said in his lectures and what he has talked about with his disciples, without much description of the contexts in which the dialogues took place. This explains the omission of the Target participant and possible Circumstances related to the verbal process. The possible aim of the compilers of the aphorisms and dialogues was to emphasize the universal truths contained in the sayings of Confucius.

In the TTs, the projecting clause is also typically realized by a verbal Process with only one Participant and without Circumstances, as shown in Table 5-1 below.

From Table 5-1, we can see that the typical realization of a projecting clause in the ST and TTs is able to achieve equivalence with similar experiential structures chosen in the TTs.

Chapter 5 Ideational Equivalence of Projection in the Lunyu and Its Translations

Table 5-1 Equivalent experiential structures of projecting clauses in the TTs

Element of experiential structure	ST	TTs
Participant	Nominal group: zǐ 子 "the Master"	The Master / Confucius
Process	Verbal group: yuē 曰 "say"	said / remarked
Circumstance	No circumstance	No circumstance

We can tentatively conclude that in the three TTs, the projecting clause is generally realized by equivalent experiential structures and achieves experiential equivalence to the ST. Although this is the case, there still exists some non-equivalence in the experiential structure of the projecting clauses. In the TTs of Legge and Xu, the experiential structure of projecting clause is similar to that of the ST. In the TT of Ku, as well as a typical realization similar to the ST, Ku uses many varied experiential structures in the projecting clauses to realize different experiential meanings to the ST. Table 5-2 shows the different experiential structures of projecting clause in KT.

Table 5-2 The experiential structure of projecting clauses in KT

Element of experiential structure	General realization of projecting clause	Variant realization of projecting clause	
Participant	Confucius	Confucius	Confucius
Process	remarked	remarked	was heard to say/exclaim
Circumstance		speaking of a favorite disciple whose name was Yen Hui	remarking on this
	general cases	15 cases	9 cases

In the three TTs, the main experiential realization for the projecting clause is "Participant + verbal Process", realizing an equivalent experiential meaning to the ST. The variant experiential structures listed in Table 5-2 construe different experiential meaning to the ST. In the experiential structure of projecting clause in the ST, there are no Circumstances or Target of the verbal process. Ku chooses to add Circumstances in the structure of the projecting clause to add circumstantial information about the verbal Process. This circumstantial information is not directly provided in the ST but can be understood by the ST readers in a Chinese context based on common knowledge. While Legge chooses to put this information in the footnotes of the translation without changing the experiential structure of the projecting clauses, Ku chooses non-experientially equivalent projecting clauses in his TT and thus realizes different experiential meanings. In the ST, the typical choice of verbal process is realized in an active voice with the Target of the verbal process omitted in the clause. Readers only know one Participant, the Sayer. Ku, in contrast, chooses the passive voice, in which two participants are included in the verbal process. The experiential meaning conveyed in the passive voice is non-equivalent to that of the ST.

As to the experiential meanings conveyed in the projecting clause, Legge and Xu achieve a great degree of equivalence. In KT, there are altogether twenty-four instances of shift realized by the different experiential structures in the projecting clause. These shifts, however, occupy only quite a small proportion of the three hundred and thirteen projecting clauses in KT so we would still claim that KT realizes a nearly equivalent experiential meaning in the projecting clause.

From this analysis we can find that the three TTs can be generally regarded as achieving equivalent experiential metafunction to the ST.

5.2.2 Logical metafunction in projection

As the logical metafunction of language concerns the relations between processes in different clauses, here we mainly examine the Taxis in the projection clause nexus. The relationship between the projecting clause and the projected clause can be either paratactic or hypotactic. In a projection relationship, as Halliday and Matthiessen (2008:521) indicate, "the two elements in a verbal projection are typically equal in status" in which the projected message is quoted as direct speech and the elements in a mental projection are typically "unequal" in which the projected message is reported as indirect thought. The other alternative relationship between the projecting clause and the projected clause is that of reported speech or quoted thought (Halliday & Matthiessen 2008:522) which are not typical and less favored in everyday English discourse.

In the ST, the projection clause nexus in the aphorisms and dialogues is typically realized as quoting (direct speech), with the projecting clause placed in front of the projected clause. In the TTs, different translators may choose different types of projection clause nexus, realizing the different logical metafunction of the projection clause nexus and conveying different logical meanings in the translated versions. In the following part, the different types of projection in different TTs are analyzed so as to investigate the different logical meanings conveyed.

In the present study, we only account for the first nine books of the *Lunyu*. In the process of studying, we recognize the aphorisms in each chapter as one projection clause nexus, while in the dialogues, we consider the structure of "one projecting clause ^ one projected message" with quotation marks as one projection clause nexus in the ST. In the TTs, in the aphorisms, we only study the first pair of projecting clause and projected clause as a projection clause nexus, omitting the remainder of the projected message. In this way the linguistic forms that realize the logical metafunction of the projection in the ST and TTs can be compared.

5.2.2.1 Logical metafunction in the ST

According to Yang (2006), in the first nine books of the ST, there are altogether 240 chapters. The descriptive passages in the chapters do not fall within the scope of the present study. We regard a pair of projecting clause with the projected message in the quotation marks in the ST as a projection clause nexus. In the 170 aphorisms[1], there are 170 projection clause nexuses, realized as

---

[1] Chapter Twenty-six of Book Seven in the ST seems to be a dialogue but is in fact two aphorisms.

quoting (direct speech). In the 57 dialogues (including the brief dialogues and complete dialogues), there are 141 projection clause nexuses realized as quoting (direct speech), and two projection nexuses realized as reporting (indirect speech). Table 5-3 below shows the logical relations between the projecting clause and the projected clause in the ST.

Table 5-3　Types of projection in the ST

Part of text	Type of projection	Number of types
aphorism	quoting	170
dialogue	quoting	141
	reporting	2

As Table 5-3 shows, the most commonly used type of projection in the ST is quoting, a paratactic relationship between the projecting clauses and the projected clauses. The logical meaning conveyed in the distinct modes of projection of quoting and reporting is different. As Halliday and Matthiessen (2004:462) point out:

> Quoting and reporting are not simply formal variants; they differ in meaning. The difference between them derives from the general semantic distinction between parataxis and hypotaxis, as it applies in the particular context of projecting. In quoting, the projected element has independent status; it is thus more immediate and lifelike, and this effect is enhanced by the orientation of the deixis, which is that of drama not that of narrative... Reporting, on the other hand, presents the projected element as dependent. It still gives some indication of mood, but in a form which precludes it from functioning as a move in an exchange. And the speaker makes no claim to be abiding by the wording.

The most commonly used mode of projection in the ST — quoting — put what Confucius said and what the other characters in the dialogues said in an independent status with the projecting clauses and convey a lively atmosphere concerning what they are talking

Chapter 5   Ideational Equivalence of Projection in the Lunyu and Its Translations

about.

5. 2. 2. 2   Logical metafunction in projection in LT

The different modes of projection chosen in the TTs realize different logical meanings. In the aphorisms, Legge mainly chooses equivalent types of projection to realize the projection clause nexus in the ST. The only one instance of non-equivalence occurs in Chapter Sixteen of Book Five, in which quoting in the ST is realized as reporting in the TT, as example 5-1 shows:

[5-1] *Zǐ wèi Zǐchǎn , "yǒu jūnzǐ zhī dào sì yān : qí xíng jǐ yě gōng , qí shì shàng yě jìng , qí yǎng mín yě huì , qí shǐ mín yě yì. "*
子谓子产，"有君子之道四焉：其行己也恭，其事上也敬，其养民也惠，其使民也义。" (ST:5/16)
The Master said of Tsze-ch'an that he had four of the characteristics of a superior man: in his conduct of himself, he was humble; in serving his superiors, he was respectful; in nourishing the people, he was kind; in ordering the people, he was just. (LT:5/16)

In the dialogues, only a few projection clause nexuses are realized by non-equivalent types of projection clause nexus, in which quoting in ST is realized as reporting in the TT as shown in example [5-2]:

[5-2] *Jì Kāngzǐ wèn : "shǐ mín jìng , zhōng yǐ quàn , rú zhī hé ?"*
季康子问："使民敬、忠以劝，如之何？" (ST:2/20)
Chî K'ang asked how to cause the people to reverence *their ruler*, to be faithful to him, and to go on to nerve themselves to virtue. (LT:2/20)

For the two instances reporting (indirect speech) in the ST, Legge translates them as equivalent reporting (indirect speech).

[5-3] *Chén sībài wèn Zhāogōng zhīlǐ hu ?*
陈司败问昭公知礼乎 (ST:7/31)
The minister of crime of Ch'ǎn asked whether the duke Chao

knew propriety, (LT:7/31)

[5-4] *Mèng Wǔbó wèn Zǐlù rén hu？*
孟武伯问子路仁乎？(ST:5/8)
Măng Wû asked about Tsze-lù, whether he was perfectly virtuous. (LT:5/7)

In summary, Legge realized most instances of projection in the ST as the equivalent quoting in the TT with only a few shifts in the types or modes of projection chosen in the TT. Legge's translation achieves comparatively the highest degree of equivalence in the logical aspect of projection. Table 5-4 shows the equivalence and shifts in the types of projection chosen in Legge's translation:

Table 5-4 Types of projection in LT

Part of text	Type of projection	ST	LT	Equivalence	Shifts
aphorism	quoting	170	169	169	1
	reporting	0	1		
dialogue	quoting	141	134	134	7
	reporting	2	9	2	

5. 2. 2. 3　Logical metafunction in projection in KT

In the aphorisms of KT, all the projection clause nexuses are realized as quoting in the TT, which is equivalent to the ST. In the dialogues, most of the projection clause nexuses are realized by the equivalent types. There are a few instances of non-equivalence in which quoting in the ST is realized as reporting in the TT, as shown in example 5-5:

[5-5] *Jì Kāngzǐ wèn：" shǐ mín jìng，zhōng yǐ quàn，rú zhī hé？"*
季康子问："使民敬、忠以劝，如之何？"(ST:7/20)
A noble who was the minister in power in the government in Confucius' native State asked him what should be done to inspire a feeling of respect and loyalty in the people, in order to make them exert themselves for the good of the country. (KT: 2/20)

Chapter 5   Ideational Equivalence of Projection in the Lunyu and Its Translations

For the two instances of reporting (indirect speech) in the ST, Ku translates them into equivalent reporting.

[5-6] *Chén sībài wèn Zhāogōng zhīlǐ hu?*
陈司败问昭公知礼乎? (ST:5/8)
A minister of justice in a certain State enquired of Confucius, while he was in that State on his travels, if the reigning prince in Confucius' native State was a man of propriety in his life. (KT: 7/31)

[5-7] *Mèng Wǔbó wèn Zǐlù rén hu?*
孟武伯问子路仁乎? (ST:5/8)
A member of a powerful family of nobles in Confucius native State asked Confucius if his disciple the above mentioned Chung Yu, was a moral character. (KT:5/8)

In the aphorisms as well as in the dialogues, *Ku* chooses the equivalent projection types (quoting / direct speech) to realize the projection in the ST. There are only a few instances of shift in the types of projection in the TT. We can conclude that Ku's translation also achieves a high degree of logical equivalence with the equivalent types of projection chosen in the TT, as shown in Table 5-5.

Table 5-5   Types of projection in KT

Part of text	Type of projection	ST	KT	Equivalence	Shifts
aphorism	quoting	170	170	170	0
	reporting	0	0		
dialogue	quoting	141	129	129	12
	reporting	2	14	2	

5. 2. 2. 4   Logical metafunction in projection in XT

In the aphorisms in XT, most of the projection clause nexuses are realized as free direct speech, which is not equivalent as to the modes of projection in the ST.

[5-8] *Zǐ yuē : "dìzǐ rù zé xiào , chū zé tì , jǐn ér xìn , fàn ài zhòng , ér qīn rén. xíng yǒu yúlì , zé yǐ xué wén. "*
子曰:"弟子入则孝,出则悌,谨而信,泛爱众,而亲仁。行有余力,则以学文。"(ST:1/6)

A young man, said the Master, should be filial at home and respectful abroad, cautious and trustworthy, affectionate towards all and intimate with the good. If he has time to spare when his duties are done, he may use it to learn arts. (XT:1/6)

As example [5-8] shows, the interdependent relationship between the projecting clause and the projected clause is that of parataxis, equivalent to that of quoting / direct speech in the ST. The speech is given an independent status in relation to the projecting clause but without the use of quotation marks. As the original text of the *Lunyu* contains no punctuation (in the form of quotation marks), we still consider that the choice of free direct speech in XT maintains logical equivalence with the choice of quoting in the ST.

One instance of quoting in the ST is realized as reporting in the TT, which conveys different logical meaning to the ST.

[5-9] *Zǐ wèi Sháo : "jìn měi yě , yòu jìn shàn yě. "*
子谓《韶》:"尽美也,又尽善也。"(ST:3/25)

The Master said of the Inauguration Music as perfectly beautiful and perfectly good. (XT:3/25)

In the dialogues, Xu realizes projection in the ST with varied projection types in the TT. For the dominant quoting / direct speech in the dialogues of the ST, Xu chooses to realize them as equivalent quoting, or non-equivalent reporting speech, as when- clauses with a reporting speech embedded, or metaphorically realized as projection within a clause, which can be shown in example [5-10], [5-11], [5-12].

[5-10] *Zě wèi Rǎn Yǒu yuē : "rǔ fú néng jiù yǔ ?"*
子谓冉有曰:"女弗能救与?"
Duì yuē : "bùnéng. "
对曰:"不能"。

Chapter 5 Ideational Equivalence of Projection in the Lunyu and Its Translations

> Zǐ yuē : "wū hū ! zēng wèi tàishān bù rú Línfàng hū ?"
> 子曰:"呜呼!曾谓泰山不如林放乎?" (ST:3/6)
> The Master asked Ran You if he could prevent it, and Ran You answered he could not. Then the Master said, "Alas, does Mount Tai not know what Lin Fang does about the rites?" (XT:3/6)

In example 5-10, Xu chooses to realize the quoting in the ST as reporting in the TT in translating the first two turns in the dialogue.

> [5-11] Jì Kāngzǐ wèn : "shǐ mín jìng , zhōng yǐ quàn , rú zhī hé ?"
> 季康子问:"使民敬、忠以劝,如之何?" (ST:2/20)
> When Ji Kangzi asked how the people could be induced to be respectful and faithful, the Master replied, "If you maintain dignity, people will respect you. If you are dutiful towards your parents and kind towards all, they will have faith in you. If the worthy are employed and the incompetent are trained, they will be induced to be respectful and faithful." (XT:2/20)

In example 5-11, the first turn of asking in the dialogue is realized in the TT as reporting embedded in a when-clause, which is dependent on the projecting clause *the Master replied*. The logical metafunction realized in the projection of the ST has been changed and the independent relationship between the different turns in the dialogue has also been changed. The projection in the asking turn of dialogue is positioned in a dependent clause in the projection clause nexus indicating what the Master said, and what he said in the dialogue is highlighted with the use of quotation marks.

> [5-12] Zǐxià wèn yuē : " 'qiǎoxiào qiàn xī , měimù pàn xī , sù yǐ wéi xuàn xī. ' Hé wèi yě ?"
> 子夏问曰:"'巧笑倩兮,美目盼兮,素以为绚兮。'何谓也?"
> Zǐ yuē : "huì shì hòu sù. "
> 子曰:"绘事后素。" (ST:3/8)
> Zi Xia asked about the meaning of the following verse: "Ah, dark on white her speaking eyes, her cheeks with smiles and

dimples glow. Colored designs are made on plain silk." The Master said, "Colors should be put on the plain ground." (XT: 3/8)

In example 5-12, the quoting in the asking turn of the ST is metaphorically realized as a projection in a clause " Zi Xia asked about the meaning of the following verse."

Of the two reporting / indirect speeches in the dialogues of the ST, in XT one is realized by the equivalent reporting / indirect speech and the other is realized by a when- clause.

[5-13] *Mèng Wǔbó wèn Zǐlù rén hu ?*
孟武伯问子路仁乎？(ST:5/8)
Meng Wu asked whether Zi Lu was a man of men. (XT:5/8)

[5-14] *Chén sībài wèn Zhāogōng zhī lǐ hū ?*
陈司败问昭公知礼乎？(ST:7/31)
The Minister of Crime of the State of Chen asked whether Duke Zhao of Lu knew the ritual system. (XT:7/31)

Table 5-6 shows the different types of projection chosen in XT and the equivalence and shifts as compared to that of the ST.

Table 5-6　Types of projection in XT①

Part of text	Type of projection	ST	XT	Equivalence	Shifts
aphorism	quoting (DS)	170	24	24	146
	FDS	0	145		
	reporting	0	1		
dialogue	quoting	141	108	108 1	34
	reporting	2	13		
	when clause	0	17		
	MPC	0	5		

In XT, a great portion of the projection clause nexuses are

---

① In Table 5-6 and Table 5-7, DS stands for "direct speech", FDS stands for "free direct speech", MPC stands for "metaphorically realized projection in clause".

realized by the different kinds of projection, among which free direct speech can function as logically equivalent to the quoting in ST, both of which have a paratactic relationship between the projecting clause and the projected clause. In the dialogues, the quoting / direct speech of the ST is realized in Xu's translation either as a projection clause nexus of reporting / indirect speech, or metaphorically as projection within a clause, or as a when- clause dependent on the main projection clause nexus. The logical meaning conveyed in these different choices of types of projection is not equivalent to that of the ST. Table 5-7 shows the equivalence and shifts in the logical metafunction of projection in XT as compared to the ST.

Table 5-7 Equivalence and shifts in the logical metafunction in projection in XT

Part of text	Types of projection	ST	XT	Equivalence	Shifts
aphorism	quoting (DS)	170	24	24 145	1
	FDS	0	145		
	reporting	0	1		
dialogue	quoting	141	108	108 1	34
	reporting	2	13		
	when clause	0	17		
	MPC	0	5		

We can find that XT can achieve general logical equivalence to the ST with thirty-five shifts of logical meaning conveyed in the TT. The degree of logical equivalence is a little bit lower as compared to the TTs of Legge and Ku.

5.3 Degrees of ideational equivalence in projection

According to the experiential and logical analysis of projection in the ST and TTs, we can make an evaluation of the degree of equivalence of projection in the ST and TTs. From the experiential analysis of projecting clauses, we have found that the three TTs nearly achieved experiential equivalence of projection to the ST, although there are some shifts in the TT by Ku with the choice of different structures for the projecting clause.

From the logical analysis of the different types of projection in the TTs as shown in Tables 5-5, 5-6, 5-7, we found that the three TTs generally achieved logical equivalence of projection to the ST, although there are still some shifts in the TTs with the choice of different types of projection. The TT by Legge achieved comparatively higher logical equivalence to the ST and the TTs of Ku and Xu achieved comparatively lower degree of logical equivalence to the ST.

Taking the experiential and logical analysis of the projection clause nexus together, we can get a picture of the overall ideational equivalence of the TTs to the ST in this area. The ideational equivalence and shifts in the different TTs as compared to the ST are shown in Table 5-8 below.

Table 5-8　The ideational equivalence of projection achieved in the TTs

Text	Equivalence in the logical metafunction (No.)	Shifts in the experiential metafunction (No.)	Shifts in the logical metafunction (No.)	Ratio of ideational equivalence (%)
LT	305	0	8	97.4
KT	301	24	12	89.5
XT	278	0	35	88.8

As Table 5-8 shows, Legge has chosen the largest proportion of equivalent types of projection to the ST, and thus the highest degree of logical equivalence, which together with the experiential equivalence achieved in the choice of projecting clause and the shifts in the choice of projection types, gives the highest degree of the ideational equivalence of all three TTs.

Ku has also chosen a large proportion of equivalent types of projection to the ST, which together with the experiential equivalence achieved in the choice of projecting clause and the shifts in the choice of projection types and in the variant structure of projecting clauses, gives a degree of the ideational equivalence achieved second to that of Legge.

Xu has chosen the most different types of projection in his TTs.

Chapter 5   Ideational Equivalence of Projection in the Lunyu and Its Translations

But as we have discussed, the choice of free direct speech in XT can realize an equivalent logical meaning to the ST. The placement of the projecting clause in the middle of the projected message does, however, cause the significant place of the projecting clause at the beginning of every chapter of aphorisms to be lost in the translation, which may convey a different interpersonal and textual meaning in the translation (which will be studied in Chapter 6 and Chapter 7). Considering the shifts of logical metafunction in the choice of projection types in which the quoting in the ST is realized either as reporting / indirect speech or a when-clause dependent on the main projection clause nexus, the logical equivalence achieved in XT is comparatively lower than that in the TTs of Legge and Ku.

From this analysis, we can find that there is only a small proportion of ideational shifts of projection in the three TTs and we can conclude that the three translated texts have generally achieved ideational equivalence to the ST, with Legge showing comparatively the higher, Ku and Xu a little lower degree of equivalence, as shown in Table 5-8 above.

5.4   Reasons for the different realizations of projection

5.4.1   Different interpretations of the ST

The first probable reason for the different realization of projection in the TTs is the different interpretations by the translators of the ST. There are no punctuation marks in the old Chinese texts and the translators will add the necessary punctuation marks while they are interpreting the ST. For example, for the text in Chapter Sixteen of Book Five, there can be two ways of adding the punctuation marks as Examples [5-15] and [5-16] show:

> [5-15] Zǐ wèi Zǐchǎn, "yǒu jūnzǐ zhī dào sì yān: qí xíng jǐ yě gong, qí shì shàng yě jing, qí yǎng mín yě huì, qí shǐ mín yě yì."
> 子谓子产："有君子之道四焉：其行己也恭，其事上也敬，其养民也惠，其使民也义。" (Qian 2011:5/16)

[5-16] Zǐ wèi Zǐchǎn yǒu jūnzǐ zhī dào sì yān: qí xíng jǐ yě gōng, qí shì shàng yě jìng, qí yǎng mín yě huì, qí shǐ mín yě yì.
子谓子产有君子之道四焉：其行己也恭，其事上也敬，其养民也惠，其使民也义。(Lau & Yang 2008:5/16)

The first interpretation of the ST (in example 5-15) regards the ST as quoting (direct speech) and the second (in example 5-16) as reporting (indirect speech), which results in the different choices of projection in the different translations.

[5-17] Confucius remarked of a famous statesman (the Colbert of the time), saying, "He showed himself to be a good and wise man in four ways. In his conduct of himself he was earnest, and in serving the interests of his prince he was serious. In providing for the wants of the people, he was generous, and in dealing with them he was just." (KT:5/15)

[5-18] The Master said of Zi Chan, "He is a cultured man in four respects: modest in his conduct, respectful in serving his superiors, beneficial to the people and just in employing his inferiors." (XT:5/16)

[5-19] The Master said of Tsze-chǎn that he had four of the characteristics of a superior man: in his conduct of himself, he was humble; in serving his superiors, he was respectful; in nourishing the people, he was kind; in ordering the people, he was just. (LT:5/15)

Ku and Xu choose to realize the sayings of Confucius in this chapter as quoting / direct speech, while in contrast Legge chooses to realize them as reporting / indirect speech. The different choices of projection in the different texts result from the different interpretation by different translators of the original text.

Different interpretations of the ST resulting in different choices of projection in the TT can also be seen in example [5-20]:

[5-20] Zǐzhāng xué gān lù. Zǐ yuē: "duō wén quē yí..."

Chapter 5 Ideational Equivalence of Projection in the Lunyu and Its Translations

子张学干禄。子曰:"多闻阙疑……"(ST:2/18)

According to Yang (2006), the interpretation of Zǐzhāng xué gān lù (子张学干禄) in modern Chinese is Zǐzhāng xiàng Kǒngzǐ xué qiú guān qǔdé fēnglù de fāngfǎ (子张向孔子学求官取得俸禄的方法 "Zizhang is learning from Confucius about how to become an official"), which can be interpreted as a description of Zizhang's action. In the TTs, Legge translates it as "Tsze-chang was learning with a view to official emolument"; Ku translates it as "a disciple was studying with a view to preferment". Both of the translations of Legge and Ku take the ST as a description of the behavior of Tszechang and recreate it in the TTs. In XT, by contrast, the corresponding translation of the clause is "When Zi Zhang asked about official emolument". It shows that the translator interprets the material process xué (学 "study") in the ST as a verbal process and that is why he chooses "asked about" in his translation.

As we have discussed in Section 1.5, Legge translated the Lunyu in close collaboration with a Chinese scholar named Wang Tao while Ku and Xu are translators skilled in both Chinese and English. It is natural for the different Chinese living in different historical periods to have different interpretations of the Lunyu. The shifts resulting from the different interpretations by the translators of the ST only occupy quite a small proportion of the shifts in the different realizations of projection in the TTs, which can not weaken the comparability of the three TTs.

5.4.2 Translators' meaningful choices

Some of the variety in the realization of projection of the TT is caused by the meaningful choices of the translators. As Jennings (1895:35) says in his translation:

> In the Chinese text, in perhaps three-fourths of the number of paragraphs, a sentence is introduced by the formula, "The Master said", which in English after a while becomes wearisome. I have thought it best to resort to little tricks of inversion, *oratio obliqua*, or, when a number of sayings of the Master follow immediately upon each other, of

combining them under one head, as "other sayings of the Master", and "*Obiter dicta* of the Master" where the sayings have no connection with each other."

Jennings (1895: 35) clearly indicates that the reason why he chooses renderings of the projecting clauses other than "The Master said" is to achieve variety. In XT, readers will recognize many examples of the translator's meaningful choice to modernize his translated version as Xu aims to achieve a modern translation of the *Lunyu*. In his introduction to his translation of the *Lunyu* at the First International Symposium on the Translation of the *Lunyu* held at Sun Yat-sen University, Xu said that he aimed to add something new to the interpretation of the *Lunyu* and its translation. For example, in translating *yŏu péng zì yuǎn fāng lái , bú yì yuè hu*？(有朋自远方来不亦说乎) he thinks he had better translate it as "is it not a pleasure to meet friends coming from far and near?" because with the convenience of the modern transportation, friends coming from afar in ancient China may now be regarded as friends coming from nearby. The meaningful choice of the different types of projection in XT is another way for Xu to modernize his translation. They may weaken to some extent the ideational equivalence in projection between the TT and the ST, but may achieve better interpersonal and textual equivalence, issues which will be discussed in the following two chapters.

5.5 Summary

This chapter examined the different degrees of ideational equivalence achieved in the three TTs. An experiential analysis of the projecting clauses in the TTs found that the TTs generally chose equivalent projecting clauses to the ST. Added to the logical analysis of the different choices of projection in the TTs, we can make an evaluation concerning the different degree of ideational equivalence achieved in the different TTs. We can conclude that based on the general equivalence of the ideational meaning in the TTs, Ku and Xu made variations in the experiential structures of projecting clauses and the choice of the projection types, which results in the different

Chapter 5 Ideational Equivalence of Projection in the Lunyu and Its Translations

degrees of ideational equivalence achieved in the three translated texts, from comparatively the higher degree to the lower degree: LT-KT-XT.

Chapter 6
Interpersonal Equivalence of Projection in the *Lunyu* and Its Translations

6.1 Introduction

In the previous chapter, the ideational equivalence of projection between the ST and TTs was probed through an examination of the different lexicogrammatical choices made by the different translators. In this chapter, we will study the interpersonal meanings conveyed in the different choices from the systems of Mood, Modality, and Person in order to evaluate the interpersonal equivalence in projection in the ST and TTs.

6.2 Speech functions realized in projection

As discussed in Chapter 3, the clause in SFL is a composite entity, constituted of three structures, each of which realizes a distinctive type of meaning: ideational, interpersonal, and textual.

The interpersonal aspect of the projection clause nexus is realized by the projection of propositions or proposals. The projection of propositions includes the projection of statements and questions; the projection of proposals includes the projection of offers and commands (Halliday 1994a: 257-258).

Both propositions and proposals can be projected paratactically (quoted) or hypotactically (reported). With propositions, the reported clause is finite; with proposals, the reported clause may be finite or non-finite, as shown by the following examples:

Chapter 6   Interpersonal Equivalence of Projection in the Lunyu and Its Translations

[6-1] The philosopher Tsăng said, "I daily examine myself on three points." (LT:1/4) (quoted proposition)

[6-2] The Master said: "A youth, when at home, should be filial, and, abroad, respectful to his elders." (LT: 1/6) (quoted proposal)

[6-3] Măng Î asked what filial piety was. (LT: 2/5) (reported proposition)

[6-4] The chief of the Chî family sent to ask Min Tsze-ch'ien to be governor of Pî. (LT:6/9) (reported proposal, non-finite)

Both propositions and proposals can be projected verbally or mentally. When propositions are projected mentally, they are projected by processes of cognition — thinking, knowing, understanding, wondering, etc. When proposals are projected mentally, they are projected by affective processes of reaction: wishing, liking, hoping, fearing and so on:

[6-6] She knew he was going. (mental projection of proposition)
[6-7] Mary hopes to go to Sweden next year. (mental projection of proposal)
[6-8] I wish they would keep quiet. (mental projection of proposal) (Halliday 1994a:259)
[6-9] The Master was wishing Chî-tiâo K'âi to enter on official employment. (LT:5/6) (mental projection of proposal)

6. 2. 1   Equivalence of speech functions realized in projection

Here we will first study the equivalence in speech functions realized in projection of the ST and TT. According to our analysis (as shown in Appendix II), in the aphorisms from Book 1 to Book 9, most of the projections are of propositions and only a few are of proposals. In two instances, in Chapters Thirteen, Book 8 and Chapter 25, Book 9, because of the ambiguity of old Chinese, projections can be interpreted either as a projection of statement or projection of command. The majority of projections of propositions

89

are of statements, and the majority of projections of proposals are of commands. The numbers of projections of propositions and proposals in the ST and TTs are listed in Table 6-1 below.

As shown in Table 6-1, projection in the ST is realized by a similar amount of projections of propositions and projections of proposals in the TTs, and in general, the three TTs realize equivalent speech functions to the ST. The dominant realization of projection as propositions in both ST and TTs indicates that the TTs convey the equivalent interpersonal meaning to the ST. In the interactive events represented by the aphorisms, the commodity exchanged is primarily information, and the main speech role of the speakers is giving information.

Table 6-1 Speech functions of projection in the ST and TTs[①]

Text	Projection of propositions	Projection of statements	Projection of proposals	Projection of offers
		Projection of questions		Projection of commands
ST	147	123	21	1
		24		20
LT	145	120	24	1
		25		23
KT	145	125	24	1
		20		23

① The number of projection clause nexuses counted in the ST was 170, 2 of which could be interpreted as projection either of proposition or proposal. The number of projection clause nexuses counted in the TTs of Legge and Ku is 169 because their English translations are not based on the intralingual translation of B. J. Yang (2006) and they combine chapters 6/1 and 6/2 in Yang's version into one chapter. So in the study, the number of projection clause nexus counted in their TTs is less than that of Xu.

(continued)

Text	Projection of propositions	Projection of statements	Projection of proposals	Projection of offers
		Projection of questions		Projection of commands
XT	145	116	25	1
		29		24

6.2.2 Shifts of speech functions realized in projection

The analysis given in the previous section shows that the overall realization of speech functions achieves equivalence between the ST and TTs. However, when we analyze the speech functions of specific projection clause nexuses in different TTs, we can identify shifts in speech functions. Table 6-2 below shows the different speech functions realized in different TTs in relation to the same ST.

As Table 6-2 shows, projection clause nexuses in the ST can be realized either as projection of propositions or projection of proposals in the different TTs, something that may be caused by the ambiguity of the old Chinese text. One of the intralingual translations for the ST is *bié rén bù liǎojiě wǒ, wǒ bù jí; wǒ jí de shì zìjǐ bù liǎojiě bié rén* (别人不了解我，我不急；我急的是自己不了解别人) (Yang 2006), which can be interpreted as a projection of statement. Another intralingual translation for the ST is *bú yào chóu biérén bù zhī wǒ, gāi chóu wǒ bù zhī rén* (不要愁别人不知我，该愁我不知人) (Qian 2011), which can be interpreted as a projection of command. Of the three TTs, Ku translates it into projection of proposal, specifically, command, in the form of a suggestion and obligation to an unspecified third person, while Legge and Xu translate it into a projection of statement. The interpersonal meanings conveyed here are different: Legge and Xu's translations represent information concerning what "I" will do in the situation, whereby the Master is only giving information instead of giving suggestions or commands to the students.

Table 6-2 Shifts of speech functions in TTs

Text	Realization of projection clause nexus	Speech functions
ST	Zǐ yuē : "bú huàn rén zhi bù jǐ zhī , huàn bù zhī rén yě." 子曰:"不患人之不己知,患不知人也。"	Projection of proposition OR proposal
KT	Confucius remarked, "One should not be concerned not to be understood of men; one should be concerned not to understand man."	Projection of proposal
LT	The Master said, "I will not be afflicted at men's not knowing me; I will be afflicted that I do not know men."	Projection of proposition
XT	I care less, said the Master, to be understood and recognized by other people than to understand and recognize others.	Projection of proposition

Old Chinese often omits the Subject of the clause. The different understandings of the omitted Subject in the projected message must be made explicit in English because of the difference in Mood systems between Chinese and English. Thus translators may realize the projection clause nexus as either a proposition or a proposal based on their own understanding, as can be shown in the different TTs for Chapter Fourteen of Book Eight:

[6-10] *Zǐ yuē : "bú zài qí wèi , bù móu qí zhèng."*
子曰:"不在其位,不谋其政。"(ST:8/14)

[6-11] The Master said, "He who is not in any particular office, has nothing to do with plans for the administration of its duties." (LT:8/14)

[6-12] Confucius remarked, "A man who is not in office in the government of a country, should never give advice as to its policy." (KT:8/14)

[6-13] Do not interfere, said the Master, into the matter you are not in a position to. (XT:8/14)

In the ST, there is no Subject for the projected clause. Translators of the ST can interpret it as a projection either of a proposition or of a proposal by adding an indefinite third-person or a second-person pronoun in their translation.

6.3 Mood elements in the projecting clause

In 3.3.3.2, we saw that the Mood is the main grammatical system that realizes the different speech functions in language, and presents the clause either as a proposition or as a proposal. The Mood structure, which consists overall of Mood and Residue, realizes the interpersonal metafunction of the clause. The Mood consists of the functions Subject and Finite, the different selection and order of which realizes different Mood types.

In the previous section, we analyzed the speech functions realized in the projection clause nexus of different TTs. Here we will analyze the Mood of the projecting clause in the projection clause nexus from the viewpoint of the interpersonal meanings conveyed by the different choices in the functions of the Mood structure, focusing on the aphorisms of the ST.

6.3.1 Equivalence in Mood in the projecting clause

The projection clause nexuses of the ST are mainly projection of propositions, which realize the speech function of giving information in the interactive event. The main projecting clause takes the form of Subject ⌢ Finite ⌢ Predicator, no matter whether the projection clause nexus is a projection of propositions or proposals. In the Mood structure of the projecting clause, the Mood is composed of the Subject and the Finite operator and the Predicator realized in the projecting verb. In Table 6-3, we can see the realization of the Mood in the projecting clause of the different TTs for the most commonly used projecting clause zǐ yuē (子曰 "the Master said") in the ST.

Table 6-3 Equivalence in Mood in a projecting clause

Text	Mood structure	
ST	*zǐ* 子	*yuē* 曰
LT	The Master	said (did + say)
KT	Confucius	remarked (did + remark)
XT	The Master	said (did + say)
	Subject	Finite operator + Predicator

In the Mood structure of the projecting clause in the ST, the Mood is composed of *zǐ* (the Subject) and *yuē* (the Predicator). In old Chinese, readers can only interprete the tense in the co-text. Tense of the projecting clause *zǐ yuē* in the ST is implicit and it can be interpreted as past tense since the *Lunyu* is a composition of what Confucius has said to his disciples in the past. The mood types chosen in the ST is declarative, realizing the speech function of giving information.

In the TTs, the Mood is realized by the combination of Subject, Finite operator and Predicator, which realizes the interpersonal function of giving information. The Finite operators in the Mood structures are "did", which indicates the primary tense of the proposition. The three translated versions have chosen the equivalent Mood types — the declarative mood types to realize the interpersonal metafunction of giving information.

6.3.2 Shifts in the Mood elements of the projecting clause

6.3.2.1 Shifts in the Subject

The three TTs generally realize equivalent interpersonal meanings in the Mood of the projecting clause. On the other hand, the different choice and configuration of Subject, Finite and the Predicator in the Mood structure can express different interpersonal meanings. Table 6-4 shows the different choice of Subject and Predicator in the Mood elements of different TTs.

Table 6-4 Shifts in the choice of Mood elements in projecting clauses

Text	M E①			
	Subject			Finite operator + predicator
ST	子 Zǐ	曾子 Zēngzǐ	子贡 Zǐgòng	曰 yuē
LT	The Master	the philosopher Tsăng	Tsze-kung	said (did +say)
KT	Confucius	a disciple of Confucius	a disciple of Confucius	remarked (did +remark)
XT	The Master	Master Zeng	Zi Gong	said (did +say)

The different choice of Subject in the Mood structure can realize different interpersonal metafunction in the interaction as Subject is the main part "responsible for the functioning of the clause as an interactive event" and is responsible for the validity of the proposition (Halliday 1994a: 76). In the TTs, different choice of the Subject can realize the attitude of the translator to the speaker, the source of the projection.

According to the Chinese dictionary, zǐ (子) is an honorific title when it is used together with the surname, such as Kǒngzǐ (孔子) and Zēngzǐ (曾子). It is used to show respect to the person of higher social status or to the Master. In the ST, the writer uses zǐ (子) to refer to Kǒngzǐ (孔子), indicating the respect of the students to their Master. When referring to the outstanding students of Confucius, such as Zēng Shēn (曾参) and Yǒu Ruò (有若), the compilers address them as Zēngzǐ (曾子) and Yǒuzǐ (有子) to show their respect. According to the study of Yang (2013), of Confucius' students only Zēng Shēn (曾参) and Yǒu Ruò (有若) are addressed as Zēngzǐ (曾子) and Yǒuzǐ (有子), putting the honorific title after their surnames. The other students mentioned in the Lunyu are addressed by their courtesy name instead of the given name. The courtesy name, zì (字) in Chinese, is a name bestowed upon a person at adulthood in addition to one's given name, or míng (名) in

---

① ME is the abbreviation for the Mood element.

Chinese. In ancient China, the courtesy name① would replace a male's given name when a man turned twenty, as a symbol of adulthood and respect. The given name can only be used by the superiors to the juniors or used as a humble address for oneself. Addressing the students of Confucius by their courtesy name and addressing *Zēng Shēn* (曾参) and *Yǒu Ruò* (有若) using *zǐ* (子) in the ST, is a style set by all the compilers of the *Lunyu* and shows that in the long period of compilation, *Zēng Shēn* (曾参) and *Yǒu Ruò* (有若) have taken a leading right of speech (Yang 2013: 34 - 45) and won respect from later compilers. That is the interpersonal meaning realized in the choice of Subject in the projecting clauses of the ST.

In LT, he translates *zǐ* (子) as "the Master", *Zēngzǐ* (曾子) as "the philosopher Tsǎng", and *Yǒuzǐ* (有子) as "the philosopher Yû?". The other students mentioned in the text are addressed by the courtesy names, which is in accordance with the ST. According to the footnotes to his translation (Legge 1971: 137), Legge chooses "the Master" to translate *zǐ* (子) because he understands *zǐ* (子) in Chinese to be the common designation of virtuous males and he thinks that in conversation it is used the same way as "Sir" and "Mr." in English and may thus be rendered "the philosopher", "the scholar" etc. He also understands that when *zǐ* (子) follows the surname, it indicates that the person spoken of was the Master of the writer. He explains in the footnotes that if he follows the preceding translators to translate *zǐ* (子) as "Confucius", he will miss the interpersonal meaning of "reverence which it bespeaks" for Confucius (Legge 1971: 137). Legge's choice of the Subject of the projecting clause can realize the equivalent interpersonal meaning to the ST.

Xu follows Legge's choice of translating *zǐ* (子) into "the Master", which conveys similar equivalent interpersonal meaning to the ST. He uses "Master Zeng" and "Master You" to refer to *Zēngzǐ* (曾子) and *Yǒuzǐ* (有子) in the ST, which can also realize similar interpersonal meanings to the ST. In translating the names of

---

① The list of courtesy names and given names for the disciples of Confucius is given in the appendix.

other disciples functioning as the Subject of the projecting clause, Xu also uses the courtesy name, which is equivalent to the ST.

In KT, he translates zǐ (子) as "Confucius", a Latinized version of Kǒng Fūzǐ (孔夫子) "Master Kong" used by early Roman Catholic missionaries from Europe. The Chinese Kǒng Fūzǐ (孔夫子), by removing the lightly pronounced-g and appending the Latin masculine ending -us, becomes "Confucius". The other Subjects in the projecting clause of the ST are translated as "a disciple of Confucius", with the specific names of the disciples of Confucius omitted. In the TTs of Ku, the readers can get the information that the projected signals come from Confucius and his disciples, but can't get the interpersonal meaning conveyed with their names. The meaningful choice of Ku concerning the Subject of the projecting clause may convey different interpersonal meaning to the ST. Ku aims to show the profound influence of Chinese culture to the westerners in his translation and he thinks in his translation the most important thing is the ideas conveyed by Confucius. To achieve the target, he meaningfully omits the unfamiliar and troublesome names of Chinese in the translation and makes the readers focus on the ideas in the *Lunyu* (Jin 2009). Choosing *Confucius* to render Kǒng Fūzǐ (孔夫子) conveys more ideational meaning than *the Master*. With the use of *Confucius* in the translation, the name Kǒng Fūzǐ (孔夫子) becomes more and more familiar to Western readers, which helps to achieve Ku's aim of conveying the Confucian philosophy to the world. With the choice of *Confucius* and a *disciple of Confucius* as Subject of each projecting clause, the interpersonal relationship between the Subjects in each chapter is made clearer than that of the other two TTs.

6.3.2.2 Shifts in the projecting verbs

The Mood structure, which consists overall of Mood and Residue, realizes the interpersonal metafunction of the clause. The Mood element contains the Finite and Predicator, as realized by the projecting verbs. The different choice of projecting verb, whether verbal or mental, can reflect the attitude of the Subject of the projecting clause towards the projected message (Zeng 2008).

Halliday and Matthiessen (2004: 448) also point out that different projecting verbs can convey different meanings. The projecting clauses in the ST and TTs are realized by the verbal process, but the choice of the projecting verbs varies in different translations.

The projecting verbs in the ST are simplex and the most frequently used projecting verb is *yuē* (曰). Some other less frequently used projecting verbs in the ST are *wèi* (谓) and *wèi yuē* (谓……曰) in aphorisms; and *wèn* (问), *wèn yuē* (问曰), *duì yuē* (对曰) in dialogues. *Yuē* (曰) is one of the most common projecting verbs in ancient Chinese. It is used to quote sayings and it is fairly neutral in terms of interpersonal connotations not showing the attitudes and aims of the speaker (Wang 2004). The choice of projecting verbs in the English TTs varies in different contexts. In Table 6-4, we can see that in the TTs of Legge and Xu, the translators choose the verb *say* as the corresponding main projecting verb in the projection clause nexus. As Halliday (1994a: 252) observes, *say* is the general member of the class of verbs used in quoting clauses. It is a neutral projecting verb which can project any kind of verbal clauses and does not specify the speaker's purpose, attitude and way of speaking. In their translations, Legge and Xu choose the projecting verb to convey the equivalent interpersonal meanings to the ST. In the aphorisms, Legge mainly chooses "the Master said" while Xu chooses "said the Master" to translate *zǐ yuē* (子曰). The choice of projecting verbs in Ku's translation is different. Firstly, he always chooses "remark" instead of "say" as the projecting verb. According to the explanation provided in the *Oxford Advanced Learners' English-Chinese Dictionary*, "remark" means "say or write by way of comment". Halliday (1994a: 252) points out that the projecting verb "remark" is specific to statements and questions. Ku uses "remark" to project most of the sayings of Confucius and his disciples, no matter whether they are statements, questions, offers or commands in the part of aphorism. The other projecting verbs used in Ku's translation include "observed" and "said to", "went on to say" etc. Compared to the simplex projecting verbs used in the aphorisms of the ST, Ku's varied choice of projecting verbs has not achieved full equivalence of the interpersonal metafunction to the ST.

There are at least two turns of asking and answering in the dialogues. The projecting verbs in the ST vary from those in the aphorisms such as *wèn* (问) and *yuē* (曰), *wèn yuē* (问曰), *gào zhi yuē* (告之曰), *duì yuē* (对曰) etc. In the TTs, while Legge and Xu still use "say" to translate *yuē* (曰), Ku uses different verbs to project the answers in the dialogue. For example, in the brief dialogues in which there is an indirect question and a direct answer, Legge and Xu choose the verbs of "ask" and "say" to project the two turns. Ku chooses "ask" and "answer" to specify the different speech functions performed by the speakers. As for the complete dialogues, the use of projecting verbs becomes more varied, such as "said to", "ask", "enquire", "answer", "reply", "rejoined", "went on to say", "enquired of Confucius saying" etc. The varied selection of verbs in different contexts in the TT of Ku can convey specific interpersonal meaning in the context which is not specifically realized in the ST and it seems to make the TT of Ku livelier than the ST.

6. 3. 2. 3 Shifts in the structure of projecting clause

In the ST, the structure of the projecting clause is very simple and almost always the same, realized as "Subject +projecting verb (which realizes Finite ^ Predicator)". In the TTs, Legge chooses similar simple-structured projecting clauses to the ST and Ku chooses many varied structures in his projecting clauses, as we have analyzed in the section of 5. 2. 1. Different choices for the structures of projecting clauses may not only cause the shifts in the experiential meanings but also in the interpersonal meanings. For example, the projecting clause with the structure of "Subject +was heard to + projecting verbs" is chosen in the TT of Ku. The experiential meaning it conveys is that it indicates two participants in the verbal process. The shifts in the experiential meaning result in the change in the interpersonal meaning conveyed in the projecting clause: the interpersonal relationship between the speakers in the TT of Ku is made clearer than that in the ST.

Xu chooses equivalent simple structures for the projecting clause in the aphorisms, and a variety structures in the dialogues. For example, in dialogues, seventeen projecting clauses of the asking turn are embedded in a hypotactic enhancing *when*- clause dependent on the main projection clause nexus which realizes the speaking turn taken by the Master. This choice of the structure of projecting clauses highlights the unequal status of speaking between Confucius and other speakers, an interpersonal meaning that is not realized by the projecting clause of the ST.

The different interpersonal meanings conveyed in the different realization of the projecting clauses of the different TTs can be seen in example [6-14] below.

[6-14] *Mèng Wǔbó wèn Zǐlù rén hu?*
孟武伯问子路仁乎?
Zǐ yuē : "bù zhī yě."
子曰:"不知也。"
Yòu wèn.
又问。
Zǐ yuē : "yóu yě , qiān shèng zhī guó , kě shǐ zhì qí fù yě , bù zhī qí rén yě."
子曰:"由也,千乘之国,可使治其赋也,不知其仁也。"
"Qiú yě hé rú?"
"求也何如?"
Zǐ yuē : "qiú yě , qiān shì zhī yì , bǎi shèng zhī jiā , kě shǐ wéi zhī zǎi yě , bù zhī qí rén yě."
子曰:"求也,千室之邑,百乘之家,可使为之宰也,不知其仁也。"
"Chì yě hé rú?"
"赤也何如?"
Zǐ yuē : "Chì yě , shùdài lì yú cháo , kě shǐ yǔ bīnkè yán yě , bù zhī qí rén yě."
子曰:"赤也,束带立於朝,可使与宾客言也,不知其仁也。" (ST:5/8)

LT
1. Măng Wŭ asked about Tsze-lû, whether he was perfectly virtuous. The Master said, "I do not know."
2. He asked again, when the Master replied, "In a kingdom

Chapter 6 Interpersonal Equivalence of Projection in the Lunyu and Its Translations

of a thousand chariots, Yû might be employed to manage the military levies, but I do not know whether he be perfectly virtuous."

3. "And what do you say of Ch'ih?" The Master replied, "In a city of a thousand families, or a house of a hundred chariots, Ch'ih might be employed as governor, but I do not know whether he is perfectly virtuous."

4. "What do you say of Ch'ih?" The Master replied, "With his sash girt and standing in a court, Ch'ih might be employed to converse with the visitors and guests, but I do not know whether he is perfectly virtuous." (LT:5/7)

KT:

A member of a powerful family of nobles in Confucius' native State asked Confucius if his disciple, the above mentioned Chung Yu, was a moral character. "I cannot say," answered Confucius. But on being pressed, Confucius said, "In the government of a State of even the first-rate power the man could be entrusted with the organization of the army. I cannot say if he could be called a moral character."

The noble then put the same question with regard to another disciple. Confucius answered, "In the government of a large town or in the direction of affairs in a small principality, the man could be entrusted with the chief authority. I cannot say if he could be called a moral character."

The noble went on to put the same question with regard to another disciple. Confucius answered, "At court, in a gala-dress reception, he could be entrusted with the duty of entertaining the visitors. I cannot say if he could be called a moral character." (KT:5/7)

XT:

Meng Wu asked whether Zi Lu was a man of men. The Master said, "I do not know." When asked again, he said, "In a country of a thousand chariots, Zi Lu might serve in the military field, but I do not know how he could be a man of men." When asked about Ran Qiu, the Master said, "In a city of a thousand families or a baronial house of a hundred chariots, Qiu might serve as an administrator, but I do not know how he could be a man of men." When asked about Gongxi Chi, the Master said, "Standing at court with a sash around the waist, Chi might serve in the intercourse with honorable guests, but I do not know how he could be a man of men." (XT:5/8)

Table 6-5 below shows the different realizations of projecting clauses in the ST and different TTs in Example [6-14]. As we can see in Table 6-5, the dialogue in the ST includes four turns of asking and answering between Meng Wubo and Confucius. The dialogue consists of seven projection clause nexus realized as quoting, two of which omitted the projecting clauses. The projecting verbs used in the projection clause nexuses are *wèn* (问 "ask") and *yuē* (曰 "say").

Table 6-5 Different realizations of projecting clauses in Example [6-14]

ST	LT	KT	XT
Mèng Wǔbó wèn 孟武伯问	Mǎng Wǔ asked	A member of a powerful family of nobles in Confucius' native State asked	Meng Wu asked
zǐ yuē 子曰	The Master said	answered Confucius	The Master said
yòu wèn 又问	He asked again	on being pressed	When asked again
zǐ yuē 子曰	When the Master replied	Confucius said	he said
omitted	omitted	The noble then put the same question	When asked about Ran Qiu
zǐ yuē 子曰	The Master replied	Confucius answered	the Master said
omitted	omitted	The noble went on to put the same question	When asked about Gongxi Chi
zǐ yuē 子曰	The Master replied	Confucius answered	the Master said

The corresponding projecting clauses in LT are "Mǎng Wǔ asked", "The Master said", "He asked again", "when the Master replied" and "the Master replied". For the two projecting clauses omitted in the ST, Legge chooses also to omit them in his translation. From Table 6-5 we can see that Legge has tried to maintain the equivalence in the Mood elements of the projecting clauses: the equivalent choice of Subject of the projecting clause [Mèng Wǔbó (孟武伯) to Mǎng Wǔ ; Zǐ (子) to the Master]; the equivalent choice of projecting verbs with only a few variations to the ST.

In Ku's translation, the projecting clauses are realized respectively as "A member of a powerful family of nobles in Confucius' native State asked", "answered Confucius", "on being pressed", "Confucius said", "The noble then put the same question", "Confucius answered", "The noble went on to put the same question", "Confucius answered". The first projecting clause carries much more information than the ST by realizing the Subject in the ST (which is realized as a proper name) with a noun explaining the status of the Subject in the ST. The extra information added in the projecting clause is based on Ku's own understanding of the ST and makes the readers easier to understand the relationship between the speakers in the dialogue. The projecting clauses omitted in the ST are supplied in the TT of Ku to make the source of the projected message clearer to the readers and make the TT as a coherent dialogue with clear turns of asking and answering. The TT of Ku carries more interpersonal meaning than the ST, with a much clearer relationship between the persons involved in the dialogue and more readers-friendly to the target readers.

In XT, the seven projection clause nexuses are realized as five projection clause nexuses, with the projecting clause realized as "Meng Wu asked" and "the Master said". The three turns of asking in the dialogue are put in the hypotactic enhancing *when-* clause dependent on the projecting clause "the Master said". With the asking turns put in the subordinated clauses, the projection clause nexuses with the projecting clause of "the Master said" are highlighted. The readers will pay more attention to the part concerning the sayings said by the Master. Thus the unequal status of speaking between Confucius and Meng Wu is highlighted, an interpersonal meaning that is not realized by the projecting clause of the ST. This interpersonal meaning conveyed in Xu's translation is based on Xu's understanding of the status of the teacher in the eyes of the disciples. Wu (2011) has found that the dialogues of the *Lunyu* are usually composed of questions asked by the disciples or other speakers and the answers given by the Master without further argument and discussion. The main reason for this is that in the eyes of the compilers of the *Lunyu*, the Master is omniscient with the ability to answer all the questions they propose. The compilers of the *Lunyu* record what the Master said word for word like taking notes in the classroom, not daring to add nor to delete anything from their Master's sayings. Wu (2011) points out that in the *Lunyu*, even in the dialogue, the dialogues look like aphorisms of the Master. Xu in his TTs specifies this implied interpersonal meaning in the ST with his unique choice of projecting clauses by placing the projection in the asking turn in a *when-* clause dependent on the answering turn taken by the Master.

The analysis of example [6-14] shows that in the translations, Legge tries to maintain equivalence of interpersonal meaning realized in the choice of the projecting clause with his similar choice of projecting clauses in the TT; Ku and Xu use different structures of projecting clauses to the ST and convey certain interpersonal meanings different from that in the ST.

In summary, in the three TTs of Legge, Ku and Xu, all the translators choose the combination of Subject and Finite to realize the declarative Mood types in the TTs, which realized the equivalent speech function of giving information to the ST. The different choice of the Mood elements of the projecting clauses can convey different interpersonal meanings in different TTs. Legge chooses the equivalent Mood elements in the projecting clauses and maintains the equivalence of interpersonal meaning to the ST. Ku chooses variant projecting verbs and structures of projecting clause to make the TT more lively in different contexts of speaking, while his choice of Subject in the projecting clauses makes the relationship of each chapter clearer to the readers. Xu realizes the projecting clauses of asking turns in the dialogues with the dependent *when-* clauses to highlight the unequal status of speaking between Confucius and the others, an interpersonal meaning that is not realized by the projecting clause of the ST.

6.4 Modality in the projected clauses

As discussed in Section 6.2.1, in the aphorisms from Book One to Book Nine in the ST and the TTs, the three translated versions achieve general equivalence to the ST in the speech functions realized in the projection clause nexuses. There are, however, shifts caused by different choices in the modality system in the projection of different TTs.

6.4.1 Modality realizing different speech functions in projection

The System of Modality can be divided into two types: Modalization, realizing different degrees of probability and usuality in propositions; and Modulation, realizing different degree of obligation and inclination in proposals.

System of orientation, the distinction between subjective and objective modality and between the explicit and implicit variants (Halliday 1994a: 357), provides a range of realizations for each type of Modality. Table 6-6 shows examples of combining the system of orientation with the types of modality.

Table 6-6　Types and orientation in Modality (Halliday & Matthiessen 2004: 620)

Types	Orientation			
	Explicit subjective	Implicit subjective	Implicit objective	Explicit objective
Modalization: probability	I think Mary knows.	Mary'll know.	Mary probably knows.	It's likely that Mary knows.
Modalization: usuality		Fred'll sit quite quiet.	Fred usually sits quite quiet.	It's usual for Fred to sit quite quiet.

(continued)

Types	Orientation			
	Explicit subjective	Implicit subjective	Implicit objective	Explicit objective
Modulation: obligation	I want John to go.	John should go.	John's supposed to go.	It's expected that John goes.
Modulation: willingness		Jane'll help.	Jane's keen to help.	

The choice of modality in the translation may result in the different realization of projection as propositions or proposals, which conveys different interpersonal meaning in the TTs. The choice of modality in the projected clause represents the angle of the Subject of projecting clauses, usually the speaker. Example [6-15] can show how the different choice of Modality in the projected clause realizes different interpersonal meanings in the TTs.

[6-15] Zǐ yuē: "jūnzǐ bú zhòng, zé bù wēi, xué zé bú gù."
子曰:"君子不重，则不威；学则不固。"
　　　Projection of proposition (ST:1/8)

The Master said, "If the scholar be not grave, he **will**① not call forth any veneration, and his learning will not be solid."
　　　Projection of proposition (LT:1/8)

Confucius remarked, "A wise man who is not serious will not inspire respect; what he learns will not remain permanent."
　　　Projection of proposition (KT:1/8)

An intelligentman, said the Master, should not be frivolous, or he would lack solemnity in his behavior and solidity in his learning.
　　　Projection of Command (XT:1/8)

As example [6-15] shows, the ST is a projection of statement concerning the proper behaviors of the *jūnzǐ* (君子) and the

---

① Emphasis added by the present writer.

probable results it may cause. In the three TTs, the projection of statement in the ST is realized respectively as projection of a statement or of a command, realized by different choices in the Modality system. The implicit subjective form of modality, *will*, chosen in the TTs of Legge and Ku represents the degree of probability held by "the Master" towards the proposition / statement in the projected clause. The implicit subjective form of modality, *should*, chosen in XT represents the degree of obligation that "the Master" applies to the projected clause: the pressure on the part of listener to carry out the requirement of being an intelligentman. The different choice in the modality system results in different speech functions realized in the TTs.

6.4.2 Modality realizing different values in the projected clause

Even when the ST is rendered using the same types of projection in the different TTs, the different modality used in the projected clauses of TTs can convey different interpersonal meanings.

First, the different choice of Finite modal operators in the modality system can realize different values of the degree of certainty towards the validity of a proposition or the degree of obligation towards the necessity of a proposal as shown in Table 6-7 below.

Second, different choices of Modal adjuncts or the expansion of the Predicators[1] also expresses different values of modality as shown in Table 6-8 below (Halliday & Matthiessen 2004:620).

Third, the different forms of modality used in the clause can express "how far the speaker overtly accepts **responsibility** for the attitude being expressed" (Thompson 1996b: 70). The speaker can express the different scale of "modal responsibility" as "explicit subjective, implicit subjective, implicit objective or explicit objective" with different forms of modality used, as shown in the previous Table 6-6.

---

[1] "expansion of the Predicator": one way of expressing obligation and inclination proposed in Halliday and Matthiessen (2004:147), typically realized by a passive verb, e.g. you're supposed to know that, or typically by an adjective, e.g. I'm anxious to help them.

Table 6-7　Different values of Finite modal operators in English（based on Halliday & Matthiessen 2004:116）

Value	Low	Median	High
positive	can, may, could, might (dare)	will, would, should, is / was to	must, ought to, need, has / has to
negative	needn't, doesn't / didn't + need to, have to	won't, wouldn't, shouldn't, (isn't / wasn't to)	mustn't, oughtn't to, can't, couldn't, (mayn't, mightn't, hasn't / hadn't to)

Table 6-8　Different values in the Modal adjuncts or the expansion of the predicators（Halliday & Matthiessen 2004:620）

value	Probability	Usuality	Obligation	Inclination
high	certain	always	required	determined
median	probable	usually	supposed	keen
low	possible	sometimes	allowed	willing

The different degrees of value and responsibility conveyed by the choice of modality can be demonstrated with an example taken from Chapter Twenty-three of Book Nine as shown in Example [6-16].

[6-16] Zǐ yuē: "hòushēng kě wèi..."
子曰:"后生可畏……"(ST:9/23)
The Master said, "A youth is to be regarded with respect." (LT:9/22)
Confucius remarked, "Youths should be respected." (KT:9/22)
Respect the young, said the Master. (XT:9/23)

In Example [6-16], all the three translated versions realize the projection clause nexus in the ST as a command. The different choices in the modality realize differing degrees of pressure on the listeners to carry out this command and differing degrees of responsibility accepted by the speaker towards the projected message as shown in Table 6-9 below.

Chapter 6　Interpersonal Equivalence of Projection in the Lunyu and Its Translations

Table 6-9　Different values realized in the choice of modality in [6-16]

Text	Choice of modality	Speech function	Orientation	Degree of pressure	Responsibility taken by the speaker
LT	is to be regarded with respect	command	implicit objective	medium	low
KT	should be respected	command	implicit subjective	medium	medium
XT	respect the young	command	explicit subjective	high	high

As Table 6-9 shows, the Finite modal operators used in the projected clause of LT and KT are respectively "is to", "should"; while in XT, being in the imperative mood, there is no Finite modal operator. The modal operators "is to" and "should" carry the medium pressure on the listeners to carry out the command of "respect the youth". The imperative clause "respect the youth" carries the highest degree of pressure on the listeners to carry out the command as the "imperative clause" is the typical choice of clause type in making a command to family and friends in informal situations (Eggins 1994: 67). The use of modality to modulate the request and command such as "is to" and "should" in LT and KT can reduce the pressure of the command on the listeners as the use of modality is a way to express politeness towards the other person.

In LT, the choice of "is to be respected" realizes the "implicit objective" orientation that the speaker of the projected message accepts because "is to be respected" means "is supposed to be respected". In KT, the choice of "should be respected" realizes the "implicit subjective" orientation of the speaker in the projection clause nexus. In XT, the choice of an imperative clause without any use of modality realizes the modal responsibility accepted by the speaker as explicit subjective because it can be interpreted as "I want you to respect the youth." In the TT of Xu, the speaker takes the highest responsibility for the command.

The different degrees of value and responsibility realized in the different choice of modality in the projected clause can also be shown in the difference choices of modality in the TTs of Chapter Thirteen of Book Six.

[6-17] *Zǐ wèi Zǐxià yuē : "rǔ wéi jūnzǐ rú ! wú wéi xiǎorén rú !"*
子谓子夏曰："女为君子儒！无为小人儒！"(ST: 6/13)

The Master said to Tsze-hsiâ, "Do you be a scholar after the style of the superior man, and not after that of the mean man." (LT:6/11)

Confucius said to a disciple, "Be a good and wise man while you try to be an encyclopedic man of culture. Be not a fool while you try to be an encyclopedic man of culture." (KT:6/11)

The Master said to Zi Xia, "You should be an intellectual of the higher class, not one of the lower class." (XT:6/13)

In example [6-17], all three TTs construe the projection as projection of commands but with different choices in the modality system in the projected clauses. LT realizes the projected command with an old-fashioned form of an imperative clause with explicit Finite and Subject. XT realizes the projected command with the modal operator *should* which carries medium pressure on the listeners and the use of an "implicit subjective" orientation shows the speaker's acceptance of the responsibility. KT realizes the projected command with an imperative clause. The imperative clause shows the speaker putting the highest pressure on the listener to carry out the command and the use of an "explicit subjective" orientation shows the speaker taking the highest responsibility for the command.

6.4.3 Understanding of modality in the ST resulting in different choices in the TTs

We have discussed in Section 6.2.2 above how the ambiguity contained in the omission of Subject in the ST can result in shifts in the interpersonal meaning of the TTs. The use of modality in the ST may also lead to various interpretations among different translators, resulting in different choices of modality in the TTs and conveying different interpersonal meaning. The differing renderings of the projection clause nexus in Chapter Twenty-four of Book Four give an example of this.

[6-18] *Zǐ yuē : "Jūnzǐ yù nè yú yán , ér mǐn yú xíng. "*
子曰:"君子欲讷于言，而敏于行。"(ST:4/24)

The Master said, "The superior man wishes to be slow in his words and earnest in his conduct." (LT:4/24)

Confucius remarked, "A wise man wants to be slow in speech and diligent in conduct." (KT:4/24)

A cultured man, said the Master, may be slow in word but prompt in deed. (XT:4/24)

According to the Chinese dictionary, *yù* (欲) in old Chinese can be interpreted as *xiǎng yào dé dào* (想要得到 "wants to get") or *xīwàng* (希望 "wishes"), *jiāngyào* (将要 "will"). The ambiguity in the modality of *yù* (欲) makes it possible for the ST to be interpreted either as a projection of a proposition describing the ideas of a *Jūnzǐ* (君子 "man of virtue") or as a projection of proposal which shows the requirement for being a *Jūnzǐ* (君子). The different choice of modality in each TT shows the differing interpretations by the translators of the modality in the ST.

In Legge's translation, the modality is realized by the expansion of the Predicator *wishes to be*, which shows the willingness or inclination of "the superior man" to "be slow in his words and earnest in his conduct". In Ku's translation, the modality is realized by *wants to be*, which shows a higher degree of willingness and inclination of "a wise man" to "be slow in speech and diligent in conduct". In Xu's translation, the modality is realized as *may*, the Finite modal operator shows a low probability of "a cultured man" to "be slow in word but prompt in deed". All three renderings can be analyzed as projections of propositions with different choices of modality, with two of them showing different degrees of inclination and one showing a low degree of probability

Example [6-19] can also show that the different understanding of the modality used in the ST may result in the different choice of modality in the TTs.

[6-19] *Zǐ yuē : "mín kě shǐ yóu zhī , bùkě shǐ zhī zhī. "*
子曰:"民**可**①使由之,不可使知之。"(ST:8/9)

The Master said, "The people **may** be made to follow a path of action, but they **may not** be made to understand it." (LT:8/9)

Confucius remarked, "The common people **should** be educated in what they ought to do; not to ask why they should do it." (KT:8/9)

The common people, said the Master, **may** be made to follow, but **not** to understand the reason why. (XT:8/9)

In the ST of example [6-19], the positive and negative form of the Modal operators *kě* (可) and *bùkě* (不可) are used to convey a pressure of command on the speakers, with *kě* (可) carrying a low degree of pressure on the listener and *bùkě* (不可) carrying a much higher degree of pressure to fulfill the requirement on the speakers. In the three translated versions, Legge and Xu choose the Finite modal operator *may* to realize a similar low degrees of pressure on the listeners as *kě* (可) in the ST and choose *may not* (*may* omitted in Xu's translation) to realize the similar highest degree of values on the command of the listeners as *bùkě* (不可) in the ST. Ku's choice of the Finite modal operator *should* in the TT carries a higher degree of value than *kě* (可) in the ST and his choice of *should not* (*should* is omitted) carries a lower degree of value than *bùkě* (不可) in the ST according to Halliday and Matthiessen's (2004:116) study on the different values in the Finite modal operators as shown in Table 6-8.

The translators' choice of modality in the projected clause is important to achieve interpersonal equivalence to the ST. The different choice of modality in the projected message may result in the different realization of the projection clause nexus as a proposition or a proposal and it may also cause difference in the value of validity or obligation of the projection clause nexus.

---

① Emphasis added by the present writer.

Chapter 6   Interpersonal Equivalence of Projection in the Lunyu and Its Translations

6.5   Person system in projection

As discussed in Section 3.3.3.2, the Person system is another important system that construes interpersonal meaning. Different choices in the person system realizing the Subject of the projecting clause, or as vocatives in the projected clause, can be used in different TTs to convey different interpersonal meanings.

In the ST, the disciples functioning as Subject of the projecting clause are addressed by their courtesy names except *Zēng Shēn* (曾参) and *Yǒu Ruò* (有若). The given name can only be used as vocatives while the Master is speaking to the disciples or the disciples use it as a humble way to refer to themselves as example [6-20] shows.

[6-20] *Zǐgòng yuē*: "*pín ér wú chǎn, fù ér wú jiāo, hé rú?*"
子贡曰:"贫而无谄,富而无骄,何如?"
Zǐ yuē: "*kě yě. wèi ruò pín ér lè, fù ér hào lǐ zhě yě.*"
子曰:"可也;未若贫而乐,富而好礼者也。"
Zǐgòng yuē: "*Shī yún*: '*rú qiē rú cuō, rú zhuó rú mó*', *qí sī zhī wèi yǔ?*"
子贡曰:"诗云:'如切如磋,如琢如磨',其斯之谓与?"
Zǐ yuē: "*Cì yě, shǐ kě yǔ yán Shī yǐ yǐ, gào zhū wǎng ér zhī lái zhě.*"
子曰:"赐也,始可与言《诗》已矣,告诸往而知来者。"
(ST:1/15)

[6-21]
1. Tsze-kung said, "What do you pronounce concerning the poor man who yet does not flatter, and the rich man who is not proud?" The Master replied, "They will do; but they are not equal to him, who, though poor, is yet cheerful, and to him, who, though rich, loves the rules of propriety."
2. Tsze-kung replied, "It is said in the Book of Poetry, 'As you cut and then file, as you carve and then polish.' — The meaning is the same, I apprehend, as that which you have just expressed."

3. The Master said, "With one like Tsze, I can begin to talk about the Odes. I told him one point, and he knew its proper sequence." (LT: 1/15)

A disciple of Confucius said to him, "To be poor and yet not to be servile; to be rich and yet not to be proud, what do you say to that?"
"It is good," replied Confucius, "but better still it is to be poor and yet contented; to be rich and to be courteous."
"I understand," answered the disciple.
"We must cut, we must file."
"Must chisel and must grind."
"That is what you mean, is it not?"
"My friend," replied Confucius, "now I can begin to speak of poetry to you. I see you understand how to apply the moral." (KT:1/15)

Zi Gong said, "What do you think of a poor man who does not flatter and a rich man who does not swagger?" The Master said, "Not bad, but not so good as a poor man who is cheerful and a rich man who is respectful." Zi Gong said, "Are such men *like polished ivory and stone and jade refined*, as said in the Book of Poetry?" The Master said, "My dear Zi Gong, now I may begin to talk with you about poetry. For when I told you about the past, you can anticipate the future." (XT:1/15)

In example [6-20], when *Duānmù Cì* （端木赐）is used as the Subject of the projecting clause, he is addressed by the courtesy name as Zǐgòng （子贡）to show respect, while when his Master addresses him, he uses instead his given name Cì （赐）as a vocative.

Of the three TTs as shown in example [6-21], Legge specifies the different use of the given name and the courtesy name in different situations in accordance with the ST: the courtesy name used as a Subject in the projecting clause, and the given name used as a vocative by superiors to the inferiors.

Ku omits all the courtesy names and given names while referring to the disciples of Confucius, all of the disciples being referred as "a disciple of Confucius". In the dialogue, he uses "my friend" as a

Chapter 6 Interpersonal Equivalence of Projection in the Lunyu and Its Translations

vocative used by the Master to his disciples to show the closeness of the Master and the disciples.

XT chooses the courtesy name to realize the names functioning as Subject of projecting clauses as well as the vocatives used by the Master to address his disciples, which cause shifts in the interpersonal meaning. In the last turn taken by the Master in the dialogue, the vocative used is "My dear Zi Gong", using the courtesy name of Duanmu Ci. The choice of courtesy name in this context has changed the interpersonal meaning conveyed in the ST and cannot convey an equivalent interpersonal meaning to the ST.

Different choices from the person system in the TTs result from ambiguity in the person system of the ST. In the ST, the person system is simple and less various than that of modern Chinese and the readers can only understand the meaning by referring to the context, while in English, the person system is much more varied and the choice of person must be clear in each situation. The choice of person system in the TTs is based on the translator's understanding of the ST, and different interpretations of the ST can result in different person choices of system in the TTs. Take the last projection clause nexus in [6-20] for example:

[6-22] *Zǐ yuē : "Cì yě , shǐ kě yǔ yán Shī yǐ yi , gào zhū wǎng ér zhī lái zhě. "*
子曰:"赐也,始可与言《诗》已矣,告诸往而知来者。"

In [6-22], the person system used includes the vocative *Cì* (赐) and the personal pronoun *zhū* (诸) which can normally be interpreted as a combination of pronoun *zhī* (之) and preposition *yú* (于). The personal pronouns which in a fuller version would proceed the verb *shǐ* (始) and follow the proposition *yǔ* (与) are omitted as retrievable from the context, as is common in old Chinese. The omission of the personal pronoun in the ST can result in the different interpretation of the translators and the different realization in the TTs. With the different personal pronouns used in the TTs, the readers can understand the interpersonal relationship between the speaker and the listener and specify the persons involved in the dialogue, as shown in Table 6-10.

Because of the omission of personal pronouns in the ST, the projected message in the ST can be interpreted as a comment made by the Master on *Duanmu Ci* to the disciples around or interpreted as what the Master said to *Duanmu Ci*. The persons involved in the dialogue could be *Duanmu Ci* and the Master or the Master and *Duanmu Ci* and other disciples. In the TTs of Ku and Xu, *Cì* (赐) is respectively realized as "my friend" and "Zi Gong". The vocative used in KT expresses an equivalent interpersonal meaning as the ST. While the use of "Zi Gong" as a vocative in XT does not realize the similar interpersonal meaning as that of the ST, as the courtesy name in ancient Chinese is used to show respect, and is not necessarily used in the situation of the Master addressing a disciple, and hence Xu's choice of vocative is not equivalent to the ST.

Table 6-10　Different choices from the person system in ST and TTs

Text	Example [6-22]	Person pronoun	Vocative	Interactants involved
ST	"*Cì yě, shǐ kě yǔ yán Shi yǐ yi, gào zhū wǎng ér zhī lái zhě.*" "赐也，始可与言《诗》已矣，告诸往而知来者。"	*zhū* 诸	*Cì* 赐	Confucius and Duanmu Ci / other disciples
KT	"My friend", "now I can begin to speak of poetry to you. I see you understand how to apply the moral."	I, you	My friend	Confucius and Duanmu Ci
XT	"My dear Zi Gong, now I may begin to talk with you about poetry. For when I told you about the past, you can anticipate the future."	I, you	Zi Gong	Confucius and Duanmu Ci
LT	"With one like Ts'ze, I can begin to talk about the odes. I told him one point, and he knew its proper sequence."	I, he, him	Ts'ze (not as vocative)	Confucius and other disciples

For the personal pronouns omitted in the ST before and after the verb *yán* (言 "speak") in the ST — both Ku and Xu render them as "I" and "you". The persons involved in the dialogue are Confucius and Duanmu Ci. In LT, they are respectively realized as *I* and *him*, and the personal pronoun *Ci* (赐) in the ST is realized as *With one like Tsze*. As Li (2009) observes, in a situation where the second person pronoun can be used, using the third person pronoun indicates an unfamiliar relationship or shows the distance between the individuals. Legge's choice of personal pronouns realizes an objective comment and judgment made by the Master on Duanmu Ci's ability, which is one of the possible interpretations of the ST. The readers of LT can identify at least three persons involved in the dialogue, as the last projection clause nexus, with the use of third person pronouns, indicates that Confucius is making comments on Duanmu Ci to those present. The interpersonal meaning conveyed in Legge's translation is different from that in the TTs by Ku and Xu.

As is commonly known, if one hundred people read *Hamlet*, there will be one hundred different kinds of Hamlet (Huang 2012a: 20). There is great scope of interpretation in the classical Chinese text such as the *Lunyu*, and the ambiguity in the person system of the ST is realized clearly in the different TTs with different interpersonal meanings conveyed in the different texts.

6.6 Summary

In this chapter, we have found that generally in the aphorisms, the different TTs achieve a similar degree of interpersonal equivalence to the ST. With further study on the Mood structure of the projecting clauses, it is found that all the three translated versions choose equivalent declarative Mood types to realize the interpersonal metafunction of the ST. Different choices of the Mood elements in different TTs show shifts between the ST and TTs. It is also found that different choices of modality in the projected clauses realize the different speech functions of the projection clause nexus in the TTs and differing values of validity and obligation in the projected message. Finally, the study of personal pronouns in the projection clause nexus can also shed lights on the different interpersonal meanings conveyed in the TTs.

This chapter has shown that the different translated versions, against a background of generally equivalent interpersonal meanings, can convey different interpersonal meanings by varying choice in the Mood elements, and the systems of Modality and Person.

Chapter 7
Textual Equivalence of Projection in the *Lunyu* and Its Translations

7.1 Introduction

This chapter will analyze the textual meaning in the projection clause nexuses of the *Lunyu* and its translated versions. As discussed in the previous section, the resources of thematic structure and cohesion are the most important grammatical means of realizing textual meaning. In the following section, the thematic structure and cohesion system of the projection clause nexus in the *Lunyu* and its translations will be analyzed.

7.2 System of Theme in the projection clause nexus

The system of Theme in clause complexes has been studied in Halliday (1994a), Halliday and Matthiessen (2004) and Eggins (2004), but there is some controversy concerning the system of Theme in the projection clause nexus. Thompson (1996b) has discussed Theme in reported clauses, and in relation to identifying Theme and Rheme in the projection clause nexus, finds still some issues unsettled.

Halliday (1994a: 53-58) suggests two patterns for representing the thematic structure of clause complexes. One pattern is to regard the clause put at the beginning of the clause nexus as Theme and the latter part of the clause nexus as Rheme. The other pattern is to identify the thematic structure of each of the constituent clauses of the clause complex. The two patterns of thematic structure can be shown in Figure 7-1:

If	winter	comes	can	spring	be far behind
Theme 1			Rheme 1		
structural	topical	Rheme 2	finite	topical	Rheme 3
Theme 2			Theme 3		

Figure 7-1　Theme in the clause complex
(Halliday 1994a:57)

Eggins (2004: 313-316) analyses the thematic structure of paratactic clause complexes and hypotactic clause complexes respectively. Following Eggins, in analyzing the thematic structure of paratactic clause complexes, we need to analyze separately the thematic structure of each individual independent clause. However, there are two different ways of analyzing the thematic structure of hypotactic clause complexes: first, when the main clause comes first and the dependent clause follows, simply to analyze the thematic structure respectively in each clause; second, when the main clause follows the dependent clause, to recognize two levels of thematic structure operating, the first to analyze the thematic structure of each clause, and second to regard the whole dependent clause as Theme of the clause complex.

In analyzing the thematic structure of the reported clause, Thompson (1996b) points out that in analyzing quotes, the Themes both in the projecting clause and the projected clause are important in the development of the text and should be analyzed separately. We can show this as in Figure 7-2.

He	said	"Some people	won't like it."
"What deters them	is the likelihood of being caught,"	he	said.
Theme	Rheme	Theme	Rheme

Figure 7-2　Theme in quotes (Thompson 1996b:161-162)

He also points out that it is sometimes difficult to analyze the thematic structure of indirect speech.

> With indirect speech, on the other hand, it is difficult to decide whether to treat the projected (reported) clause as forming a T-unit with its projecting clause — in which case the Theme need not be shown separately — or as a separate message on a different "level" — in which case the Theme should appear separately (Thompson 1996b: 162).

Thompson prefers to identify the Themes in the projecting clause and projected clause separately. Figure 7-3 gives an example of his way of analysis.

Baker (1999)	suggests	that certain features	might be observed more systematically using corpora
Strike action	puts teachers' hopes of winning reduction at risk,	the education secretary	will warn today.
Theme	Rheme	Theme	Rheme

Figure 7-3 A possible analysis of Theme in the indirect speech
(Thompson 1996b: 162)

Although there is no agreement on how to analyze the thematic structure in projection clause nexus, we can conclude two points from the research discussed above. First, in analyzing the thematic structure of the clause complex, the clause coming first can be regarded as Theme of the clause complex. Second, the Theme of the clause complex is different from the respective Themes of its constituent clauses (Fang 2001:57). In the study, Theme is regarded as the projecting clause or projected clause put in the first place of the projection clause nexus, as the "starting point" of the clause nexus. As shown in Figure 7-4, the projecting clause put in first place in a projection clause nexus functions as Theme while the projected clause functions as Rheme: this is the typical unmarked thematic structure of the projection clause nexus.

Zǐ yuē 子曰：	" qiǎo yán lìng sè , xiǎn yǐ rén. " "巧言令色，鲜矣仁。" (ST:1/3)
The Master said	Fine words and an insinuating appearance are seldom associated with true virtue (LT:1/3)
Projecting clause	Projected clause
Theme	Rheme

Figure 7-4　Unmarked thematic structure of projection
clause nexuses in the *Lunyu*

When the projected clause is put in first place in a projection clause nexus, this gives a marked thematic structure, as shown in Figure 7-5.

Few who respect their parents and their elders,	said Master You,	would do anything against their superiors.
part of projected clause	projecting clause	projected clause
Theme (marked)	Rheme	

Figure 7-5　The marked thematic structure of projection
clause nexus in the *Lunyu*

7.3　Thematic structure in projection

The thematic structure of projection in the ST is realized as a projecting clause ⌢ projected clause and this pattern of thematic structure is repeated in each chapter of the ST. The same Theme occurring regularly in each chapter can result in a clear focus for the text; but on the other hand, can make the text less dynamic and lacking connection between the Rhemes of the text. The text with this pattern of thematic structure is regarded as " a text which is going nowhere" and the "new information introduced in the Rhemes would not be followed up" (Eggins 2004:324).

7.3.1　Thematic structures of projection in the aphorisms

In the TTs, Legge and Ku mainly choose the unmarked

Chapter 7 Textual Equivalence of Projection in the Lunyu and Its Translations

thematic structure of "projecting clause ⌃ projected clause". Xu chooses the marked nested thematic structure "part of projected clause ⌃ projecting clause ⌃ part of projected clause" as the main thematic structure. The different choice of thematic structure in the three TTs can be shown in Figure 7-6 below.

ST	Zǐ yuē 子曰:	" Jūnzǐ bú qì. " "君子不器。" (ST:2/12)
LT	The Master said	"The accomplished scholar is not an utensil." (LT:2/12)
KT	Confucius remarked	"A wise man will not make himself into a mere machine fit only to do one kind of work." (KT:2/12)
	projecting clause	projected clause
	unmarked thematic structure	
XT	An intelligent man,	said the Master, is not a mere implement. (XT:2/12)
	part of projected clause	projecting clause ⌃ projected clause
	marked thematic structure	

Figure 7-6 Unmarked and marked thematic structure in the TTs

Our study on the thematic structure of projection in the aphorisms of TTs has gained the following findings. First, in KTs, the thematic structures for all the projection clause nexuses in the aphorisms are "projecting clause ⌃ projected clause", equivalent to that of the ST. Second, in LT, most of the projection clause nexuses show the unmarked thematic structure of "projecting clause ⌃ projected clause" equivalent to that of the ST, with the single exception of one projection clause nexus whose thematic structure is analyzed in Example [7-1].

[7-1] "I did not think," he said, "that music could have been made so excellent as this." (LT:7/13)
"part of projected clause ⌃ projecting clause ⌃ part of projected clause"

Third, in XT, only a small portion of thematic structures in the projection clause nexus are equivalent to that in the ST. For the most part, Xu chooses a nested thematic structure "part of projected clause ⌒ projecting clause ⌒ part of projected clause" or in a small number of cases the marked structure "projected clause ⌒ projecting clause" as shown in Examples [7-2] and [7-3]:

[7-2] Few who respect their parents and their elders, said Master You, would do anything against their superiors. (XT:1/2)
"part of projected clause ⌒ projecting clause ⌒ part of projected clause"

[7-3] How can an untrustworthy man be employed? said the Master. (XT:2/22)
"projected clause ⌒ projecting clause"

Table 7-1 gives the exact numbers of the unmarked and marked thematic structures chosen in the projection clause nexus of the ST and TTs in the aphorisms, showing the proportion of equivalence and shifts.

Table 7-1 Number of unmarked and marked thematic structures of projection in the aphorisms

Text	Unmarked thematic structure (No.)	Marked thematic structure (No.)
ST	168	0
LT	167	1
KT	168	0
XT	28	140

Table 7-1 shows that in the aphorisms, Legge and Ku have chosen the equivalent thematic structure of projection to the ST and achieved textual equivalence to the ST. Xu has chosen a large portion of marked thematic structure and has not achieved the textual equivalence to the ST.

The different choices in the thematic structure of the projection clause nexus demonstrate the different interpretations of textual meaning on the part of translators. Legge and Ku choose equivalent thematic structure to the ST and convey equivalent textual meaning to the ST: the starting point of information for each projection clause nexus is the source of projection, to be specific, the projecting clause of the projection clause nexus. There is no connection between the Rhemes of each projection clause nexus but the repeating of the projecting clause in each chapter of aphorisms can serve as a means of cohesion over the whole text. Xu chooses part of the projected clause or the whole projected clause as Theme of the projection clause nexus, so that the starting point of information is not the source of the projection message but part or the whole of the projected message. The information in the projected clause realized as Theme of the clause nexus is highlighted. Readers of the chapters can acquire a whole new array of information from the outset. Xu chooses the different thematic structure to the ST and realizes a different textual metafunction in his TT.

7.3.2 Thematic structures of projection in the dialogues

In the dialogues, the main thematic structure for the projection clause nexus chosen by Legge is the unmarked thematic structure "projecting clause ^ projected clause". For KT, a large proportion of the projection clause nexuses have marked thematic structures, such as "part of the projected clause ^ projecting clause ^ part of the projected clause" and "projected clause ^ projecting clause". For XT, a small portion of the clause nexuses have marked thematic structures: e.g. a hypotactic enhancing *when-* clause with an embedded projection clause nexus functioning as Theme; or part of the projected clause functioning as Theme in the projection clause nexus. The marked thematic structure of projection chosen in the TTs is shown in Table 7-2 below.

Table 7-2 Marked thematic structures in the dialogues

Text	Form of marked thematic structure	Marked thematic structure (No.)
LT	Part of P-ed C ^ P-ing C P-ed C ^ P-ing C	5
KT	Part of P-ed C ^ P-ing C P-ed C ^ P-ing C	69
XT	When-clause ^ P-ing C Part of P-ed C ^ P-ing C	32

As we can see in Table 7-2, LT chooses the largest proportion of equivalent unmarked thematic structure to the ST, with only a few variations in thematic structures. The marked thematic structures include the structure of "part of the projected clause functioning as Theme" and "the projected clause functioning as Theme". In XT, a large proportion of the marked thematic structure take the form of *when* clause ^ projecting clause ^ projected clause. In the *when*- clause, a projection clause nexus functioning as the asking turn of the dialogue is embedded, as seen in example [7-4].

[7-4] When Zi Zhang asked if the ritual systems of ten generations to come could be foreseen, the Master said, "The Yin Dynasty followed and modified the ritual system of the Xia, and its modified system was known. The Zhou Dynasty followed and altered the ritual system of the Yin, and its altered system is also known. So we may predict the system of the successors of the Zhou can be foreseen even a hundred generations later." (XT:2/23)

In the ST of example [7-4], there are two projection clause nexuses functioning as the asking turn and the answering turn of the dialogue. The thematic structure for each clause nexus is "projecting clause ^ projected clause". In the TT of Xu, the projection clause nexus functioning as the asking turn is realized as a *when*- clause dependent on the projecting clause in the answering turn. The thematic structure chosen is different from that in the ST and conveys a different textual meaning. The *when*- clause functions as the Theme of the whole dialogue and tells the readers that the starting point of the message is the questions proposed by the questioner with the new message conveyed in the projection clause nexus of the answering turn. This textual meaning realized with the choice of the marked thematic structure is not present in the ST.

The other two marked thematic structures in XT are realized as "part of projected clause ^ projecting clause ^ part of the projected clause" as we can see in Example [7-5].

[7-5] "A significant question," said the Master. "In ritual performance, it would be better to be thrift than lavish; in

mourning service, it would be better to be deep in grief than minute in observance." (XT:3/4)

In these marked thematic structures, the projected clause is put before the projecting clause and makes a better connection with the information in the Rheme of the previous projection clause nexus.

Apart from the marked thematic structures which are not equivalent to the ST, Xu chooses the equivalent thematic structure "projecting clause^projected clause" as the main thematic structure in the dialogues.

Ku has chosen the most marked thematic structure in the dialogues as we can see in Table 7-2. Some of the marked Themes are realized by part of the projected clause and others by the whole projected clause, as shown in example [7-6].

[7-6] A disciple asked Confucius for the meaning of the following verse: Her coquettish smiles, How dimpling they are; Her beautiful eyes, How beaming they are; How fairest is she who is simple and plain. "**In painting**", answered Confucius, " ornamentation and colour are of secondary importance compared with the ground work." "**Then art itself**," said the disciple, " is a matter of ' secondary' consideration?" "**My friend**," replied Confucius, "You have given me an idea. Now I can talk of poetry with you." (KT:3/8)

As example [7-6] shows, the Theme in the four projection clause nexuses is respectively realized by the projecting clause, the circumstantial adjunct of the projected clause, the Subject of the projected clause and the vocative. In the marked thematic structures chosen by Ku, some parts of the projected clause are put first in the clause nexus and function as Theme. The projection clause nexus begins not from the Given information in the projecting clause but part of the New information in the projected clause. The topics being discussed are put in a prominent position thus achieve better cohesion between the different turns of the dialogue.

7.3.3 Textual meaning realized in the thematic structures

In our study of the thematic structures in the projection clause nexus in the aphorisms and dialogues, we have found marked and unmarked thematic structures in the different TTs. Table 7-3 shows the shifts of the ST and TTs concerning the thematic structures of projection.

Table 7-3 Shifts of thematic structures in TTs

Text	Shifts of thematic structure in aphorisms	Shifts of thematic structure in dialogues	Shifts of thematic structure in TTs
LT	0	5	5
KT	1	69	70
XT	140	32	172

Of the three TTs, Legge has chosen the most equivalent unmarked thematic structures and Xu has chosen the least equivalent thematic structures. Legge maintains the formal equivalence of the thematic structure of the projection clause nexus in the translation and tries to achieve the textual equivalence of the ST and TT in both form and meaning. In reading Legge's version, the readers can appreciate the simple structural characteristics of old Chinese texts. In the ST, each chapter begins with *Zǐ yuē* (子曰) and each chapter of Legge and Ku's translation begins with "the Master said" and "Confucius remarked". The projecting clauses indicating the source of the projected message are put at the beginning of each chapter and make the different chapters coherent. The information contained in the projecting clause (the unmarked theme) is taken for granted and the readers need not to pay much attention to it since it contains the given information in the context. In this aspect, Legge and Ku have achieved textual equivalence of projection in their TTs.

Based on the general equivalence of the textual meaning in the TT, Ku tries to achieve variation in the thematic structures of projection in the dialogues. By putting some part of the projected clause or the whole projected clause before the projecting clause, these marked themes can achieve better coherence between the different projection clause nexuses in the dialogues, while result in a lesser degree of equivalence in textual meaning.

In the majority of the aphorisms and dialogues, Xu chooses marked Themes that are not equivalent to the ST. In the aphorisms, Xu chooses part of the projected clause or the whole projected clause as the Theme of the clause nexus. The clause nexus begins with the information in the projected clause and the connection between the different chapters of the ST realized by the repetition of the projecting clause is lost in XT. In dialogues, the most usually used marked Theme is the *when-* clause which realizes the asking turns in an dependent clause of the projection clause nexus and makes the following projection clause nexus more prominent. The TT of Xu contains the textual meaning that is not contained in the ST. Xu's choice of thematic structures achieves the least degree of equivalence to the ST.

Table 7-4 shows the cline of textual equivalence as realized in the choice of thematic structure from high to low degree.

Table 7-4 Cline of textual equivalence realized in the thematic structure

Degree of equivalence	High	Middle	Low
TTs	LT	KT	XT

7.4 Thematic-progression patterns in projection

7.4.1 Patterns of thematic progression in the aphorisms

In the aphorisms, the thematic structure of projection in the ST takes the form of projecting clause ^ projected clause. Each chapter of aphorisms begins with the projecting clause *Zǐ yuē* (子曰) or *Subject* + *yuē* (曰). The repetition of projecting clauses in each chapter gives the thematic progression a constant-Theme pattern as shown in Table 3-2 above. The repeated projecting clause forms a cohesive pattern whereby the ST builds the cohesive ties between the different chapters of the *Lunyu*. As the *Lunyu* was compiled by different disciples from the teachings of the Master over a long period of time, there are few cohesive ties across the different chapters. The repetition of the projecting clause tells the readers that what follows the projecting clause is what the Master said on one occasion, and that the whole book is a record of what the Master said while teaching his disciples. The constant-Theme pattern of thematic progression makes the different sayings recorded by different disciples into a coherent text. This pattern comes from the tradition of the official historians recording the sayings of the king, in which they indicate the beginning of the king's sayings by repetition of the pattern *the king said ... the king said ... the king said.* This pattern, according to Zhang (2008), indicates that the message following *the king said* is the actual recording of what the king said and makes the record of the different sayings coherent.

In the aphorisms, Legge and Ku maintain the constant-Theme pattern of thematic progression with the main projecting clause "the Master said" and "Confucius remarked" repeatedly put at the beginning of each chapter. By choosing an equivalent pattern of thematic progression, they realized similar textual meanings to the ST in their TTs. Xu chooses a pattern of thematic progression different from that of the ST in the aphorisms, with most of the thematic structure in the form of "part of projected clause ⌢ projecting clause ⌢ part of projected clause". The Theme in each chapter is realized by the whole projected clause or part of the projected clause or a minor projected clause. That means that most chapters of the aphorisms begin with new message conveyed in the projected clause or part of the projected clause. This pattern of thematic progression is not equivalent to the ST and does not realize the textual meaning conveyed in the ST.

7.4.2 Patterns of thematic progression in the part of dialogues

In the dialogues, the ST maintains the constant-Theme pattern of thematic progression. For each turn in the dialogues, the projection clause nexus progresses from Theme to Rheme, from the projecting clause to the projected clause.

As for the different TTs, Legge maintains a pattern of thematic progression equivalent to the ST. The analysis of thematic structures in the TTs of Ku and Xu in Section 7.3.2 above shows that their TTs take the different patterns of thematic progression to the ST. In

KT, sixty-nine projection clause nexuses are realized with a marked thematic structure in which some of the Theme is realized by part of the projected clause and some of the Theme is realized by the whole projected clause. The derived pattern of thematic progression (Bloor & Bloor 1995) can make each projection clause nexus in the dialogue more closely related and make the whole dialogue more coherent than that of the ST.

In XT, there are 30 marked thematic structures in the projection clause nexuses realized as hypotactic enhancing *when-* clause ^ projecting clause ^ projected clause. The thematic progression pattern is constant-Theme pattern in which the Theme is realized by the *when-* clause with a projection clause nexus embedded, and realizes a textual meaning that is not equivalent to the ST. It tells the readers the starting point (and the given information) of the message is the question proposed by the questioners (usually the disciples) and the new information is contained in the Rheme, with the projection clause nexus realizing the answering turns taken by the Master. This textual meaning realized by this pattern is not equivalent to that in the ST.

7.4.3 Textual meanings realized by patterns of thematic progression

From the above analysis, we find that Legge chooses an equivalent pattern of thematic progression in both the aphorisms and the dialogues; Ku chooses an equivalent pattern in the aphorisms but not in the dialogues; and Xu chooses the least equivalent pattern of thematic progression in both the aphorisms as well as the dialogues. Their different choices of patterns of thematic progression convey different textual meaning in the text and achieve differing degrees of textual equivalence to the ST. The cline of textual equivalence realized by the choice of thematic progression patterns is shown in Table 7-5 below.

Table 7-5 Cline of textual equivalence realized in the pattern of thematic progression

Degree of equivalence	High	Middle	Low
TTs	LT	KT	XT

7.5 Study of cohesion in projection

Cohesion is another important grammatical source of realizing textual metafunction. The study of different kinds of cohesive ties in a text can show the different characteristics of the specific text.

The *Lunyu*, as Wang (1986:272) points out, is "a recording of the sayings and actions of Confucius by his disciples" after the death of Confucius. It has the characteristics of the quotation style but it is not the typical quotation style as it contains the recording of the actions of Confucius. Ban (1962:1717) also points out that the text of the *Lunyu* originates from the notes taken by the disciples in the process of Confucius' teaching and talking and after the death of Confucius the disciples came together to compile what they had heard in the Master's teaching. In the process of compiling the *Lunyu*, the compilers extracted the essence from the original records by the disciples and compile the book in a summary and concise style containing aphorisms and dialogues (Chen: 2006). Although there is still no fixed conclusion on how many disciples were involved in the compiling of the book and who the compilers are, the fact that the *Lunyu* is compiled by the different disciples of Confucius over a long period of time is certain. So it is natural for the *Lunyu* not to be as logically cohesive and compact as books compiled or written by one writer. Huang (2011) has made an incisive and detailed study on the topic of coherence and cohesion in the *Lunyu* and its translations. Huang pointed out that researchers have different opinions on whether the *Lunyu* is coherent or not. For example, Zou (2010:23) criticizes the content of the *Lunyu* as miscellaneous and lacking coherence; Tian (2010:2) praises the organization of the *Lunyu* as logically clear; Yao (2004:95) points out that the organization of the *Lunyu* is neither in disorder, because there are still cohesive ties found in the different chapters, nor in good order, as it is not a book consistently written by one writer (Huang: 2011).

Huang (2011) divides the notion of textual "coherence" into "global coherence" and "local coherence". He points out that the *Lunyu* is globally coherent as the whole text is connected with the central idea of *Rén* (仁 "kindness"). As for the local coherence of the text, Huang (2011) points out that the cohesive ties in the specific chapters lie in the numbering system of the different chapters and books in the *Lunyu*, and the genre of *quotation style* to which it belongs as the text of this genre is allowed to have no direct cohesive ties between the different chapters.

In the following part, we mainly study the cohesive ties in the projection clause nexus of the text. We aim to study the cohesive ties that the translators have built into their translated versions as the ST has so few cohesive methods to build coherence. The different kinds of cohesive ties in the TTs are studied to analyze the different degree of cohesion achieved.

7.5.1 Cohesion in the aphorisms

In the ST, no matter whether in the aphorisms or in dialogues, the repetition of *Zǐ* (子) in the text is one of the main cohesive ties in the text. As *Zǐ* (子) referring to Confucius occurs repeatedly in the text, the readers can get a coherent understanding that the text is a recording of the sayings and behaviors of Confucius. In the part of aphorisms, the repetition of *Zǐ yuē* (子曰) or *Subject +yuē* (曰) in each chapter is one of the main cohesive ties in different chapters. Readers of the ST can understand the relationship between the subjects of the projecting clauses and achieve a coherent understanding of the information conveyed in each chapter with the common sense of Chinese cultural background as the "encyclopedic knowledge" and "shared knowledge" between the writers and the readers play a decisive role in judging if a text or discourse is coherent or not (Huang 2011:90).

From a study of the Subjects of projecting clauses in the three TTs, we can get a picture on the different degree of coherence achieved in the translated texts.

In LT, the projecting clause *the Master said* appears at the beginning of every projection clause nexus, no matter whether it is an aphorism or a dialogue. In the aphorisms, other kinds of projecting clauses are also put at the beginning of each chapter. This similar pattern of thematic progression builds similar cohesive ties to the

ST. As for the Subjects of the projecting clauses, Legge translates *Zǐ yuē* (子曰) as *The Master said* and uses his Legge Romanization to represent the names of Confucius' disciples. Readers can get a detailed introduction to the different persons mentioned in the translation by referring to Section III of Legge (1971) in which Legge gives an elaborate introduction to the life stories of the disciples of Confucius. Readers who are not familiar with Chinese culture may not understand the relationship among the persons mentioned in the translation by reading just the text of Legge's translation as they do not share knowledge with Chinese readers.

In Ku's translated version, the main cohesive ties lie in the repetition of the projecting clause "Confucius remarked" and "a disciple of Confucius remarked" conveying a similar textual meaning to the ST. The different Subjects / sayers of the projecting clauses are translated into "Confucius" and "a disciple of Confucius" omitting the names of the disciples which may be difficult for the foreign readers to pronounce and recognize. The cohesive ties built by the Subjects of the projecting clauses make the different chapters of the aphorisms more coherent than that in the TT of Legge.

In XT, the projecting clauses have lost the ability to build cohesive ties across the different chapters of the aphorisms. The projecting clause is put in the middle of the projected information and every chapter begins with new information in the projected clause. As to the translation of the Subjects of the projecting clause, Xu represents the names of Confucius' disciples using the Hanyu Pinyin system to make Chinese names familiar to non-Chinese as Hanyu Pinyin is adopted as the international standard in 1982 by the International Organization for Standardization (Wikipedia). However, Xu does not provide any explanation of the names of the people mentioned in the text, which may make it difficult for foreign readers to achieve a coherent understanding of the relationships between them.

Table 7-6 shows the cohesive methods used in the projecting clauses of the ST and different TTs in the aphorisms. As Table 7-6 shows, the cohesive ties built across the projecting clauses of the different TTs are different. With the repetition of the projecting clause in the aphorisms, the TTs by Legge and Ku build similar cohesive ties to the ST, while XT does not build any cohesive ties of that kind. In the projecting clauses, Legge uses notes and an explanatory appendix to build cohesive ties between the Subjects of the projecting clauses, while Ku uses lexical cohesion between the Subjects of the projecting clauses. Xu does not use any cohesive methods in the projecting clause to build cohesion in the TT.

Table 7-6 Cohesive methods used in the projecting clauses of the ST and TTs

Text	Projecting clause	Subjects of projecting clause	Cohesive methods
ST	Subject + yuē (曰)	Zǐ (子), Yǒuzǐ (有子), Zēngzǐ (曾子), Zǐxià (子夏), Zǐqín (子禽), Zǐgòng (子贡)	Repetition of projecting clause, the Subjects understood from the common knowledge of Chinese culture
LT	Subject + said	the Master, the philosopher Yǔ, the philosopher Tsǎng, Tsze-hsiâ, Tsze-ch'in, Tsze-kung	Repetition of projecting clause, Section III introducing the Subjects
KT	Subject + remarked	Confucius, a disciple of Confucius	Repetition of the projecting clause, lexical cohesion between the Subjects
XT	said + Subject	The Master, Master You, Master Zeng, Zi Xia, Zi Qin, Zi Gong	The projecting clauses build no cohesive ties, no introduction to the names functioning as Subjects

The cohesive ties built in the projected clauses are mainly realized by the connection of the main ideas conveyed in them. As Huang (2011) and Yang (1999) point out, the projected message in the projection clause nexus is all conveyed around the main idea of rén (仁). In a global sense, rén (仁) refers to practicing a gentle and kind policy; in a narrower sense, it refers to loving people, being loyal and forgiving, being filial to parents (Yang 1999: 19, cited in Huang 2011: 93). The sayings, discussions and descriptions in the Lunyu are mainly about the main idea ren and Huang (2011) suggests that this renders the Lunyu semantically coherent. In this sense, the three translated versions have all built cohesive ties in the projected clause and achieved the semantic cohesion among the information conveyed in the different chapters.

In summary, in the aphorisms, the TTs of Legge and Ku achieve better coherence than that of Xu by the choices made in the projecting clauses.

7.5.2　Cohesion in the part of dialogues

In the dialogues, the chapters consist of at least two turns of asking and answering. Following Huang (2011:91), we regard the co-occurrence of the adjacency pair of asking and answering in the dialogue as the main cohesive method used in these segments of the *Lunyu*.

The dialogue parts of the three translated versions studied all show the co-occurrence of the adjacency pair of asking and answering and the dialogues are coherent in this global sense. But in the different translated versions, there are different cohesive ties built and different degree of cohesion achieved in the text, as will be studied here.

Example [7-7] shows the different cohesive methods used in the dialogue. The ST is a dialogue between Confucius and one of his disciples and they are remarking on a person named "Guan Zhong".

[7-7] *Zǐ yuē : "Guǎn Zhòng zhī qì xiǎo zāi."*
　　　子曰："管仲之器小哉。"
Huò yuē : "Guǎn Zhòng jiǎn hu?"
或曰："管仲俭乎？"
Yuē : "Guǎnshì yǒu sān guī, guān shì bú shè, yān dé jiǎn?"
曰："管氏有三归，官事不摄，焉得俭？"
"Rán zé Guǎn Zhòng zhīlǐ hu?"
"然则管仲知礼乎？"
Yuē : "bāng Jūn shù sāi mén, Guǎnshì yì shù sāi mén. Bāng Jūn wéi liǎng jūn zhī hǎo, yǒu fǎn diàn, Guǎnshì yì yǒu fǎn diàn. Guǎnshì ér zhīlǐ, shú bù zhīlǐ?"
曰："邦君树塞门，管氏亦树塞门。邦君为两君之好，有反坫，管氏亦有反坫。管氏而知礼，孰不知礼？"(ST:3/22)

Chapter 7 Textual Equivalence of Projection in the Lunyu and Its Translations

LT:
1. The Master said, "Small indeed was the Capacity of Kwan Chung!"
2. Some one said, "Was Kwan Chung parsimonious?" "Kwan," was the reply, "had the *San Kwei,* and his officers performed no double duties; how can he be considered parsimonious?"
3. "Then, did Kwan Chung know the rules of propriety?" The Master said, "The princes of states have a screen intercepting the view at their gates. Kwan had likewise a screen at his gate. The princes of states on any friendly meeting between two of them, had a stand on which to place their inverted cups. Kwan had also such a stand. If Kwan knew the rules of propriety, who does not know them?" (LT:3/22)

KT:
Confucius, speaking of a famous statesman (the Bismarck of the time) remarked, "Kuan Chung was by no means a great-minded man!"
"But," said somebody, "Kuan Chung was simple in his life: was he not?"
"Why," replied Confucius, "Kuan Chung had that magnificent Sansouci Pleasaunce of his. Besides, he had a special officer appointed to every function in his household. How can one say that he was simple in his life?"
"Well," rejoined the enquirer, "but still, Kuan Chung was a man of taste who observed the correct forms; was he not?"
"No," answered Confucius, "The reigning princes have walls built before their palace gates. Kuan Chung also had a wall built before his door. When two reigning princes meet, each has a special *buffet.* Kuan Chung also had his special buffet. If you say Kuan Chung was a man of taste, who is not a man of taste?" (KT:3/22)

XT:
The Master said, "Guan Zhong was not a great minister." When asked if Guan Zhong was frugal, the Master said, "Guan Zhong had three granaries while his official duties were not performed, how could he be considered frugal?" When asked if Guan

Zhong knew the rites, the Master said, "Only the prince may build a wall to screen the gate of his mansion, but Guan Zhong had one before his. Only the prince may use a stand for cups to entertain his guests, but Guan Zhong used one. If he knew the rites, who does not?" (XT:3/22)

Table 7-7 can show the equivalent methods of building cohesion used in the ST and TTs and the methods used in specific TTs that are not equivalent to that of the ST.

Table 7-7 Cohesive methods in the dialogues of the ST and TTs

Text	Equivalent cohesive methods	Different cohesive methods
ST	Co-occurrence of the adjacency pair; repetition of P-ing C; the repetition of *Guan Zhong* in the P-ed C	
LT	Co-occurrence of the adjacency pair; repetition of P-ing C; the repetition of *Kwan Chung* in the P-ed C	Arabic numerals used to indicate the different adjacency pairs
KT	Co-occurrence of the adjacency pair; repetition of projecting clause; Repetition of *Kuan Chung* in the P-ed C	Use of various projecting verbs indicating the different adjacency pairs; adding the omitted P-ing C; the anaphoric reference in the subject of the projecting clause; the conjunctive expressions
XT	Repeated occurrence of the projecting clause; repetition of *Guan Zhong* in the P-ed C;	Lack of co-occurrence of the adjacency pair of asking and answering; the repetition of "when asked"

In this dialogue, the first projection clause nexus is a comment made by Confucius on Guan Zhong. The following four projection clause nexuses form two pairs of asking and answering between the Master and the disciples. The third and fifth projection clause nexuses omit the projecting Subject and the third one omits the whole projecting clause. Readers can achieve cohesion among the different turns of asking and answering based on their shared knowledge and the context of the dialogue although there are few

Chapter 7   Textual Equivalence of Projection in the Lunyu and Its Translations

conjunctives used in the dialogue except the term *ránzé* (然则 "but").

In Legge's translation, the translator takes the similar structure of projection clause nexus and chooses to omit the projecting Subject and the projecting clause in the third and fourth projection clause nexuses. To make the turns of asking and answering clear-cut, Legge uses Arabic numerals to indicate the different adjacency pairs in the dialogue and so readers can achieve a coherent understanding concerning the source of the projection clause nexuses, even though the projecting clauses in the third and fourth projection clause nexus are omitted, as the ST. In Legge's translated version, few conjunctives are used in the dialogues, just as in the ST.

In Ku's translation, the translator makes the structure of the third and fourth projection clause nexus clearer by adding the omitted Subjects and the projecting clause. The added subject of the projecting clause, *Confucius*, in the third projection clause nexus builds cohesive ties with the subject of the first and the fifth projection clause nexus through repetition. The subject in the fourth projection clause nexus, the *enquirer*, builds cohesive ties with that in the second, *somebody*. The use of the projecting verbs *remarked, said, replied, rejoined*, and *answered* makes the adjacency relation of the asking and answering clearer than in the ST. The lexical cohesion in the repetition of *Confucius* and the anaphoric reference of *the enquirer* to *somebody* make the dialogue more coherently structured and easier to understand for the English readers. In Ku's translation, the cohesive devices also take the form of the conjunctions *but, why, well, but, still*, the cohesive relation between the projected message in the asking and answering turns is made clearer and more coherent. The conjunctive expression *but* indicates an adversative relation between what Confucius said and what the disciple said, which has a cohesive effect that the ST lacks. The continuative *well* is cohesive in function as it indicates that the following is a response to what precedes and means that "I acknowledge the question, and will give a considered answer" (Halliday & Hasan 1976: 269). *No* in the last projection clause nexus functions as part of a textual Theme and it is used as a continuative signaling that "a new move is beginning"

(Halliday & Matthiessen 2004: 145) and has the cohesive power to connect the asking and answering turns in the two projection clause nexuses, in contrast to the ST, where no definite answers are given in the last projected clause. In a word, in Ku's translation, the translator makes the dialogue achieve a greater degree of coherence than the ST by adding the omitted projecting subject and projecting clause, as well as adding conjunctive items that are not present in the ST.

In Xu's translation, the five projection clause nexuses in the ST are realized in his translation as three projection clause nexuses. The turn of asking questions by the disciple is put in a *when-* clause dependent on the projection clause nexus realizing the answer by Confucius. The lack of co-occurrence of the adjacency pair of asking and answering makes the text less characteristic of a dialogue. With the repetition of the projecting clause *the Master said* and the repetition of *Guan Zhong, frugal, the prince* in the projected clause as the main cohesive device in the dialogue, the readers can also get the coherent textual meaning of the translated text: the text is about what Confucius said about Guan Zhong. The conjunctive *when* is used to connect the asking and answering turns in the dialogue. The readers cannot, however, get the textual meaning that the text is a dialogue between a disciple of Confucius and Confucius himself. Xu's translation text does not achieve the same degree of coherence as a dialogue to the ST, but more as a description of what Confucius said in the situation.

In summary, as for the cohesive devices used in the dialogues, Legge has chosen the similar methods of achieving coherence to the ST and the coherence built in the dialogue of LT is no less or more coherent than the ST. Ku in his TT has chosen more methods to build coherence in the dialogue than the ST thus making the dialogue more coherent than the ST. Xu has not chosen a similar method of building cohesive ties to the ST and the turns of asking and answering taken by the different speakers are not as clear as that in the ST. The TT of Xu is coherent in his own way as a description of sayings instead of as a dialogue.

7.5.3 Textual meaning realized in the cohesive methods

The different choices of cohesive methods used in the TTs convey different textual meanings. To summarize the study of cohesion in the aphorisms and dialogues: Legge has chosen similar cohesive ways to the ST and build an equivalent degree of coherence in his TT to the ST; Ku has chosen more cohesive methods in his TT to build a higher degree of cohesion than the ST, but giving KT a lesser degree of equivalence to the ST; while Xu has chosen the least equivalent methods to build cohesion as compared to the ST with the text realized as a description rather than as a collection of quotations, thus giving XT the least degree of equivalence to the ST.

The cline of textual equivalence realized by the choice of cohesive methods can be shown in Table 7-8.

Table 7-8 Cline of textual equivalence realized in the cohesive methods

Degree of equivalence	High	Middle	Low
TTs	LT	KT	XT

7.6 Summary

In this chapter, we have studied the textual meaning realized in the projection clause nexuses of the ST and the three TTs. In terms of the thematic structure, the patterns of thematic progression, and the cohesive ties built in the projection clause nexus, translators have made different choice in the different TTs and realized different degree of textual equivalence to the ST. Legge has chosen a similar thematic structure and pattern of thematic progression to the ST and he has chosen similar cohesive methods in his TT to build an equivalent degree of cohesion to the TT, thus achieving the highest degree of equivalence. Ku has also chosen a similar thematic structure to the ST in the aphorisms but there are some instances of shifts in the dialogues in the choice of patterns of thematic progression. Ku has chosen similar methods of building cohesion to the ST as well as adding some new ways to make the TT more cohesive than the ST, thus giving KT the second degree of equivalence to the ST. Xu has chosen different thematic structures and patterns of thematic progression to the ST and the cohesive ties in his TT are different from that in the ST, thus achieving the lowest degree of equivalence to the ST.

The different TTs achieve different degree of textual equivalence to the ST. We can conclude that Legge's translation achieves the highest degree of textual equivalence to the ST, while Xu's translation achieves the lowest and Ku's translation stands in the middle.

Chapter 8
Equivalence of Projection in the *Lunyu* and Its Translations in Context

8.1 Introduction

The analysis in the previous four chapters has shown that different translators make different choices in the lexicogrammatical realization of projection in their translated versions and thus convey different ideational, interpersonal and textual meanings to the ST. Taking into account the equivalence and shifts in the ideational, interpersonal and textual meaning of the TTs, can we judge whether these translated versions are or are not equivalent to the ST? Is the study of equivalence at the metafunction perspective enough for the study of equivalence of the *Lunyu* and its translated versions? These questions will be studied in the present chapter.

8.2 Equivalence in context

As discussed in 3.4.3, the study of equivalence in projection based on theory of "discourse analysis" in SFL consists in making links between the text and its context.

In the previous chapters, the linguistic study of the translation equivalence in projection between the ST and the TTs was carried out along the dimension of metafunction which, as pointed out by Matthiessen (2001) and Halliday (2009), "has long been recognized ... in translation studies but has seldom been addressed systematically" (Halliday 2009:18). The lexicogrammatical realizations of the three metafunctions of language, which are the "fundamental property of every language system" and "the basis for the organization of meaning" (Halliday 2009: 18), were studied by identifying the different choices made by translators concerning the different types and structures of projection in the TTs. After this study of the texts from the stratum of semantics downward to the stratum of lexicogrammar, in this chapter the equivalence study of the *Lunyu* and its translated versions will work upwards from the text to the context including the context of situation and the context of culture, to study the differential value that the different kinds of metafunctional equivalence have in both these contexts in order to evaluate the different TTs. In order to evaluate whether a translated version is or is not an effective translation, we need to interpret the "systemic relationship between context and text." (Halliday 1994a: F41)

In previous chapters, we have analyzed the correspondence and divergence between the ST and the TTs from the perspectives of three metafunctions of language, on which basis we can now go on to analyze the context of situation or register of each translated text. Correspondence and divergence in the relationship between text and context will be jointly considered in making judgments concerning the equivalence between the ST and TTs. The different TTs are to be regarded as closely related registerial variants (Steiner 2001:169) of each other.

8.3 Register analysis for the ST and TTs

Register as "a semantic concept" (Halliday & Hasan 1985:38-39) is determined by the variables in the context of situation and realized in the lexicogrammatical choices of the text. When we interpret a particular text in relation to its context, we assign it to some register, in other words, a semantic configurations typically associated with a particular social context, defined in terms of Field, Tenor and Mode (Halliday & Hasan 1985:42).

In previous chapters, we analyzed the ideational, interpersonal and textual meanings realized in the choices of types and structures

Chapter 8   Equivalence of Projection in the Lunyu and Its Translations in Context

of projection in the *Lunyu* and its translated versions. On the basis of this analysis, we can now go on to analyze the register variables corresponding to the three metafunctions in the different target texts and predict the context of situation in which they function.

8. 3. 1   Register analysis of the ST

By analyzing the transitivity structures and the lexical choices, we can find that the Field of the ST is: the morals taught by Confucius, the sayings of Confucius and the behaviors of Confucius. It is a text of Chinese traditional ideas. There are many technical terms in the text that only the contemporaries of the compilers or the researchers on Confucius or Chinese traditions can understand and the understanding of the text requires a high degree of technical explicit knowledge among the modern readers about the relationship between the participants, and about the main ideas in the Chinese philosophy. The ST uses the technical terms, abbreviations and abbreviated syntax that only " insiders " understand. It can be regarded as a technical text characterized "by a significant degree of assumed knowledge among the interactants about the activity focus" (Eggins 1994:71). The text is mainly narrative in terms of the genre and sets out to describe the sayings and actions of the Master.

In the ST of the *Lunyu*, the interactants include the Master and the disciples, in the "fictional" context created by the text itself; the compilers of the text and the unknown readers, in the context of reading involving the writers and readers. The Master and the disciples are joined by an unequal and hierarchical power relationship, with frequent contact and highly affective involvement. This unequal power relationship between the Master and the disciples can be reflected in the repetition of the projecting clause *Zǐ yuē* (子曰), by the fact that most of the sayings are in the form of aphorisms and there is seldom discussion in the dialogues, and there are few ideas that go against the Master. Even in the dialogues, the sayings of the disciples take shortened forms and there are few instances of interruptions and overlapping in the dialogues. The colloquial lexis and given names used by the Master to address the disciples reflects the frequent contact and highly affective involvement among the participants. Besides, the typical mood choices (without any incongruent mood choices) in the text reflect an informal spoken language. The other interactants in the text, such as the compilers of the book and the unknown and unseen readers, have infrequent contact and low affective involvement. The task of the compilers of the text are to record the actual sayings of Confucius and his disciples word by word without any adjustment to the common readers not familiar with Confucius' ideas.

The Mode of the ST can be described as follows: written language recording the sayings and dialogues. The language used in the text is said to be read by the unknown readers. The function of language in the text is didactic to the unknown readers and language is being used to reflect the experience instead of enacting it. There is no expectation of the compilers of the face to face feedback from the readers and there are no direct contacts between the compilers of the text and the unknown readers.

To summarize, the register of the ST can be described as follows: a technical record of Confucius' sayings and actions, a recording of Confucian philosophy, the participants of the interactions are unequal in status and there is a low affective involvement of the compiler of the book to the unknown readers. The language used is the spoken language recorded to be read by unknown readers to perform a didactic function for those readers.

8.3.2 Register analysis of the TTs

8.3.2.1 Field in the TTs

In Chapters 5 to 7, we studied the equivalence and shifts between the ST and TTs concerning the metafunctional meanings in the projection clause nexus in the *Lunyu*. From the lexicogrammatical choices made by the different translators, the different translations can realize the same or different metafunctional meanings. As we have discussed, the field correlates with ideational meanings. The experiential subtype of meanings is realized through transitivity structures and lexical choices. In the TTs the transitivity of the projecting clause is mainly realized as verbal processes. The

Chapter 8   Equivalence of Projection in the Lunyu and Its Translations in Context

logical subtype of meanings are realized in the choice of the types of projection clause nexus, mainly realized as quotes / direct speech in LT and KT, and free direct speech in XT. We found that the TTs by Legge and Ku achieved a great degree of ideational equivalence to the ST and constructed a similar Field to the ST: the description of the sayings and dialogues of Confucius and his disciples and descriptions of the actions of Confucius. From the analysis of the structures of the projecting clauses, we found that Legge chose the equivalent simple structure of " Subject + said" to introduce the projected message, without any information concerning the receivers of the speaking, or the environment in which the sayings take place etc. , which indicates that the Field constructed in LT is as technical as the ST. In KT, the varied structures of projecting clauses other than the simple structure of " Subject + said / remarked" add necessary information concerning the receiver of the speaking, and the environment in which the conversation occurs etc. The added information concerning the background of the sayings and the dialogues can make it easier for readers to understand the sayings and dialogues, which constructs a more reader-friendly and less technical Field for the readers. Legge and Xu's choice of realizing the Subject of the projecting clause by *the Master* and the courtesy name of the disciples and, Ku's choice of referring to him as *Confucius* and omitting the proper names of all the disciples simply referring to them as *a disciple of Confucius* also indicate that KT has constructed a less technical Field. In the study of ideational meaning in the TTs, we found that in XT there were some shifts in ideational meaning compared to the ST: the large amount of free direct speech, the choice of reporting / indirect speech to realize quotations, the choice of dependent *when-* clause embedding a projection clause nexus to realize quotations. The Field constructed in Xu's translation is still a description of the sayings of Confucius, and of the dialogues of the Master with his disciples and descriptions of Confucius' behavior, but the Field is more like a narrative of the translator to the unseen readers than the mere recording of the disciples on the sayings and dialogues of the Master.

8.3.2.2　Tenor in the TTs

Tenor correlates with the interpersonal meanings realized through the lexicogrammatical systems of Mood, Modality and Person. The interactants in the TTs not only include Confucius and his disciples in the aphorisms and dialogues, the compilers of the book, but also include the translators and target readers of the translated versions. By analyzing the amount of projection of propositions versus proposals in the ST and different TTs, we found that in the TTs, there are similar amount of projection of propositions and proposals to the ST, realizing the interpersonal functions of giving information and demanding services in the TTs. By examining the Mood element in the projecting clauses, the choices made by Legge and Xu in realizing *zǐ* （子） by "the Master" and the other Subjects in the projecting clause by the courtesy name of them indicate that they have constructed a similar Tenor to the ST: Confucius, the Master stands in an authoritarian role towards the disciples. The interactants in the TT — the Master and the disciples — are in a relationship of unequal power, but with frequent contact and highly affective involvement. Both Legge and Xu in their TTs keep the respectful relationship of the compilers to their Master. In XT, Xu's choice of putting the asking turn of the dialogue in the hypotactic enhancing *when-* clause dependent on the projecting clause "The Master said" highlights the turns taken by the Master in the dialogue and also indicates the relationship of unequal power among the speakers in the dialogue. With the study of person system in the TTs, Xu chooses the courtesy name of the disciples as vocatives used in the dialogue by the Master to address the disciples, which carries a relationship of occasional contact and low affective involvement among the Master and the disciples, which is not equivalent to the ST.

From analyzing the choice of structures for the projection clause nexus, we have the following findings. In LT, the pattern of word-by-word recording of the sayings of Confucius is strictly kept, with additional information that helps readers' understanding reserved for the notes and appendix. The relationship of the translator with the unseen readers is unequal and less friendly in Legge than in Ku's translation, who omits names to unfamiliar western readers and adds necessary information in the structure of the projection clause nexus which helps readers understand. XT builds the friendliest relationship between the translator and the readers. Xu is mainly aimed at modern readers interested in Confucian philosophy and puts the repeated pattern of the projecting clause zǐ yuē （子曰） in the middle of the projected message, which builds a friendliest relationship to the readers.

8.3.2.3 Mode in the TTs

Mode is realized by the textual meaning in the semantics, reflected in lexicogrammatical features that carry the textual meanings: Theme, thematic progression, and cohesive relations etc. From the analysis of the thematic structure in the aphorisms, we found that the TTs by Legge and Ku chose a similar thematic structure to the ST of "projecting clause ⌢ projected clause" and a similar thematic progression pattern of constant theme to the ST, which constructs a typical quotation style of the spoken mode — a written representation of the spoken mode. The cohesive ties in LT are built mainly through the repetition of the projecting clause, and cohesive ties built in the dialogue are through the clear-cut turn taking by speakers, which also constructs a spoken mode.

In the dialogues, Legge chooses the similar pattern of thematic structure to the ST while Ku chooses a large proportion of marked thematic structures in which the Theme is realized by part of the projected message, or the whole projected message. With some part of the projected clause or the whole projected clause put before the projecting clause, the marked theme chosen by Ku in the dialogues is able to achieve better cohesion between the different projection clause nexuses. Considering the choices made in the aphorisms and dialogues, Ku has constructed a Mode which blends quotation and narrative, in other words, a blend of spoken and written modes.

From the analysis of thematic structure, we find that Xu has chosen a thematic structure which is not equivalent to the ST. In the aphorisms, the information begins with the new information contained in the projected message instead of with the projecting clause. It constructs a Mode more like written narrative than the spoken quotation mode of the ST, which has the typical linguistic feature of "Subject +said" at the beginning of each chapter. From the analysis of thematic structures in the dialogues, it is found that Xu has chosen a marked thematic structure of "*when* clause ⌒ the projection clause nexus" whereby the information in the dialogue begins with the asking turn of the disciples and ends with the answering turn of the Master. These marked Themes are quite common in the TTs of Xu and "appear to be one realization of a careful written mode, in which the writer has planned the rhetorical development of the text to allow the foregrounding of Circumstantial information" (Eggins 1994:319). With the asking turn taken by the disciples put in the *when-* clause, the clear-cut turn taking of the quotation mode is lost. From the linguistic features studied, we can conclude there is a written oriented mode in XT. In this Mode, the translator describes to the unseen readers the main ideas contained in the *Lunyu* as said by Confucius, instead of recording the quotations said by Confucius.

8.3.2.4 Description of register in the TTs

Based on the study on the three register variables in the different TTs, we can describe the register in the three TTs as shown in Table 8-1 below.

Table 8-1 Register description of the TTs

Register variables	LT	KT	XT
Field	Recording what Confucius said with his disciples Technical	Recording and describing what Confucius said with his disciples Less technical	Describing by narrating what Confucius said with his disciples Less technical

Chapter 8 Equivalence of Projection in the Lunyu and Its Translations in Context

(continued)

Register variables	LT	KT	XT
Tenor	Unequal power relationship between the Master and disciples Medium affective involvement and frequent contact among the speakers Relatively formal and didactic relationship between the translator and the readers	Unequal power between the Master and disciples High affective involvement among the speakers Readers-friendly Less didactic	Unequal power between the Master and disciples Low affective involvement among the speakers Reader-friendly Tenor Less didactic
Mode	Spoken mode to be read	Spoken mode to be read Blend of spoken and written	The most oriented to the written mode

From Table 8-1, we can see that the register of LT is technical quotations of the sayings of Confucius and his disciples and their dialogues, a spoken register written to be read by the readers who are interested in doing some research on Confucian philosophy. The relationship between the interactants in the sayings and dialogues is of unequal power but with frequent contact and a highly affective involvement. The relationship between the translator and the unseen target readers is didactic. Following the Mode dimension described in Martin (1984:26), the TT of Legge has the furthest spatial distance between the translator and the readers, without visual or aural communication and expecting no feedback from the readers. Language is used to reflect on the past experience.

The register of KT can be summarized as less technical quotations of the sayings of Confucius and his disciples and their dialogues, a spoken register written to be read with more features of written mode. The relationship among the speakers in the aphorisms and dialogues is closer than that in the ST. The relationship between the translator and the unseen readers is friendlier and less didactic than that in the ST.

The register of XT can be described as a less technical description and narrative of the sayings and talking of Confucius and his disciples. It is in a spoken register written to be read with the most orientation towards written mode. The relationship between the translator and the unseen readers is the friendlier and less didactic than that in the ST.

8.4 Equivalence study of projection in the context

From the register analysis of each TT, we can evaluate whether the register is kept constant across the different TTs and if there are any variations. As Steiner (2001:166) proclaims, "a relative stability of register across source texts and target texts" is assumed to be a criterion in translation and the more the register variables change, the less the translated texts will be regarded as a translation in a narrow sense.

From the previous analysis of register in the TTs, we find that the three TTs have maintained stability in Field to the ST, without which a translation cannot be regarded as a translation. In the other two register variables, there are different degrees of variation from the ST. LT maintains the highest degree of stability in Field, Tenor and Mode to the ST, while KT and XT vary to different degrees in Tenor and Mode. Table 8-2 shows the degree of equivalence in the three variables of register in different TTs.

As we have discussed, between register and the context in which the text functions, there is a relationship of double-directional prediction: from the variables of the context, we can make a prediction of the linguistic forms and features of the text; and from the linguistic forms and features of the text, we can also make a prediction of the variables of context (Halliday 1978:110). The fact that Tenor and Mode variables in the TTs do not achieve full equivalence to those of the ST shows that the translators have not fully reflected the context of situation in the ST but rather reconstructed in the TTs their own context of situation. The different degrees of equivalence in the register of the TTs can be explained in

Chapter 8   Equivalence of Projection in the Lunyu and Its Translations in Context

the context in which the TTs function.

Table 8-2   Equivalence and variation in the register of the TTs

Register variables	ST	LT	KT	XT
Field	Recording what Confucius said with his disciples Technical	Recording what Confucius said with his disciples Technical Greatest degree of equivalence of Field with ST	Recording and description of what Confucius said with his disciples Less technical Mid-degree of equivalence of Field	Describing what Confucius said with his disciples Least technical Lower degree of equivalence of Field
Tenor	Unequal power between the Master and the disciples Relatively formal and didactic to the readers	Unequal power between the Master and disciples Relatively formal and didactic relationship between the translator and the readers Highest degree of equivalence	Unequal power between the Master and disciples Reader-friendly Tenor Medium degree of equivalence in Tenor	Unequal power between the Master and disciples Reader-friendly Lower degree of equivalence in Tenor
Mode	Spoken mode to be read	Spoken mode to be read Highest degree of equivalence	Blend of spoken and written to be read Medium degree of equivalence	The most oriented to the written mode Lower degree of equivalence

8.4.1   Equivalence study of projection in the context of situation

As discussed in Section 3.4.1, following Halliday's model of context (Halliday 1978; Halliday & Hasan 1985), context is a complete level above language that includes two forms of expression: the context of situation and the context of culture. They are at the two poles of the continuum of instantiation. The context of situation is at the instantial point and represents the immediate situation in which the text takes place; while the context of culture is at the potential point and represents a more abstract level of context which potentially controls the use of language.

From the comparison of the registers in the different TTs, we can identify changes in the variables of the context of situation in which the text functions. With the change in the Tenor and Mode of the TTs, the translators have reconstructed a context of situation in their translated versions. As the three register variables are in accordance with the three variables in the context of situation, we can identify different degrees of equivalence of the TTs in the context of situation. LT constructs a context of situation of the highest degree of equivalence to the ST, maintaining the highest degree of equivalence in Field, Tenor and Mode. KT constructs a context of situation of a medium degree of equivalence to that of the ST, maintaining a medium degree of equivalence in Field with some variations in Tenor and Mode. XT constructs a context of situation of the lowest degree of equivalence to that of the ST, maintaining comparatively lower degree of equivalence in Field and large variations in Tenor and Mode.

The reconstruction of context of situation results from the changes of the interactants taking part in the interactions of the texts: in the ST, the interactants are Confucius and his disciples, the compilers and readers in ancient Chinese; in the TTs, the interactants are Confucius and his disciples, the translator and his target readers. The different relationship between the translator and his target readers reconstructs the Tenor in the context of situation in the TTs. Legge aims to help western missionaries know more about Chinese culture so the target readers are not the ordinary readers in English but missionaries who have the need and responsibility to do some research on Chinese culture. The target readers of Ku's translation are the ordinary people in the western world as Ku claims that the main aim of his translation is to correct the mistranslations in

Legge's translation and help more people in the West know more about Chinese Confucianism. Ku (1898: vii-x) points out that the purpose of his translation is to translate the sayings and dialogues of Confucius according to the ways that an educated Englishman speaks. Since his target readers are ordinary people, he omits proper names that may seem to be strange and hard to understand for English speakers and builds a more reader-friendly Tenor. The target readers for XT are modern Chinese or English readers as Xu points out in the title of his translated versions: *Confucius modernized, thus spoke the Master*. To make his target readers more interested in reading the ancient Chinese book, Xu in his TT adopts many variations in the choice of the linguistic forms and construes a more reader-friendly Tenor. To make the text more coherent and readable, both Ku, particularly in his translation of the dialogues, and Xu construct a written-oriented mode and use many cohesive methods to make the TTs coherent.

The changes in the variables of context of situation in which the different TTs function determine the variations in the register and the different lexicogrammatical choice made by the translators in the TTs. The reconstruction of the context of situation in different TTs can explain the different degree of equivalence of register, and the changes in Field, Tenor, and Mode in the different TTs.

8.4.2 Evaluation of different TTs in the context of culture

Based on the SFL theory of translation, we have analyzed the equivalence in projection in the ST and TTs at the levels of lexicogrammar, semantics, and context. As Steiner (2001: 185) points out, a translation which preserves the features of the ST at the level of lexicogrammar can be regarded as a literal translation; and a translation which only preserve the features of the ST at the level of register or context can be regarded as relatively free. With the study of the three TTs at the three levels, we can conclude that the translated version of Xu is the freest one and that of Legge is the most literal one, while Ku's translation stands in the middle.

As Huang (2012a: 20) points out, in evaluating a translated text, many factors should be considered, including the purpose of translation, the reconstruction of context in the translated texts, the attitudes of the translators, the target readers, etc. The different choices made in the different translated versions are determined by the context of culture in which the translated text functions. The context of culture in which the different texts function includes the different periods of historical time in which the different translators lived, the different purposes of translation, the systematic variations between the SL and the TL, in this case Chinese and English, the ambiguity of old Chinese ST, and the different interpretation of the ST by the different translators.

In our study of equivalence in projection in the *Lunyu* and its translated versions from the text and context, from the levels of lexicogrammar, semantics and context, we have found that Legge in his translation preserves the features and structures of the ST at the level of lexicogrammar so as to convey the equivalent meaning at the level of semantics and achieve equivalence at the level of context. Legge's translation can be regarded as a literal translation. This is determined by the context of culture in which Legge translated the *Lunyu*. Legge lived in China as a missionary and stayed in Hong Kong for nearly 30 years. Legge translated the Chinese classics into English as he was convinced of the need for missionaries to be able to comprehend the ideas and culture of the Chinese. In his *Confucian Analects*, Legge maintains the equivalence to the ST from the level of lexicogrammar up to the level of context. Each page of the book is made up of the ST, the TT and the notes. The notes occupy almost half of the page. At the beginning of the book, there is a long prolegomenon, which introduces the different editions of the *Lunyu*, the commentaries upon the book, and the life and influence of Confucius and his immediate disciples. With the purpose of introducing the Chinese classic to Western missionaries, Legge himself claims that his translation has always tried to be faithful to the original Chinese rather than to grace of composition (Legge 1971: vi). This explains why Legge's translation has been granted a high academic status but it is the hardest for common readers to understand. Our study of projection in his translated version can draw a similar conclusion. In old Chinese, the words can usually be

Chapter 8 Equivalence of Projection in the Lunyu and Its Translations in Context

interpreted differently in diffreat contexts and there are few connectives used in sentences. To translate an old Chinese text into English without adding necessary connectives and background information, the text would be "practically unreadable" (Lin 1938: 36). Legge chooses to achieve equivalence at the level of lexicogrammar as well as the context of situation (the way of literal translation) to maintain the originality of the Chinese classic and leave the interpretation of book to the readers, so that the ambiguity of the ST and multiple possible interpretations of it are maintained in the TT.

In relation to Ku's translated version, we have found that Ku makes some variations as compared to the ST. Ku thinks Legge's stiff translation of the *Lunyu* and his narrow mentality have distorted the meaning of the Confucian classics (Ku 1898: vi-viii). He, as a Singapore-born Chinese who is an advocate of monarchy and Confucian values, aims to help ordinary Westerners know more about Confucian philosophy. Ku thus adopts the method of "domestication" in his translation. This context of culture determined the choices he made in his translation, such as the variations in the choice of types and structures of projection at the level of lexicogrammar: Ku maintains equivalence in Field but makes some variations in the Tenor and Mode to build a more reader-friendly relationship between the translator and the target Western readers. He adds some necessary connectives and background information within the text of the translation to make his texts smooth and readable. The choice of projection in his translation is in accordance with his purpose in translating the *Lunyu*.

Xu advocates creative rewriting in his translation of the *Lunyu, Confucius modernized, thus spoke the Master* published in 2005 when the translator was in his eighties. XT shows the most variations in the types and structures of the projection at the level of lexicogrammar and realizes comparatively the lowest degree of equivalence on the metafunctional meanings of the text. The register of XT shows the least degree of equivalence to that of the ST, with variations mostly in Tenor and Mode. Xu's choices in his translation are also determined by the context of culture in which he translates the *Lunyu*. Xu translates the book for contemporary modern readers no matter whether they are Westerners or Chinese. The translator tries to rewrite the ancient book of Chinese as a modern reader-friendly book of philosophy in which modern readers can get some ideas about Confucian philosophy. This explains why he chooses to abandon the typical but somewhat wearisome style of quotation in order to focus on the ideas conveyed by Confucius. At the level of lexicogrammar, Xu achieves the least degree of equivalence as well as including in his translated text some interpersonal and textual meanings not contained in the ST. We can conclude that the translation of Xu can be regarded as a free translation in the three TTs studied in the present study. In Xu's literary translations, he advocates the method of making the most of the advantage of the target language and recreating a translated version that is "competitive" to the ST. Xu thinks that literary translation is like an art and in his translation he can abandon the original structure of the ST and recreate a translated version in the target language. Xu's translation aims and methods can explain why in XT there is such a large portion of variations in Tenor and Mode, in contrast to the relative equivalence achieved in Field.

As discussed before, there is no guarantee of absolute equivalence in translation and equivalence is constructed out of a diversity of similarities. What kind of similarity we are prepared to accept as equivalence is determined by a particular context for a particular purpose. As Halliday (2001:17) puts it while discussing the different values of equivalence in different strata:

> In strata, likewise, equivalence is typically most valued at the highest stratum within language itself, that of semantics (where again the lower strata may be allowed to vary); value may also attach explicitly to the level of context, especially when equivalence at lower strata is problematic.

In evaluating the relative equivalence achieved in the different translated versions, value will be attached to the level of context. The variations in the context of culture have determined the different choices made in the different translated versions.

8.5 Summary

Translation texts are "instantiations of language systems, their grammars and their semantics, according to particular contextual requirements" (Teich 2001:218). With this study of the translated texts of the *Lunyu* from the pole of instance to that of system, from text to context, we have found the different degrees of equivalence achieved in the different texts.

Legge achieves the highest degree of metafunctional equivalence in the text and he has reconstructed a highly equivalent context of situation in his TT.

Ku achieves a middle-degree of metafunctional equivalence in the text and he has reconstructed a context of situation in which the Tenor is more reader-friendly and the Mode is more written-oriented than that of the ST.

Xu achieves relatively the lowest degree of metafunctional equivalence in the text and he has reconstructed a context of situation in which the Tenor is more reader-friendly and the Mode is the most written-oriented compared to that in the ST.

The different degrees of equivalence of projection achieved in the different TTs can be explained in the context of culture and the evaluation of the translation quality of the TTs should also be conducted in the context of culture, which will be further discussed in Chapter 9.

Chapter 9
Discussion

9.1 Introduction

The observation, interpretation, description, analysis and explanation of projection in the three translated texts were conducted from the perspectives of metafunction and context in Chapters 4 to 8 above. In the present chapter, we will bring together these issues in a general discussion as to what extent the equivalence analysis of projection can contribute to the evaluation of the translation qualities of the three translated texts of the *Lunyu*. We will also make a general comment and evaluation of the three translated texts.

9.2 Observation and description of projection choices

In the study of translation based on FDA, the first two steps are the observation and description of the different choices at the lexicogrammatical level made in the translation process. Translation, as discussed in Section 3.4, is the "**recreation of meaning in context through choice** — choice in the interpretation of the original text and choice in the creation of the translated text" (Matthiessen 2014: 271). From an SFL viewpoint, choice is meaning. The meanings conveyed through the different choices in different translations may be equivalent to the meanings in the ST or they may not. In Section 5.3.3, it is argued that there is no absolute equivalence between the ST and its TTs. The equivalence achieved by the TTs can only be equivalence of various degrees.

The different projection choices observed in the ST and TTs are different types and structures of projection in the *Lunyu* and its

Chapter 9 Discussion

three translated texts, described with examples taken from the ST and the three TTs in Chapter 4. As shown in Section 4.2, projection in the ST is realized in the following different forms:

1) congruent realization of projection in a clause nexus;
2) projection realized metaphorically in a paragraph; and
3) projection realized metaphorically in a clause.

In Section 4.2, we clarified the research target of the study by confining the study of projection in the ST and TTs to the level of clause complex, in the aphorisms and dialogues (except the descriptions) from Book One to Book Nine of the *Lunyu*.

The types of projection in the ST were identified as quoting (direct speech), with the structure of "projecting clause + projected clause". In the three TTs, various types and structures of projection were chosen by the different translators. The types of projection identified in the three TTs were described as follows (see Sections 4.2, 4.3, 4.4 and 4.5):

1) Quoting (direct speech)
2) Free indirect speech
3) Reporting speech
4) A hypotactic enhancing *when-* clause

The different structures of projection were identified in the three TTs as:

1) Projecting clause ^ Projected clause
2) Projected clause ^ Projecting clause
3) Part of projected clause ^ Projecting clause ^ the other part of Projected clause
4) Minor projected clause ^ Projecting clause

The different choices of types and structures of projection are made consciously or unconsciously by the translators in the process of translating. An systemic functional linguist aims to investigate "the particular types of functions or meanings" connected with particular types of wordings (Thompson 1996b: 30), such as the different logical features realized in the choice between quoting and reporting in the TTs, or the different textual features realized in the choices of structures "projecting clause ⌒ projected clause" or "projected clause ⌒ projecting clause". To study the translated text from a SFL perspective, as discussed in Section 3.2, is to discover the metafunctional meanings conveyed by the different lexicogrammatical choices of projection in the different TTs and to compare and analyze the equivalence and shifts of meaning in the context. As discussed in Section 3.2, as a general and appliable linguistics, SFL can function as a sound basis for the analysis of projection in the ST and TTs.

9.3 The value of a metafunctional analysis of projection

Texts in SFL consist of different modes of meaning and people can understand texts from an overall understanding of the following different modes of meaning: logical, experiential, interpersonal, and textual. In studying projection in the translated texts, one may study whether the rendering of projection in the translated texts is metafunctionally equivalent to the ST or not. In the SFL model of analysis given in Section 3.6, projection is analyzed in text and context as well on the basis of different choices in the lexicogrammar from the perspective of the four metafunctions. In Chapters 5 to 7 we analyzed whether "the translated text is experientially equivalent, logically equivalent, interpersonally equivalent, and / or textually equivalent" (Huang 2013:265). In Chapter 8 the different degrees of equivalence achieved in the different TTs were compared in the context of different target texts. The issue that needs to be discussed now is: Is the analysis of projection from the perspectives of metafunction and context sufficient for evaluating the quality of the translated texts of the *Lunyu*?

9.3.1 Value of the ideational analysis of projection

The ideational meanings realized by the different choices of projection in the TTs are studied in Chapter 4 in two parts: first, describing the different choices in the TTs of experiential structure of projecting clauses; second, studying the logical aspects of projection in the TTs.

In SFL, different experiential meanings are construed by the configuration of the three elements of the experiential structure of the clause: the Process, the Participant(s) involved in the Process; and the Circumstances associated with the Process (Halliday & Matthiessen 2004: 175-176: see the analysis in Section 5.2.1). Chapter 5 analyzes the experiential structure of projecting clauses in the ST and TTs, and it is found that the Process used in the projecting clauses in both the ST and TTs is typically a verbal Process, with only one Participant, i.e. a Sayer, and with no Receiver and no Circumstances. The experiential structure of projecting clauses in both the ST and TTs usually contains no circumstance of the process, which conveys the equivalent experiential meaning in the ST and TTs. The experiential meaning conveyed in the equivalent experiential structure of projecting clauses in the ST and TTs is: what the projection clause nexus in the ST and TTs conveys is a recording of what the Master said, without any specific information concerning to whom the Master said and or in what situation he said it. With the choice of similar experiential structure of projecting clauses in the TTs, it is found in Chapter Five that projection in the TTs can convey equivalent experiential meaning. The TTs studied are found to have maintained the experiential meaning conveyed in the ST and nearly achieved experiential equivalence of with projection in the ST and TTs.

In Section 5.2.2, the logical aspect of projection in the TTs is studied by investigating the taxis in the projection clause nexus. In the ST, the projection clause nexus in the aphorisms and dialogues is typically realized as quoting (direct speech), with a paratactic relationship between the projecting clause and the projected clause. In the TTs, different translators have chosen different types of projection for the projection clause nexus: in the TTs by Legge and Ku, there are only a few instances of non-equivalence as to the modes of projection chosen; in XT, a great portion of the projection clause nexus is realized by free direct speech, which is not equivalent to the ST as to the types of projection chosen but realizes an equivalent paratactic relationship between the projecting clause and projected clause to that of the quoting (direct speech) in the ST. In the dialogues, the quoting / direct speech of the ST is realized in Xu's translation either as reporting / indirect speech in a projection clause nexus, or metaphorically realized as projection within a clause, or realized as a *when-* clause hypotactically dependent on the main projection clause nexus. The logical meanings conveyed in these different choices of projection are not equivalent to that of the ST. For example, with the choice of reporting instead of quoting (direct speech) in XT, the equal status of projecting clause and projected clause in the ST is changed into unequal status in the TT; the hypotactic enhancing *when-* clause dependent on the following projection clause nexus puts the asking turn of the dialogue in a dependent status to the main clause nexus, etc.

From the study of the experiential and logical aspects of projection in the ST and TTs, we can evaluate the experiential and logical equivalence in projection between the ST and the TTs. The three TTs generally achieved ideational equivalence in projection to the ST but the degree of ideational equivalence varied across the TTs. Shifts resulted from the varying choices in the experiential structures of projecting clauses and the types of projection.

Based on the ideational analysis of projection in the ST and TTs, we can ask: what does the analysis of ideational equivalence of projection tell us about the characteristics of the translated texts? Is the ideational analysis of projection sufficient to evaluate the quality of the translation, and for us to make meaningful comments on the quality of the translated works? According to Section 2.3.5.2, Halliday (2001)argues that the "equivalence at different strata carries differential values", the higher the stratum is, the more value it carries. As to metafunctions, Halliday (2001:16) proposes that the ideational equivalence is a must-be, without which the translation cannot be regarded as a translation.

The study of experiential equivalence and logical equivalence of projection in the ST and TT in Chapter 5 shows that the must-be requirement of ideational equivalence is generally met in these three translated texts. Based on the background of generally equivalent ideational meanings, we should discuss what the shifts of ideational meaning of projection in the translations of Ku and Xu imply and why they choose the non-equivalent forms among the available equivalent forms of projection. Can we conclude that their TTs are not good translations because of their comparatively low degree of ideational equivalence compared to the TT of Legge? These questions can only be answered when we further study the interpersonal metafunction and textual metafunction and evaluate the four metafunctional meanings together to get a clear picture on the translation quality of the three TTs. As Halliday (2001: 16) proposes, " in metafunction, high value may be accorded to equivalence in the interpersonal or textual realms — but usually only when the ideational equivalence can be taken for granted" (Halliday 2001:17).

9.3.2 Value of the interpersonal analysis of projection

The interpersonal meaning of projection can be seen in the analysis of the different choices of Mood element: i. e. Subject and Finite in the projecting clauses, and from the modality system and person system in the projection clause nexus.

The interpersonal aspect of the projection clause nexus is realized by the projection of propositions (statements and questions) and the projection of proposals (offers and commands). Section 6.2.1 examined the speech functions realized in projection in the aphorisms. The numbers of propositions and proposals projected in the ST and TTs were counted and it was found there were a similar number of propositions and proposals in both. That indicates the TTs generally realized equivalent speech functions to the ST. In both ST and TTs, the majority of projections were realized as propositions and only a few as proposals. The majority of propositions were statements and the majority of proposals were commands. Both the ST and the three TTs conveyed the equivalent interpersonal meanings in the choice of projection: the aphorisms consist of the sayings of Confucius and some of his disciples. The commodity exchanged is primarily information, and the main speech roles of the speakers are giving information.

With the study of interpersonal metafunction of projection

realized in the different choices of the mood elements of projecting clauses, the structures of the projecting clauses, the different choices in the modality system and person system in the projected clauses, we can find the specific interpersonal meanings realized in the TTs which are not equivalent to the ST and the analysis can help interpret the specific characteristics of the translated text.

For example, in studying the mood elements of projecting clauses, we find both Legge and Xu chose "the Master" and the courtesy name of the disciples as Subjects of projecting clauses. The interpersonal meaning realized in the choice of Subjects in TTs is equivalent to that of ST. The subjects chosen in KT are respectively "Confucius" and "a disciple of Confucius", the interpersonal meaning of disciples showing respect to the Master is less but the interpersonal relationship between the lexical items realizing Subjects of projecting clauses is made clearer.

Another example is the choice of projecting verbs. The projecting verbs used in the TTs of Legge and Xu are simple and general projecting verbs equivalent to those used in the ST, while the projecting verbs used in KT are more specific to each situation than those of the ST.

Another instance comes from the study of structures in the projecting clauses. Ku in his TT has chosen some structures of "Subject + *was heard to* +projecting verbs" to specify the Subject of a passive verb and makes the interpersonal relationship between the speakers clearer than that of the ST.

The interpersonal meanings realized in the different choices from the Modality and Person systems in the projected clauses were also analyzed in Section 6.4 and Section 6.5. These choices result from a different interpretation of the corresponding systems used in the ST.

From the study of the speech functions, mood elements, the structure of projecting clauses, and the modality and person system in projection, we can analyze the interpersonal equivalence and shifts. On the whole, all three TTs have realized the equivalent speech functions to the ST, but still conveyed different interpersonal meanings in their specific texts. The specific equivalence and shifts in each translated text are as follows.

The mood elements chosen in the projecting clauses of LT realized an equivalent interpersonal meaning to the ST. The different projecting verbs and structures of projecting clauses chosen in KT made the TT more lively in different contexts of speaking, and his choice of Subjects in the projecting clauses made the relationship of each chapter clearer to readers and built a more reader-friendly relationship between the translator and the target readers. Xu chose to realize the projecting clause of the asking turns in dialogues with hypotactic enhancing *when-* clauses dependent on the projection clause nexus of the answering turn of the Master, thus highlighting the unequal status between Confucius and his disciples, and realizing an interpersonal meaning not contained in the ST.

The analysis of the interpersonal metafunction of the translated texts helps readers to further understand and interpret the special qualities of the TTs.

9.3.3 Value of textual analysis in projection

The textual meaning of projection in the ST and TTs has been studied through the choice of thematic structure, patterns of thematic progression and choices from the system of cohesion in projection clause nexuses. This analysis can reveal the degree of textual equivalence of projection in the ST and TTs and the textual characteristics of the different translated texts.

The different thematic structure of projection in the ST and TTs was described in Section 7.3. It was found that in the three TTs, Legge chose the most equivalent unmarked thematic structure ("the projecting clause ^ the projected clause") thus achieving the highest degree of equivalence in the textual meaning conveyed in the TT; Xu chose the least equivalent thematic structure in the three TTs and the least degree of equivalence in textual meaning.

LT is the most equivalent to the ST, both of which have a clear focus of the text by repeating the same thematic structure in each chapter, but at the same time lack dynamism and a sense of connection between the Rhemes of the text. KT achieves the general textual equivalence in the aphorisms, while varying the thematic structures of projection in some respects in the part of dialogues. The marked Themes chosen by Ku in the dialogues achieve better cohesion between the different projection clause nexuses in the dialogues. XT shows the most shifts of textual meaning to the ST. First, in the aphorisms, the thematic structure of "projected clause ^ projecting clause" realizes each chapter with a projection clause nexus beginning with New information in the projected clause, without the repetition of the projecting clause to connect each chapter. Second, the most usually used marked Theme in the dialogues — the hypotactic enhancing *when-* clause which realizes the asking turns in an dependent clause of the projection clause nexus, puts the asking turn in a subordinate status to the answering turn of Confucius, which carries not only a textual meaning not equivalent to the ST but also a unique interpersonal meaning in his TT (see the analysis in Section 7.3.3).

The topic of cohesion in the *Lunyu* and its translation has been discussed by many researchers with different opinions on whether the *Lunyu* is coherent or not. For example, Zou (2010:23) criticizes the content in the *Lunyu* as miscellaneous and lacking in coherence; Yao (2004:95) points out that the organization of the *Lunyu* is not in disorder, because there are still cohesive ties found in the different chapters, while it is not in good order as it is not a book consistently written by one writer (Huang 2011). The main cohesive method used in the ST is the repetition of the projecting clause *Zǐ yuē* (子曰). Another way to achieve cohesion in understanding the text is the "encyclopedic knowledge" and "shared knowledge" between the writers and the readers of the ST (Huang 2011:90).

From the analysis in Section 7.5.1 of cohesive methods in the aphorisms as well as the dialogues in the different TTs, we have found that LT maintains an equivalent degree of coherence to the ST by using similar cohesive methods, such as repeating the projecting clauses, using notes and appendix to build cohesion in the subjects of the projecting clauses and achieving coherence in the dialogues through the use of the adjacency pairs of asking and answering. KT chooses some cohesive methods not equivalent to the ST besides the equivalent methods of repeating the projecting clauses in the aphorisms: for example, using methods of lexical cohesion between the Subjects of the projecting clauses, and using marked thematic structures not equivalent to the ST to achieve cohesion in the dialogues. The textual meaning conveyed with Ku's choice of cohesive methods is less equivalent to the ST but KT achieves better cohesion and coherence than the ST. Xu's choice of cohesive methods shows the least degree of equivalence to the ST. Xu neither chooses the similar method of repeating the projecting clauses to achieve cohesion nor uses the clear turn of asking and answering in dialogues to achieve coherence as in the ST. XT has lost the typical way of achieving coherence in quotations and dialogues. How can XT achieve coherence? The coherence in XT is not mainly realized in the typical realization of quotation style: the projection clause nexus. Actually, Xu purposefully omits the style of quotation by putting the projecting clause in the middle of the chapter, and by not using the quotation marks, so coherence is mainly achieved through the content of the projected clauses.

From the analysis of textual meaning in projection in Chapter Seven, we have found that Legge chooses equivalent thematic structures and cohesive methods to the ST and achieves the highest degree of textual equivalence to the ST. By choosing some cohesive methods not used in the ST, KT conveys less textual equivalence than Legge's, while XT achieves the least degree of equivalence.

However, we cannot conclude that the TTs by Ku and Xu are not as good as that of Legge. We find that KT is more coherent than the ST, while XT has lost the typical characteristics of quotations and dialogues and reads more like a description. The two translated texts vary to some extent as to the textual meaning conveyed in projection, but achieve textual meanings specific to that translation. It is the shifts in metafunctional meanings that make each translated text unique in its own way.

9.4 Evaluation of translation quality in the context

As we have discussed in 9.3, the analysis of metafunctional equivalence in projection in the ST and TT can help us understand the meaning of projection in each translated text. We find that LT achieves the higher degree of experiential, logical, interpersonal and textual equivalence, while XT shows a lower degree of equivalence for all four metafunctions. Can we then evaluate LT as the translation of higher quality and XT as the one of lower quality?

As discussed in Section 3.5.3, there are two levels of achievement in the translation studies based on FDA. The lower level of achievement is to understand the text. The metafunctional study of projection in the ST and TTs can help one understand the meanings of projection in the ST and TTs and provide a basis for the evaluation of the translation quality. The higher level of achievement in the present study is to evaluate the translation quality of the TTs, which needs to be carried out in relation to its context. As we know, in order to evaluate whether a translated text is effective or successful, people should interpret the context as well as the text and to interpret the relationship between them.

There have been some preliminary studies of the *Lunyu* and its English translations from the perspectives of the situational and cultural context (e.g. Zou 2007). The context of situation and the context of culture, however, are not easily identified, no matter how hard one tries to re-contextualize the text (Huang 2013: 267). As discussed in Section 3.5.1, there is a two-way context-metafunction hook-up between language and situation: the predictability between context and metafunctions. The study of the metafunctional meanings of projection in the ST and TTs identifies the different TTs as closely related registerial variants (Steiner 2001:169) of each other, as shown in Section 8.3. The register of LT is highly in accordance with the register of the ST, whereby the relationship between the translator and the readers are didactic. The register of KT is found to vary in Field (to be less technical than the ST), in Mode (with more features of written mode than the ST), and in Tenor (to create a friendlier and less didactic relationship between the translator and readers). The register of XT is found to vary the most: in Field, e.g. more like a narrative of the translator than the recording on the sayings and dialogues of the Master; in Mode, e.g. the most orientation towards written mode; and in Tenor, e.g.

with a friendlier and less didactic relationship between the translator and readers. This analysis shows that the three TTs have reconstructed the context of situation in which their translated texts function. The contexts of situation reconstructed in the different TTs are at different degrees of equivalence to that of the ST, with Legge's being the highest and Xu's the lowest.

The analysis of the context of situation of each translated text can provide a better understanding of the characteristics of the translated texts, but one still cannot explain why different translators choose to reconstruct different contexts of situation in which their translated text function. To fully understand the texts, the evaluation of the translated texts should be conducted in relation to the context of culture. In studying the context of culture for each TT, one can make a meaningful judgment on the translation quality of the three translated texts.

9.4.1 Purpose of the translators

The purpose of each translator is an important factor in evaluating a translated text in relation to the context of culture (see Section 8.4.2). The purpose of the translators, and the historical period in which the translation takes place, provides a more reasonable basis for making a judgment on the quality of the translated text. Take LT for example: his purpose is to help missionaries in China understand Chinese culture. This explains why he tries to maintain faithfulness to the ST in every respect, from the experiential, logical, interpersonal to the textual metafunction. He chooses to leave the interpretation of the text to the target readers. The highest degree of equivalence in the text and context fully realizes Legge's translation purpose and has had great influence on missionaries and scholars of later periods. In light of his translation purpose one can conclude that LT should be evaluated as a good translation. However, some scholars argue that LT is "practically unreadable" (Lin 1938: 36) because of the stiff faithfulness of LT which translates the ancient Chinese text literally without adding any necessary connectives and explanations in the text. Legge leaves the multiple interpretation of the *Lunyu* to his readers, which demands a great deal of efforts.

The purpose of Ku's translation is to make some variations on the "stiff translation" of Legge and to make the Confucius philosophy more easily known by ordinary Westerners, not just by scholars and missionaries, and it is this purpose that determines his translation choices. The desire for a friendlier relationship between translator and readers determines his choices in reconstructing the Tenor and the Mode of the TT through choices in the interpersonal and textual lexicogrammar. These variations make his translated text more readable and understandable: for example, by adding connectives, the omission of the courtesy name that is strange and hard to understand for Westerners, variation in the textual structures, etc. Although KT does not achieve full equivalence to the ST, he has achieved his purpose of transmitting the Chinese philosophy to the Westerners at his historical period.

Xu's purpose in translating this Chinese classic, as the title of the translated text indicates, is to modernize the ancient work for modern times. His target readers are modern readers no matter whether they are Westerners or Chinese. This explains why he varies greatly in Tenor and Mode in reconstructing the context of situation in which his translated text functions, and why he abandons the typical style of quotation of the ST. Xu's text achieves comparatively the least degree of equivalence as to the metafunctional meanings conveyed in the choice of projection, but it can still be regarded as a good translation aimed at modern readers.

9.4.2 Literal translation and free translation

The topic of literal translation and free translation has been dealt with by many researchers in the literature. From an SFL viewpoint, the translation that can preserve the features and structure of the ST at the level of lexicogrammar can be regarded as literal translation and the translation that can only preserve the features of the ST at the level of register or context can be regarded as relatively free (Steiner 2001:185). The three TTs studied can also be evaluated in this respect.

From the study of the lexicogrammatical realization of

projection in the three TTs, we have found that Legge has maintained the equivalence of form and meaning across all strands of meaning: experiential, logical, interpersonal, and textual. His TT chooses equivalent types and structures of projection at the level of lexicogrammar to achieve the highest degree of metafunctional and contextual equivalence in projection to the ST. LT can be viewed as a typical literal translation.

Xu has achieved comparatively the least degree of equivalence in the form and meaning of projection in his TT. XT chooses non-equivalent types and structures of projection so as to achieve variation in the interpersonal and textual meanings of the TT as compared to the ST. It does not achieve equivalence at the level of lexicogrammar but successfully realizes its translation purpose at the level of context. XT results from Xu's unique way of translation — rewriting, and can be viewed as a typical free translation.

Ku has maintained the medium degree of equivalence in the form and meaning of projection both metafunctionally and contextually. KT shows some variations in the metafunctional meanings, especially in the interpersonal and textual meanings, maintaining stability in Field while varying in Mode and Tenor in reconstructing the context of situation in translation. KT varies more than LT but less than XT at the level of lexicogrammar, thus resulting in a medium degree of variation in the interpersonal and textual metafunctions, and in the context. It can be viewed as a translated text which adopts both a literal and a free way of translation.

9.4.3 Role of translators

The translator's role is also an important issue in evaluating the translated text, something which has been raised in many parts of the current study: in discussing the reasons for the different choice of projection in different TTs as illustrated in 5.4; in discussing the different understanding of modality in the ST by the translators in Section 6.4.3; and in discussing the importance of the translator's role using Jennings' (1895:35) statements on why he has chosen his unique form of projecting clauses (see Section 5.4.3). Some translators aim to achieve variation from previous translators in their translations and achieve a unique identity for their own translation. This issue is something worthy of further investigation in later studies.

The translators' role functions in the process of translation in relation to their different cultural backgrounds, different motivations for translation, and different understanding and interpretation of the ST. These factors can determine translators' translation choices. Huang (2013: 265) also stresses that systemic functional linguists should pay attention to the motivation behind each choice of meaning and expression in examining translated texts.

The different interpretations and explanations of the ST is also an important factor in translation and this is something that makes the role of translator very important. The translator functions as "a reader, as an interpreter, as a text analyst, as a re-writer and as a translator" (Huang 2013:268). Sections 5.4 and 6.4.3 cite examples to show how different interpretations of the ST by different translators result in different choices in the translated texts. As shown in the Section 5.4.2, the different interpretations of the description clause *Zǐzhāng xué gān lù* (子张学干禄) by different translators results in the differing realization of the clause as the equivalent descriptive clauses in the TTs of Legge and Ku, or as a projection clause in the TT of Xu. The Chinese text of the *Lunyu* was compiled by many people over a long period of time. There are a great number of intralingual translations and interlingual translations of it. It is difficult to achieve a generally accepted interpretation either in Chinese or in English. For a systemic functional linguist, what we aim to discover is the meaning conveyed in the different choices of translators in the process of translation, and to study to what extent the systemic functional linguistics can help a researcher to evaluate a translated text.

9.5 Summary

The issues discussed in this chapter are the main issues related to the equivalence study of projection in the *Lunyu* and its translated texts. We have highlighted the main issues discussed from Chapter Four to Chapter Eight. We have also discussed how to evaluate the quality of the three translated texts based on the previous analysis of projection from the perspectives of metafunction and of context. Other issues related to the evaluation of the translated texts such as the difference between literal translation and free translation, and the issue of translators' roles was also discussed.

With the discussion of the evaluation of the quality of the three translated texts, we will bring the whole study to a conclusion in the following chapter.

Chapter 10
Conclusion

10.1 Introduction

In the previous chapters, the phenomenon of projection in the *Lunyu* and its English translations has been comprehensively studied through specific analysis of the data. The present chapter aims to bring the study to a conclusion. The purpose of the present study is to present a comprehensive description of projection in the *Lunyu* and to make a comparison of the projection in the ST and the TTs within the framework of SFL. In this concluding chapter, we will bring these descriptions and comparisons together in light of the overall objectives of the study and give an overview of the main findings of the present study. Then we will present some implications and limitations of the study and put forward some suggestions for further investigations.

10.2 An overview of the study

The present research is a linguistic-oriented study of translation based on FDA within the framework of SFL. The study has gone through the following steps.

In Chapter 2, previous studies related to the present research were reviewed. In the linguistic literature, projection has been extensively studied from different approaches but this phenomenon has received little attention in the translation studies. The present study of the translation of projection in the *Lunyu* aims to extend the scope of translation studies on the *Lunyu* within the framework of SFL.

In Chapter 3, the basic theoretical notions in translation studies within the scope of SFL are introduced to provide guidance for the present study. Based on the theoretical principles of SFL, an analytical model of projection in the ST and TTs of the *Lunyu* is built up and translation studies of projection in the *Lunyu* are explored in relation both to texts and context.

From Chapters 4 to 8, projection in the ST and TTs of the *Lunyu* is explored from a metafunctional viewpoint to find answers to the research questions proposed in Chapter 1. The ultimate purpose of the present study is to evaluate the degree of equivalence of projection achieved in the different TTs. In the actual description of the phenomenon of projection in the *Lunyu* and its translations, we set out to describe it part by part. The metafunctional meanings of projection realized in the lexicogrammatical choices were studied and compared and the evaluation of the degree of equivalence was conducted in relation to the context of situation and the context of culture.

Chapter 9 brings the issues related to the equivalence study of projection together and discusses how to evaluate the quality of the three translated texts of the *Lunyu* based on the analysis of projection from the perspective of metafunction and of context. Chapter Ten brings the whole study to a conclusion.

10.3 Main research findings

The study has found that the phenomenon of projection is important in the text of the *Lunyu* and that the translation of projection will influence the degree of equivalence that translated texts can achieve. The first chapter of the study points out that the main objectives of the present study are to widen the appliability of SFL in discourse analysis and translation studies. In order to achieve the objectives of the study, we put forward four research questions concerning the equivalence study of projection. We then begin to search for the answers to the research questions by describing and analyzing the phenomenon of projection from the angle of the grammatical choices within different metafunctional domains. The different metafunctional meanings realized in the translated texts are analyzed and the degree of equivalence the TTs achieve is calculated. Now we can conclude by providing generalized answers to the research questions.

The first three research questions put forward are about the different metafunctional meanings realized by different lexicogrammatical choices of projection in the target texts. We find that in different translated versions, translators choose different types and structures of projection, among which Legge has the most equivalent types and structures of projection while Xu has the most varying types and structures of projection as compared to that of the ST. These different choices of linguistic forms of projection can convey different metafunctional meanings in their TTs.

With regard to the ideational meanings of projection realized in the lexicogrammatical choices, we find different degrees of equivalence and shifts in the ideational metafunction between the ST and TTs at the level of linguistic expression as well as at the level of meaning potentials. Although basically the three TTs convey equivalent ideational meanings to the ST, the degree of ideational equivalence to the ST is different in the different TTs. By analyzing different choices in the structures and types of projection realizing the experiential metafunction of projecting clauses and the logical metafunction of the projection clause nexus, we find that in comparison to the ST the translated version of Legge varies slightly in the ideational meaning of projection but the translated version of Xu varies more in it. The cline of ideational equivalence from high to low in the three translated versions is: LT, KT and XT.

With regard to the interpersonal meanings of projection realized in the different TTs, we find that the three TTs realize equivalent speech functions with their choice in realizing the projection as propositions or as proposals, but the interpersonal meanings conveyed in each TT are different. Examining the different choices in the Mood, Modality and Person systems in the projecting clauses and the projected clauses, the shifts of interpersonal meaning in the ST and TTs are identified and analyzed. We find that the TTs by Ku and

Chapter 10 Conclusion

Xu add some new interpersonal meaning in their TTs through different choices of projection. The TTs by Ku and Xu convey a more reader-friendly relationship between the translators and the target readers than that in the ST. The shifts in the realization of interpersonal meanings of projection are mainly caused by different understandings of the ST, ambiguities in the systems of Modality and Person in Old Chinese, and the different target readers of the translated texts.

With regard to the textual meanings of projection in different TTs, through examining the system of Theme and the patterns of thematic progression and the cohesive methods used in the projection clause nexus, we find that different TTs have different textual meanings from different choices made in the textual lexicogrammar. The Legge's translation only makes slight shifts in the structure of Theme and the pattern of thematic progression and maintains a high degree of textual equivalence of projection to the ST. Ku makes different choices in the dialogues, while Xu makes substantial shifts in the structure of Theme and the patterns of thematic progression in the aphorisms as well as in the dialogues. The textual meanings realized in both cases are different to that of the ST. From an examination of the cohesive methods used in different TTs, we find that Legge chooses similar cohesive methods to the ST, while Ku and Xu choose more cohesive methods to make their translated versions more coherent than the ST. The cline of textual equivalence in the TTs from high to low is: LT, KT and XT.

The fourth research question is concerned with the equivalence of the projection in the ST and TT evaluated in context. From the register analysis of the ST and TTs, we discover that the TTs construct different contexts of situation through variation in the three register variables. Different TTs achieve different degrees of equivalence in the context of situation. We analyze and discuss the influence of the different periods of historical time in which different translators live, the different purposes of translation by different translators, systematic differences between the Chinese and English languages, the ambiguity of old Chinese and different interpretations of the ST by different translators. By evaluating the equivalence of projection in the context, we find that the translators only achieve relative equivalence to the ST and the degree of equivalence that readers can accept is determined by the context in which the text functions. The three TTs achieve different degrees of metafunctional equivalence to the ST because they have reconstructed the context of situation. The differences and shifts in the Tenor and Mode of the context of situation in which the texts function relate to the different choices of the translators in their process of translation.

With the equivalence study of projection from the angle of the three metafunctions based on the text and context, we find that Legge chooses the method of literal translation in his translation and tries to maintain the equivalence of projection at the level of lexicogrammar as well as the level of context. Ku and Xu choose the method of free translation and add some interpersonal and textual meanings not contained in the ST. With the change of Tenor and Mode in the context of situation of their TTs, they also achieve their purpose of translation and their translated versions of the *Lunyu* can also be regarded as successful translations.

10.4 Implications of the research

The present study has aimed to provide a systematic and comprehensive account of projection in the Chinese classic and its English translations. This proves that SFL can be a reliable framework in which to conduct a comprehensive description of the linguistic phenomenon of projection. The realization of metafunctional meanings in projection was analyzed at the rank of clause nexus. Metafunctional meanings realized in the Chinese text and English texts were compared and evaluated in the context of situation and context of culture.

The research also proves the feasibility of using SFL as a linguistic base for translation studies. The linguistic parameters defining equivalence in translation studies put forward by systemic functional linguists such as metafunction and stratification have proven critical and effective in the comparison of two languages and in translation studies. The findings from the present translation study of projection in the *Lunyu* are in accordance with the findings of studies of translating the *Lunyu* from other perspectives. For instance, in the present study of projection in James Legge's translation, we have discovered that the translated version of Legge tries to maintain the equivalence of projection at the level of lexicogrammar and at the level of metafunctional meanings so as to maintain a high degree of equivalence in the TT. This finding corresponds with the findings in the research on Legge's style of translating Chinese classics (Zhou 2011). Our present research on the equivalence of projection in the ST and TT proves that applying the notions of SFL to the study of translation is feasible and appliable and the study of projection in the translated versions of the *Lunyu* can broaden the scope of appliability of SFL in the translation studies. As Newmark (1987:293-303) suggests, " Hallidayan linguistics" provides "a serviceable tool" (Newmark 1987:293) for translation studies and the present study of projection in the translated texts can testify to the appliability of SFL as a tool in describing, analyzing and comparing the ST and TT in the process and purpose of translation.

The present study takes its goal as relative translation equivalence and regards equivalence in translation as " the accommodation of differences " (Teich 2001:218) as it accommodates "both diversity and commonality between language systems and their instantiation in texts" (Teich 2001:212). The descriptive and comparative study of the ST and TTs can gain valuable insights for the field of comparative linguistic studies and shed light on the study of relative equivalence in the product of translation. Equivalence between the ST and the TT is the perennial pursuit of translators and the equivalence study of translation is also a perennial topic of interest for the linguists. With the existence of systemic differences between languages, shifts are inevitable in the process of translating one text to another. The present equivalence study of projection in the ST and the TT of the *Lunyu* can prove the uniqueness of each translated version and also show that translation can only achieve relative equivalence in the TTs due to the change in language and in the context in which language is used. It also shows that the degree of relative equivalence that readers can accept is a kind of "similarity we are prepared to accept as equivalence in a particular context for a particular purpose." (Yallop 2001:242)

Finally, the study may shed light for translation studies on quotation style texts. There has so far been no comprehensive study on the projection of a text in quotation style. The analysis of the different metafunctions of projection realized in the text of quotation styles can deepen the understanding of readers as to how projection is used in quotation style texts.

10.5 Limitations and suggestions for further studies

The present study focuses on the study of projection at the rank of clause nexus with the hope of providing a comprehensive study on projection in the *Lunyu* and its translated texts. There are still various areas worthy of further investigation.

First, projection study at the level above clause nexus or below clause nexus: due to the limitations of this study, we have taken the first projection clause nexus in the projection paragraph as our main data for analysis, and the other projected message in the same projection paragraph has been left unstudied. The exploration of the projection paragraph can be further pursued. The study of projection that is metaphorically realized within the clause also deserves further exploration.

Second, study of projection in the simplified version of the *Lunyu* and its translated versions: the translated versions we have chosen for the present study are complete translations of the *Lunyu* in different periods of time by different translators. At the present time, there are also a number of different intralingual and interlingual simplified translations of the *Lunyu* aiming to educate the school students. The study of projection in these versions deserves to be further pursued.

Third, translation studies of projection in different genres: as the previous studies suggest, projection is prevalent in the *Lunyu* and the equivalence study of projection in the *Lunyu* is worthwhile and meaningful. Further studies can be made as to the equivalence of projection in different genres such as in the translation of modern novels.

References

Baker, M. 1992. *In Other Words: A Coursebook on Translation.* Beijing: Foreign Language Teaching and Research Press.
Ban, G. (班固) 1962. *Hanshu* (汉书, *History of Han Dynasty*). Beijing: Zhonghua Book Company.
Bassnett, M. S. 1980. *Translation Studies.* London: Methuen.
Baynham, M. 1996. Direct speech: What's it doing in non-narrative discourse? *Journal of Pragmatics* (25):61-81.
Bell, R. T. 2001. *Translation and Translating: Theory and Practice.* Beijing: Foreign Language Teaching and Research Press.
Bloor, B. & Bloor, M. 1995. *The Functional Analysis of English: A Hallidayan Approach.* Beijing: Foreign Language Teaching and Research Press.
Bowcher, W. L. 2013. Material action as choice in field. In L. Fontaine, T. Bartlett & G. O'Grady (eds.). *Systemic Functional Linguistics: Exploring Choice.* New York: Cambridge University Press, pp. 318-341.
Calvino, I. 1986. *Why Read the Classics ?* (C. Patrick, Trans.). CA: Harcourt Brace Jovanovich. (Original work published 1959)
Catford, J. C. 1965. *A Linguistic Theory of Translation.* London: Oxford University Press.
Chan, S. W. 2009. *A Chronology of Translation in China and in the West from the Legendary Period to 2004.* Hong Kong: The Chinese University Press.
Chang, H. C. 1997. Language and words: Communication in the "Analects" of Confucius. *Journal of Language and Social Psychology* 16 (2):107-131.
Cheang, A. W. 2000. The master's voice: On reading, translating and interpreting the "Analects" of Confucius. *The Review of Politics* 62 (3):563-582.
Chen, T. S. (陈桐生) 2006. Kongzi yulu de jieben he fanben —

cong *Zhong Gong* kan *Lunyu* yu qishizi houxue sanwen de xingshi chayi (孔子语录的节本和繁本——从《仲弓》看《论语》与七十子后学散文的形式差异, On the formal differences in the simplified and complicated versions of Confucius' sayings). *Kongzi yanjiu* (孔子研究, *Confucian Studies*) (2):116-122.

Chen, Y. (陈旸) 2009. *Lunyu* san ge yingyiben fanyi yanjiu de gongneng yuyanxue tansuo (《论语》三个英译本翻译研究的功能语言学探索, A functional analysis of quotations from *The Analects*). *Waiyu yu waiyu jiaoxue* (外语与外语教学, *Foreign Languages and Foreign-language Teaching*) (2):49-52.

Chen, Y. (陈旸) 2010. *Lunyu* yingyiben yanjiu de gongneng yupian fenxi fangfa (《论语》英译本研究的功能语篇分析方法, A functional discourse analysis of English translations of *The Analects*). *Waiguo yuwen* (外国语文, *Foreign Language and Literature*) (1):105-109.

Chesterman, A. 1989. *Readings in Translation Theory.* Helsinki: Finn Lectura.

Coffin, C. 2001. Theoretical approaches to written language: a TESOL perspective. In A. Burns & C. Coffin (eds.) *Analyzing English in a Global Context.* London: Routledge, 93-122.

Coulmas, F. 1985. Direct and indirect speech: General problems and problems of Japanese. *Journal of Pragmatics* (9):41-63.

Du, X. M. (杜学敏) 2009. *Lunyu zhong shuolei dongci de fanyi duibi yanjiu* (《论语》中说类动词的翻译对比研究, *A Comparative Study on the Translation of Verbs Denoting "saying" in The Analects*). Unpublished MA dissertation. Maritime Affairs University of Dalian.

Durrant, S. W. 1981. On translating *Lunyu. Chinese Literature: Essays, Articles, Reviews* 13 (1):109-119.

Eggins, S. 1994. *An Introduction to Systemic Functional Linguistics.* London: Pinter.

Fang, Y. (方琰) 2001. Lun hanyu xiaoju fuheti de zhuwei (论汉语小句复合体的主位, On theme in the clause complex in Chinese). *Waiyu yanjiu* (外语研究, *Journal of Foreign Language Research*) (2):56-58.

Fang, Y. (方琰) 2006. Constructing a harmonious world: Linguistic studies on *The Analects* of Confucius. In G. W. Huang, C. G. Chang & F. Dai (eds.). *Functional Linguistics as Appliable Linguistics*. Guangzhou: Sun Yat-sen University Press, pp. 95-112.

Gao, S. W. (高生文) 2012. Yuyu fenxi yu *Lunyu* fanyi yanjiu (语域分析与《论语》翻译研究, Register analysis and the study of *The Analects* and its translation). *Beijing keji daxue xuebao (shehui kexue ban)* [北京科技大学学报 (社会科学版), *Journal of University of Science and Technology of Beijing (Social Science Edition*] (3):34-43.

Gu, B. (顾犇) 2002. Guanyu Nuobeier yu Kongfuzi de yixie shuoming (关于诺贝尔与孔夫子的一些说明, Some explanations on Nobel and Confucius). *Zhongguo wenhua yanjiu* (中国文化研究, *Journal of Chinese Culture Study*) (11):147-148.

Guo, C. B. (过常宝) 2007. *Lunyu* de wenti yiyi (《论语》的文体意义, The significance of the literary style of *The Analects*). *Qinghua daxue xuebao (zhexue shehui kexue ban)* [清华大学学报 (哲学社会科学版), *Journal of Tsinghua University*] (6):29-34.

Gutt, E. 2000. *Translation and Relevance: Cognition and Context* (2nd ed.). Oxford: ST. Jerome Publishing.

Halliday, M. A. K. 1978. *Language as Social Semiotic: The Social Interpretation of Language and Meaning*. London: Arnold.

Halliday, M. A. K. 1991. The notion of "context" in language education. In T. Le & M. McCausland (eds.). *Proceedings of the Second International Conference of Language Education: Interaction and Development*. Launceston: Press of the University of Tasmania, pp. 7-87.

Halliday, M. A. K. 1992. Language theory and translation practice. *Rivista Internazionale di Technica Della Traduzione* (0):15-25.

Halliday, M. A. K. 1994a. *An Introduction to Functional Grammar* (2nd ed.). London: Arnold.

Halliday, M. A. K. 1994b. Systemic theory. In R. E. Asher (ed.). *The Encyclopedia of Language and Linguistics*. Oxford: Pergamon, pp. 4504-4508.

Halliday, M. A. K. 2001. Towards a theory of good translation. In E. Steiner & C. Yallop (eds.). *Exploring Translation and Multilingual Text Production: Beyond Content.* Berlin: Mouton de Gruyter, pp. 13-18.

Halliday, M. A. K. 2004. Linguistics and machine translation. In J. J. Webster (ed.). *The Collected Works of M. A. K. Halliday: Vol. 6. Computational and Quantitative Studies.* London: Continuum, pp. 20-36. (Original work published 1962)

Halliday, M. A. K. 2005a. How do you mean. In J. J. Webster (ed.). *The Collected Works of M. A. K. Halliday: Vol. 7. Studies in English Language.* London: Continuum, pp. 352-368. (Original work published 1992)

Halliday, M. A. K. 2005b. Notes on transitivity and theme in English: Part 1. In J. J. Webster (ed.). *The Collected Works of M. A. K. Halliday: Vol. 7. Studies in English Language.* London: Continuum, pp. 5-54. (Original work published 1967)

Halliday, M. A. K. 2006a. Appendix: Systemic theory. In J. J. Webster (ed.). *The Collected Works of M. A. K. Halliday: Vol. 3. On Language and Linguistics.* London: Continuum, pp. 433-441. (Original work published 1994)

Halliday, M. A. K. 2006b. Introduction: On the "architecture" of human language. In J. J. Webster (ed.). *The Collected Works of M. A. K. Halliday: Vol. 3. On Language and Linguistics.* London: Continuum, pp. 15-29.

Halliday M. A. K. 2006c. Language as system and language as instance: The corpus as a theoretical construct. In J. J. Webster (ed.). *The Collected Works of M. A. K. Halliday: Vol. 6. Computational and Quantitative Studies.* London: Continuum, pp. 76-92. (Original work published 1992)

Halliday, M. A. K. 2006d. The linguistic basis of a mechanical thesaurus. In J. J. Webster (ed.). *The Collected Works of M. A. K. Halliday: Vol. 6. Computational and Quantitative Studies.* London: Continuum, pp. 6-19. (Original work published 1956)

Halliday, M. A. K. 2006e. Some theoretical considerations underlying the teaching of English in China. *Yingyu yanjiu* (英语研究, *The Journal of English Studies*) (4): 7-20.

Halliday, M. A. K. 2008. *Complementarities in Language*. Beijing: The Commercial Press.

Halliday, M. A. K. 2009. The gloosy ganoderm: systemic functional linguistics and translation. *Zhongguo fanyi* (中国翻译, *Chinese Translators Journal*) (1):17-26.

Halliday, M. A. K. & Hasan, R. 1976. *Cohesion in English*. London: Longman.

Halliday, M. A. K. & Hasan, R. 1985. *Language, Context, and Text: Aspects of Language in a Social-semiotic Perspective*. Oxford: Oxford University Press.

Halliday, M. A. K. & Matthiessen, C. M. I. M. 2004. *An Introduction to Functional Grammar* (3rd ed.). London: Arnold.

Halliday, M. A. K. & Matthiessen, C. M. I. M. 2008. *Construing Experience through Meaning: A Language-based Approach to Cognition*. Beijing: Shijie tushu chuban gongsi (世界图书出版公司, The World-Book Press).

Han, X. W. (韩效伟) 2008. *Pingjia lilun shijiao xia de lunyu huayu fenxi* (评价理论视角下的《论语》话语分析, *A Discourse Analysis of The Analects from the Perspective of Appraisal Theory*). Unpublished MA dissertation. Qufu Normal University.

Harbsmeier, C. 1990. Confucius ridens: Humor in "The Analects". *Harvard Journal of Asiatic Studies* 50 (1):131-161.

Hasan, R. 1995. The conception of context in text. In Fries, P. & Gregory, M. (eds.). *Discourse in Society: Systemic Functional Perspectives: meaning and choice in language: studies for Michael Halliday*. Norwood: Ablex, pp. 183-283.

Hjelmslev, L. 1943. *Omkring Sprogteoriens Grundlaeggelse*. Copenhagen: Akademisk Forlag.

Hou, W. H. (侯文华) 2008. *Lunyu* wenti kaolun (《论语》文体考论, A study of the style of *The Analects*). *Zhongguo wenxue yanjiu* (中国文学研究, *Journal of Chinese Literature Study*) (3): 34-38.

House, J. 1977. *A Model for Translation Quality Assessment* (2nd ed.). Tubingen: Gunter Narr Verlag.

House, J. 1997. *Translation Quality Assessment: A Model Revised*. Tubingen: Gunter Narr Verlag.

House, J. 2001. How do we know when a translation is good? In E. Steiner & C. Yallop (eds.). *Exploring Translation and Multilingual Text Production: Beyond Content.* Berlin: Mouton de Gruyter, pp. 127-160.

Hsieh, C. H. & Jen, W. 1991. "Great Man" (chun-tzu) and "Small Man" (hsiao-jen) in the "Confucian Analects": A transformation approach. *Journal of Applied Behavioural Science* 27 (4):425-443.

Hu, H. H. (胡红辉) 2013. *Lunyu* ji yingyiben zhong toushe yuyan yupian gongneng yanjiu (《论语》及英译本中投射语言语篇功能研究, A textual approach to projection in *The Analects* and its English translations). *Beijing keji daxue xuebao (shehui kexue ban)* 北京科技大学学报（社会科学版）, *Journal of University of Science and Technology of Beijing (Social Science Edition*) (4): 44-49.

Hu, H. H. & Chen, Y. (胡红辉, 陈旸) 2013. *Lunyu* yingyiben zhong toushe yuyan gainian gongneng fenxi (《论语》英译本中投射语言概念功能分析, An analysis of the ideational function in the language of projections in English translations of *The Analects*). *Neimenggu caijing daxue xuebao* (内蒙古财经大学学报, *Journal of Inner Mongolia University*) (6):134-138.

Hu, H. H. & Zeng, L. (胡红辉，曾蕾) 2012. *Lunyu* ji yingyiben zhong toushe yuyan renji gongneng fenxi (《论语》及英译本中投射语言人际功能分析, An interpersonal approach to projection in *The Analects* and its English versions). *Beijing keji daxue xuebao (shehui kexue ban)* [北京科技大学学报（社会科学版）, *Journal of University of Science and Technology of Beijing (Social Science Edition)*] (3):44-49.

Hu, Z. L., Zhu, Y. S. & Zhang, D. L. (胡壮麟，朱永生，张德禄) 1989/2008. *Xitong gongneng yufa gailun* (系统功能语法概论, *General Introduction to Systemic-functional Grammar*). Changsha: Hunan Education Press /Beijing: Peking University Press.

Huang, G. W. (黄国文) 1988. *Yupian fenxi gaiyao* (语篇分析概要, *Essentials of Text Analysis*). Changsha: Hunan Education Press.

Huang, G. W. (黄国文) 2001. Gongneng yupian fenxi zongheng

tan (功能语篇分析纵横谈, On functional discourse analysis). *Waiyu yu waiyu jiaoxue* (外语与外语教学, *Foreign Languages and Their Teaching*) (12): 1-4.

Huang, G. W. (黄国文) 2002a. Gongneng yupian fenxi mianmian guan (功能语篇分析面面观, Aspects of functional discourse analysis). *Guowai waiyu jiaoxue* (国外外语教学, *Foreign Languages and their Teaching*) (4): 25-32.

Huang, G. W. (黄国文) 2002b. Hallidayan linguistics in China. *World Englishes*, 21 (2): 281-290.

Huang, G. W. (黄国文) 2006a. *Fanyi yanjiu de yuyanxue tansuo-gushici yingyiben de yuyanxue fenxi* (翻译研究的语言学探索——古诗词英译本的语言学分析, *Linguistic Explorations in Translation Studies: Analysis of English Translations of Ancient Chinese Poems and Lyrics*). Shanghai: Shanghai Foreign Language Education Press.

Huang, G. W. (黄国文) 2006b. Zuowei shiyong yuyanxue de xitong gongneng yuyanxue (作为适用语言学的系统功能语言学, Systemic functional linguistics as appliable linguistics). *Yingyu yanjiu* (英语研究, *The Journal of English Studies*) 4 (4): 1-6.

Huang, G. W. (黄国文) 2007. Zuowei putong yuyanxue de xitong gongneng yuyanxue (作为普通语言学的系统功能语言学, Systemic functional linguistics as a general linguistic theory). *Zhongguo waiyu* (中国外语, *Foreign Language of China*) 4 (5): 14-19.

Huang, G. W. (黄国文) 2011. *Lunyu* de pianzhang jiegou ji yingyu fanyi de jige wenti (《论语》的篇章结构及英语翻译的几个问题, Some issues in the textual structure of the English translations of *The Analects*). *Zhongguo waiyu* (中国外语, *Journal of Foreign Languages in China*) (6): 88-95.

Huang, G. W. (黄国文) 2012a. *Lunyu* yingyi yiyi fangfa yanjiu de gongneng jufa shijiao (《论语》英译意译方法研究的功能句法视角, Paraphrase as a strategy in translating *The Analects* into English: A functional linguistic perspective). *Beijing keji daxue xuebao* (*shehui kexue ban* [北京科技大学学报 (社会科学版)], *Journal of University of Science and Technology of Beijing (Social-science Edition*) (3): 16-21.

Huang, G. W. (黄国文) 2012b. Dianji fanyi: cong yunei fanyi dao yuji fanyi — yi *Lunyu* yingyi weili (典籍翻译：从语内翻译到语际翻译——以《论语》英译为例, Translating the classics: From intralingual translation to interlingual translation in translating *The Analects* into English). *Zhongguo waiyu* (中国外语, *Journal of Foreign Languages in China*) (6):64-71.

Huang, G. W. (黄国文) 2013. Analyzing the reporting clause in translating Confucius's "Lunyu" ("The Analects"). In Y. Fang & J. J. Webster (eds.). *Developing Systemic Functional Linguistics: Theory and Application.* London: Equinox, pp. 256-270.

Huang, G. W., Chang, C. G. & Dai, F. (黄国文, 常晨光, 戴凡) (eds.). 2006. *Functional Linguistics as Appliable Linguistics.* Guangzhou: Sun Yat-sen University Press.

Jacobson, R. 1985. The fundamental and specific characteristics of human language. In R. Jacobson, *Selected Writings 7: Contributions to Comparative Mythology. Studies in Linguistics and Philology. 1972—1982.* Berlin: Mouton de Gruyter.

Jennings, W. 1895. *The Confucian "Analects": A Translation with Annotation and Introduction.* London: George Routledge and Sons.

Jin, X. Q. (金学勤) 2009. *Lunyu yingyi zhi kuawenhua chanshi — yi Liyage Gu Hongming weili*(《论语》英译之跨文化阐释——以理雅各、辜鸿铭为例, *A Cross-culture Interpretation of Translating The Analects: With Special Reference to James Legge and Ku Hung-ming).* Chengdu: Sichuan University Press.

Ku, H. M. 1898. *The Discourse and Sayings of Confucius: A New Special Translation, Illustrated with Quotations from Goethe and Other Writers.* Shanghai: Kelly and Walsh.

Lang, S. W. (郎淑文) 2009. *Lunyu yingyi zhong renji yiyi de jiangou: pingjia zhi taidu xitong fenxi* (《论语》英译中人际意义的建构：评价之态度系统分析, *The Construction of Interpersonal Meaning in English Translations of The Analects: a Systemic Appraisal Analysis*). Unpublished MA dissertation. Hangzhou: Zhejiang University of Industry and Commerce.

Lau, D. C. (刘殿爵) & Yang B. J. (杨伯峻), 2008. *Lunyu zhong*

ying wen duizhao (《论语 中英文对照》, *The Analects: Chinese-English edition)*, Beijing: Zhonghua Book Company.

Leech, G. N. & Short, M. 1981. *Style in Fiction: A Linguistic Introduction to English Fictional Prose.* London: Longman.

Legge, J. 1971. *Confucius, Confucian Analects: The Great Learning & the Doctrine of the Mean.* New York: Dover Publications.

Li, G. & Li, J. Z. (李钢,李金姝) 2013. *Lunyu* yingyi yanjiu zongshu (《论语》英译研究综述, On the translation of *The Analects* : A survey). *Hunan shifan daxue xuebao (shehui kexue ban)* [湖南师范大学（社会科学版）], *Journal of Hunan Normal University. Social Sciences Edition* (1):131-135.

Li, J. Y. (李桔元) 2009. Guanggao yupian zhong rencheng daici de guanxi jiangou gongneng — yinghan duibi fenxi (广告语篇中人称代词的关系建构功能——英汉对比分析, Personal pronouns as means of relation-building in advertising discourse: An English-Chinese contrastive analysis). *Beijing keji daxue xuebao (shehui kexue ban)* [北京科技大学学报（社会科学版）], *Journal of University of Science and Technology of Beijing (Social-science Edition)* (2):104-108.

Li, Y. X. (李运兴) 2002. "Zhuwei" gainian zai fanyi yanjiu zhong de yingyong ("主位"概念在翻译研究中的应用, On the application of the concept of "Theme" in translation studies). *Waiyu yu waiyu jiaoxue* (外语与外语教学, *Foreign Languages and Their Teaching*) (7):19-22.

Lim, T. S. 2012. Observance of forms: An aesthetic analysis of "Analects" 6.25. *Dao* 11 (2):147-162.

Lin, Y. T. (林语堂) 1938. *The Wisdom of Confucius.* New York: The Modern Library.

Littlejohn, R. (2005). Recent works on Confucius and "The Analects". *Philosophy East & West* 55 (1):99-109.

Liu, W. S. (刘伟生) 2011. Yuluti yu zhongguo wenhua tezhi (语录体与中国文化特质, On the quotation style and Chinese cultural characteristics). *Shehui kexue ji kan* (社会科学辑刊, *Social Science Journal*) (6):265-268.

Lyons, J. 1968. *Introducton to Theoretical Linguistics.* Cambridge: Cambridge University Press.

Makeham, J. 2003. *Transmitters and Creators: Chinese Commentators and Commentaries on The Analects*. Cambridge: Harvard University Press.

Makeham, J. 2006. A new hermeneutical approach to early Chinese texts: The case of the "Analects". *Journal of Chinese Philosophy*. 33 (sl):95-108.

Malinowski, B. 1935. *Coral Gardens and Their Magic: A Study of the Methods of Tilling the Soil and of Agricultural Rites in the Trobriand Islands. Vol. 2: The Language of Magic and Gardening*. London: Allen and Unwin.

Manfredi, M. 2014. *Translating Text and Context: Translation Studies and Systemic Functional Linguistics. Vol. 2: From Theory to Practice*. Bologna: Asterisco.

Martin, J. R. 1984. Language, register and genre. In F. Christie (ed.). *Children Writing: Reader*. Geelong: Deakin University Press, pp. 21-29.

Martin, J. R. 1992. *English Text: System and Structure*. Amsterdam: John Benjamins.

Matthiessen, C. 1993. Register in the round: Diversity in a unified theory of register analysis. In M. Ghadessy (ed.). *Register Analysis: Theory and Practice*. London: Pinter Publishers, pp. 221-292.

Matthiessen, C. 2001. The environment of translation. In E. Steiner & C. Yallop (eds.). *Exploring Translation and Multilingual Text Production: Beyond Content*. Berlin: Mouton de Gruyter, pp. 41-124.

Matthiessen, C. 2014. Choice in translation — metafunctional considerations. In K. Kunz, E. Teich, S. Hansen-Schirra, S. Neumann & P. Daut (eds.). *Caught in the Middle – Language Use and Translation. A Festschrift for Erich Steiner on the Occasion of his 60th Birthday*. Saarbrücken, Germany: Saarland University Press, pp. 271-334.

Matthiessen, C. & Halliday, M. A. K. 2009. *Systemic Functional Grammar: A First Step into the Theory* (G. W. Huang & H. Y. Wang, Trans.). Beijing: Higher Education Press.

Matthiessen, C. M. I. M., Teruya, K. & Lam, M. 2010. *Key

Terms in Systemic Functional Linguistics. London: Continuum.

Munday, J. 2001. *Introducing Translation Studies, Theories and Applications.* London: Routledge.

Newmark, P. 1987. The use of systemic linguistics in translation analysis and criticism. In R. Steele & T. Threadgold (eds.). *Language Topics: Essays in Honour of Michael Halliday, Vol. 1.* Amsterdam: Benjamins, pp. 293-303.

Olberding, A. 2007. The educative function of personal style in the "Analects". *Philosophy East and West.* 57 (3): 357-374.

Page, N. 1973. *Speech in the English Novel.* London: Longman.

Pfister, L. 1986. Considerations for the contemporary revitalization of Confucianism: Meditations on "Te" in the "Analects". *Journal of Chinese Philosophy.* (13): 239-265.

Pound, E. 1969. *Confucius, the Great Digest, the Unwobbling Pivot, The Analects.* New York: New Directions Publishing Corporation.

Poynton, C. 1985. *Language and Gender: Making the Difference.* Geelong, Vic: Deakin University Press.

Qi, X. K. (齐宪凯) 2011. *Gongneng yufa shijiao xia Lunyu sange yingyiben de bijiao yanjiu* (功能语法视角下《论语》三个英译本的比较研究, *A Comparative Study of Three English Versions of The Analects from the Perspective of Functional Grammar*). Unpublished MA dissertation. Harbin: Harbin Engineering University.

Qian, M. (钱穆) 2011. *Lunyu xin jie* (论语新解, *A New Interpretation of the Lunyu*). Beijing: Jiuzhou Publishing Corporation.

Sakita, T. I. 2002. *Reporting Discourse, Tense and Cognition.* Kidlington: Elsevier Science.

Schaberg, D. 2001. "Sell it! Sell it!": Recent translations of "Lunyu". *Chinese Literature: Essays, Articles, Reviews* (23): 115-139.

Shen, D. (申丹) 1991. Xiaoshuo zhong renwu huayu de butong biaoda fangshi (小说中人物话语的不同表达方式, Different modes of expression in the discourse fictional characters). *Waiyu jiaoxue yu yanjiu* (外语教学与研究, *Foreign Language Teaching*

and Researching) (1):13-18.
Si, X. Z. (司显柱) 2005. Zhuli'an Haosi de "fanyi zhiliang pinggu moshi" piping (朱莉安·豪斯的"翻译质量评估模式"批评, A criticism of Julianna House's model of translation quality assessment). *Waiyu jiaoxue* (外语教学, *Foreign Language Education*) (3):79-84.
Steiner, E. 2001. Intralingual and interlingual versions of a text — how specific is the notion of translation? In E. Steiner & C. Yallop (eds.). *Exploring Translation and Multilingual Text Production: Beyond Content*. Berlin: Mouton de Gruyter, pp. 161-190.
Steiner, E. 2005. Halliday and translation theory — enhancing the options, broadening the range and keeping the ground. In Hasan, R., C. Matthiessen and J. Webster (eds.). *Continuing Discourse on Language: A Functional Perspective*. London/Oakville: Equinox, pp. 481-500.
Teich, E. 2001. Towards a model for the description of cross-linguistic divergence and commonality in translation. In E. Steiner & C. Yallop (eds.). *Exploring Translation and Multilingual Text Production: Beyond Content*. Berlin: Mouton de Gruyter, pp. 191-228.
Thompson, G. 1994. *Propositions, projections and things*. Paper presented at the 21st International Systemic Functional Congress. Gent: Belgium.
Thompson, G. 1996a. Voices in the text: Discourse perspectives on language reports. *Applied Linguistics* (17):501-530.
Thompson, G. 1996b. *Introducing Functional Grammar*. London: Arnold.
Tian, Y. (天宜) 2010. *Lunyu mingxin* (《论语》明心, *The True Nature of the Lunyu*. Nanjing: Southeast University Press.
Voloshinov, V. N. 1978. Reported speech. In L. Matejka & K. Pomorska (eds.). *Readings in Russian Poetics*. Cambridge: MIT Press.
Wang, C. (王充) 1986. *Lun heng* (论衡, *On Heng*). Shanghai: Shanghai Book Company.
Wang, C. (王诚) 2013. *Lunyu* zhong de xianjie (《论语》中的衔接,

Cohesion in *The Analects*). *Gansu lianhe daxue xuebao (shehui kexue ban)* [甘肃联合大学学报（社会科学版）], *Journal of Gansu Lianhe University (Social Sciences Edition)* (1): 85-89.

Wang, F. X. (王凤霞) 2008. Cong Xu Yuanchong shige fanyi kan wenhua zhuanjiyin de zaixian—*yi xu yuanchong xiansheng sou yi you dong tian weili* (从许渊冲诗歌翻译看文化转基因的再现——以许渊冲先生所译《游东田》为例, On the reproduction of cultural transgenes in the poetic translations of Xu Yuanchong). *Journal of Xihua University (Philosophy & Social Sciences)* (1): 101-103.

Wang, H. (王辉) 2004. Liyage, Pangde *Lunyu* yiben bijiao (理雅各、庞德《论语》译本比较, A comparison of Legge's and Pound's translations of *The Analects*). *Sichuan waiguoyu xueyuan xuebao* (四川外国语学院学报, *Journal of Sichuan International Studies University*) (5): 140-144.

Wang, K. F. & Zhang, M. F. （王克非，张美芳）2001. Introduction. In R. T. Bell (ed.). *Translation and Translating: Theory and Practice*. Beijing: Foreign Language Teaching and Research Press, pp. F25-F32.

Wang, Y. (王勇) 2006. 20 nian lai de *Lunyu* yingyi yanjiu (20 年来的《论语》英译研究, Studies of English translations of *The Analects* in the past twenty years). *Qiu suo* (求索) (5): 178-181.

Wang, Y. (王琰) 2010a. Guoneiwai *Lunyu* yingyi yanjiu bijiao (国内外《论语》英译研究比较, A comparative study of *The Analects* English translation studies in China and abroad). *Waiyu yanjiu* (外语研究, *Foreign Language Research*) (2): 70-73.

Wu, G. X. (吴国向) 2012. Jingdian fanyi yu wenhua chuancheng: shoujie *Lunyu* fanyi yantaohui jianshu (经典翻译与文化传承——"首届《论语》翻译研讨会"简述, Translation of classics and cultural transmission: A review of "The 1st conference on translating *The Analects*"). *Zhongguo waiyu* (中国外语, *Journal of Foreign Languages in China*) (1): 104-107.

Wu, L. (吴恋) 2011. Bolatu yu Kongzi de duihuati bijiao (柏拉图与孔子的对话体比较, A comparative study of the quotation style of Plato and Confucius). *Wenxue jie (lilun ban)* [文学界（理论版）, *Literature (Theory Edition)*] (5): 178-179.

Wu, X. M. 2009. Words, speech, and argument in "The Analects". *Journal of Chinese Philosophy* 36 (4):541-553.

Xia, D. K. (夏德靠) 2013. *Lunyu* wenti de shengcheng ji jiegou moshi (《论语》文体的生成及结构模式, On the generative and structural model of the style of *The Analects*). *Sichuan shifan daxue xuebao (shehui kexue ban)* [四川师范大学学报 (社会科学版)], *Journal of Sichuan Normal University (Social Sciences Edition)* (1):106-114.

Xiao, J. Y. & Li, R. S. (肖家燕, 李儒寿) 2013. Jiaoliu yu chuancheng — di'erjie *Lunyu* fanyi yantaohui zongshu (交流与传承——第二届《论语》翻译研讨会综述, Communication and inheritance: A summary of the second conference on the translation of *The Analects*). *Zhongguo waiyu* (中国外语, *Journal of Foreign Languages in China*) (1):109-111

Xiao, Y. 2007. How Confucius does things with words: Two hermeneutic paradigms in "The Analects" and its exegeses. *The Journal of Asian Studies*, 66 (2):497-532.

Xu, Y. C. (许渊冲) 2005. *Confucius Modernized, thus Spoke the Master* (《论语》). Beijing: Higher Education Press.

Yallop, C. 2001. The construction of equivalence. In E. Steiner & C. Yallop (eds.). *Exploring Translation and Multilingual Text Production: Beyond Content.* Berlin: Mouton de Gruyter, pp. 229-248.

Yang, B. J. (杨伯峻) 2006. *Lunyu yizhu* (论语译注, *The Translation and Notes of the Lunyu*). Beijing: Zhonghua Book Company.

Yang, F. B. (杨逢彬) 1999. Introduction in "The Analects" (A. Waley, Trans.). Changsha: Hunan People's Publishing House, pp. 17-35.

Yang, P. (杨平) 2009. *Lunyu* yingyi de gaishu yu pingxi (《论语》英译的概述与评析, A critical survey of English translations of *The Analects*). *Zhejiang jiaoyu xueyuan xuebao* (浙江教育学院学报, *Journal of Zhejiang Education Institute*) (5):37-46.

Yang, Y. (杨义) 2013. *Lunyu* zaoqi bianzuan guocheng ji pianzhang zhengzhixue (shang) (《论语》早期编纂过程及篇章政治学 (上), The early compilation of *The Analects* and the politics of its textual structure). *Xueshu yuekan* (学术月刊, *Academic Monthly*) (1):34-45.

Yang, Y. N. (杨延宁) 2014. Fazhan yu chuangxin — di san jie *Lunyu* fanyi yantaohui zongshu (发展与创新——第三届《论语》翻译研讨会综述, Development and creativity: A summary of the third conference on the translation of "*The Analects*"). *Zhongguo waiyu* (中国外语, *Journal of Foreign Languages in China*) (2):109-111.

Yao, J. Z. (幺俊洲) 2004. *Lunyu wenda* (《论语》问答, *Questions and Answers on* The Analects). Jinan: Qinu Pressing House.

Yu, Q. Q. (余琴琴) 2013. *Pingjia lilun shijiao xia Lunyu ji qi yingyi de duibi yanjiu* (评价理论视角下《论语》及其英译的对比研究, *A Comparative Study of The Analects and its English Translations from the Perspective of Appraisal Theory*). Unpublished MA dissertation. Jinan: Shandong University.

Yuan, J. X. (袁济喜) 2008. Cong Kongzi *Lunyu* duihua fengcai kan wenyi piping (从孔子《论语》对话风采看文艺批评, Dialogues in *The Analects* and literary criticism). *Zhongguo renmin daxue xuebao* (中国人民大学学报, *Journal of Renmin University of China*) (3):139-146.

Zeng, L. (曾蕾) 2000a. Yinghan "toushe" xiaoju fuheti de gongneng yu yuyi fenxi (英汉"投射"小句复合体的功能与语义分析, A functional and semantics approach to the projection clause nexus in English and Chinese). *Xiandai waiyu* (现代外语, *Modern Foreign Languages*) (2):163-173

Zeng, L. (曾蕾) 2000b. Cong gongneng yuyanxue jiaodu kan "toushe" yu "yupian fenxi" (从功能语言学角度看"投射"与"语篇分析", On projection and discourse analysis from an SFL perspective). *Waiyu yu waiyu jiaoxue* (外语与外语教学, *Foreign Languages and Their Teaching*) (11): 15-17.

Zeng, L. (曾蕾) 2002. Cong luoji gongneng dao jingyan gongneng — kuozhan "toushe" xianxiang de gainian gongneng moshi (从逻辑功能到经验功能——扩展"投射"现象的概念功能模式, From the logical to the experiential: An alternative ideational way into the analysis of "projection" in SFG). *Xiandai waiyu* (现代外语, *Modern Foreign Languages*) (3):269-275.

Zeng, L. (曾蕾) 2003. Lun xitong gongneng yufa zhong "toushe" gainian yinyu jugou ji qi yuyi tezheng (论系统功能语法中"投射"概念隐喻句构及其语义特征, A study of the syntactic and semantic features of "projection" from the perspective of ideational metaphor in SFG). *Xiandai waiyu* (现代外语, *Modern Foreign Languages*) (4):352-357.

Zeng, L. (曾蕾) 2005. Yinghan toushe fuhao de yupian fanyi celüe (英汉投射符号的语篇翻译策略, On the discourse translation methods of projecting signals in English and Chinese). In G. W. Huang, C. G. Chang, J. X. Ding (eds.). *Gongneng yuyanxue de lilun yu yingyong* (功能语言学的理论与应用, *Functional Linguistics: Theory and Application*). Beijing: Higher Education Press, pp. 411-420.

Zeng, L. (曾蕾) 2006a. *A Functional Interpretation of "Projection"*. Guangzhou: Sun Yat-sen University Press.

Zeng, L. (曾蕾) 2006b. Toushe yuyan fanyi zhong de zhuwei shijiao (投射语言翻译中的主位视角, A study of the translation of projection from the perspective of Theme). In D. F. Wang (王东风) (ed.). *Gongneng yuyanxue yu fanyi yanjiu* (功能语言学与翻译研究, *Functional Linguistics and Translation Studies*. Guangzhou: Sun Yat-sen University Press, pp. 161-175.

Zeng, L. (曾蕾) 2007. Cong yufa yinyu kan xueshu yupian zhong de "toushe" (从语法隐喻视角看学术语篇中的"投射", A study of projection in academic discourse from the perspective of grammatical metaphor). *Waiyu Xuekan* (外语学刊, *Foreign Language Research*) (3):46-49.

Zeng, L. (曾蕾) 2008. Yingyu xueshu yupian zhong toushe dongci shitai de yufa yinyu (英语学术语篇中投射动词时态的语法隐喻, An approach to the metaphorical meanings of the tense of projecting verbs in English academic discourse). *Beijing keji daxue xuebao (shehui kexue ban)* [北京科技大学学报 (社会科学版)], *Journal of University of Science and Technology Beijing (Social Sciences Edition)* (2):104-108.

Zhang, H. T. (张怀通) 2008. "Wang Ruo yue" xin shi ("王若曰"新释, A new interpretation of "Wang Ruo said"). *Lishi yanjiu* (历史研究, *History Studies*) (2):182-188.

Zhu, X. (朱熹) 1983. *Lunyu jizhu* (论语集注, *Commentaries on the Lunyu*). Beijing: Zhonghua Publishing House.

Zhou, X. L. (周晓玲) 2011. *A Corpus-based Study of the Translator's Style: A Case Study of James Legge's Style in his Translation of Chinese Classics*. Unpublished doctoral dissertation. Changsha: Hunan Normal University.

Zhu, Y. S. & Yan, S. Q. (朱永生, 严世清) 2001. *Xitong gongneng yuyaxue duowei sikao* (系统功能语言学多维思考, *A Multidimensional Study of Systemic Functional Linguistics*). Shanghai: Shanghai Foreign Language Education Press.

Zou, C. M. (邹春媚) 2007. *The Genre Analysis of The Analects of Confucius from the Systemic Functional Perspective.* Unpublished MA dissertation, Guangzhou: South China Normal University.

Zou, J. M. (邹纪孟) 2010. *Qing Lunyu zouxia shen tan* (请《论语》走下神坛, *The Analects: Walking down the Altar*). Beijing: China City Press.

Appendix I

The courtesy names and given names of Confucius' main disciples

Surname + given name	courtesy name
颜回 (Yán Huí)	子渊 (Zǐyuān)
冉耕 (Rǎn Gēng)	伯牛 (Bóniú)
冉雍 (Rǎn Yōng)	仲弓 (Zhònggōng)
冉求 (Rǎn Qiú)	子有 (Zǐyǒu)
仲由 (Zhòng Yóu)	子路 (Zǐlù)
宰予 (Zǎi Yǔ)	子我 (Zǐwǒ)
端木赐 (Duānmù Cì)	子贡 (Zǐgòng)
颜偃 (Yán Yàn)	子游 (Zǐyóu)
卜商 (Bǔ Shāng)	子夏 (Zǐxià)
曾参 (Zēng Shēn)	子舆 (Zǐyú)
澹台灭明 (Tántái Mièmíng)	子羽 (Zǐyǔ)
宓不齐 (Fú Bùqí)	子贱 (Zǐjiàn)
公冶长 (Gōngyě Cháng)	子长 (Zǐcháng)
司马耕 (Sīmǎ Gēng)	子牛 (Zǐniú)
漆雕开 (Qīdiāo Kāi)	子开 (Zǐkāi)
公西赤 (Gōngxī Chì)	子华 (Zǐhuá)
有若 (Yǒu Ruò)	子有 (Zǐyǒu)
冉季 (Rǎn Jì)	子产 (Zǐchǎn)

Appendix II

Translations of the examples given in Chapter 4

[4-1]
The Master said, "Parents are anxious lest their children should be sick." (LT:2/6)
Confucius answered, "Think how anxious your parents are when you are sick, and you will know your duty towards them." (KT:2/6)
(When the son of Meng Yi Zi asked about filial duty,) the Master said, "Do not let your parents worry about their health." (XT:2/6)

[4-2]
1. The Master said, "Is it not pleasant to learn with a constant perseverance and application?"
2. "Is it not delightful to have friends coming from distant quarters?"
3. "Is he not a man of complete virtue, who feels no discomposure though men may take no note of him?" (LT:1/1)

Confucius remarked, "It is indeed a pleasure to acquire knowledge and, as you go on acquiring, to put into practice what you have acquired. A greater pleasure still it is when friends of congenial minds come from afar to seek you because of your attainments. But be is truly a wise and good man who feels no discomposure even when he is not noticed of men." (KT:1/1)

Is it not a delight, said the Master, to acquire knowledge and put it into practice? Is it not a pleasure to meet friends coming from afar? Is he not an intelligentleman, who is careless alike of being known or unknown? (XT:1/1)

[4-3]
Tsze-yew asked what filial piety was. (LT:2/7)

A disciple of Confucius asked him the same question as the above. (KT:2/7)

When Zi You asked about filial duty, (XT:2/7)

[4-4]
1. He sacrificed to the dead, as if they were present. He sacrificed to the spirits, as if the spirits were present.
2. The Master said, "I consider my not being present at the sacrifice, as if I did not sacrifice." (LT:3/12)

Confucius worshipped the dead as if he actually felt the presence of the departed ones. He worshipped the Spiritual Powers as if he actually felt the presence of the Powers.

He once remarked, "If I cannot give up heart and soul when I am worshipping, I always consider as if I have not worshipped." (KT:3/12)

Sacrifice to the dead as if they were living, and to the divinities as if they were present. If I do not think they are present, said the Master, I had better not sacrifice at all. (XT:3/12)

[4-5]
The duke Ai asked which of the disciples loved to learn. Confucius replied to him, "There was Yan Hui; He loved to learn. He did not transfer his anger; he did not repeat a fault. Unfortunately, his appointed time was short and he died; and now there is not such another. I have not yet heard of any one who loves to learn as he did." (LT:6/2)

The reigning prince of Confucius native State asked him which one of his disciples he considered a man of real culture. Confucius answered, "There was Yen Hui. He never made others suffer for his own annoyances. He never did a wrong thing twice. But unfortunately he died in the prime of his life. Now there is no one, none who can be said to be a man of real culture." (KT:6/2)

Duke Ai of Lu asked Confucius, "Which of your disciples are eager to learn?" Confucius said, "There was Yan Hui who was eager to learn. He did not shift the blame on to others, nor would he make the same mistake again. But it was a pity that he died early. Now there is none like him. I have never again heard of anyone so eager to learn." (XT:6/3)

[4-6]
Tsze-hea asked what filial piety was. The Master said, "The difficulty is with the countenance. If, when their elders have any troublesome affairs, the young take the toil of them, and if when the young have wine and food, they set them before their elders, is THIS to be considered filial piety?" (LT:2/8)
Another disciple asked the same question. Confucius answered, "The difficulty is with the expression of your look. That merely when anything is to be done the young people do it, and when there is food and wine the old folk are allowed to enjoy it, do you think that is the whole duty of a good son?" (KT:2/8)
When Zi Xia asked about filial duty, the Master said, " It is difficult to appear happy in trouble. If the young serve the old and feed them with wine and food before themselves, but with troubled looks, could they be call filial sons?" (XT:2/8)

[4-7]
Mang Woo asked what filial piety was. The Master said, "Parents are anxious lest their children should be sick." (LT:2/6)
A son of the noble mentioned above put the same question to Confucius as his father did. Confucius answered, "Think how anxious your parents are when you are sick, and you will know your duty towards them." (KT:2/6)
When the son of Meng Yi Zi asked about filial duty, the Master said, "Do not let your parents worry about their health." (XT:2/6)